Hemingway's Spain

Hemingway's Spain

Imagining the Spanish World

Edited by Carl P. Eby
and Mark Cirino

The Kent State University Press
Kent, Ohio

"Bulls, Art, Mithras, and Montherlant" was originally published in a slightly different form as chapter 4 of *Hemingway and French Writers,* by Ben Stoltzfus (The Kent State University Press, 2009), and appears courtesy of the author.

ISBN 978-1-60635-242-7
Manufactured in the United States of America

Cataloging information for this title is available at the Library of Congress.

20 19 18 17 16 5 4 3 2 1

For Linda and Paco

For Kristen

Contents

Acknowledgments

We are deeply grateful to the many friends who helped make this book possible. The essays in this volume originated in presentations at the Twelfth Biennial International Hemingway Conference in Málaga and Ronda, Spain, in June 2006, and this volume wouldn't have been possible without the help of everyone who contributed to that conference. Carl wants to begin by thanking James Meredith, then president of the Ernest Hemingway Foundation and Society, and Susan Beegel, then editor of the *Hemingway Review*, for their wisdom, good humor, and tireless assistance during the planning of the conference. As program director for the conference, Carl received extensive and crucial help from conference the site director, Diane Pérez Buck, and the assistant site director, Miriam Mandel. Excellent advice and very welcome assistance was provided by a host of Hemingway scholars, including Andrés Arenas Gómez, Jackson Bryer, Nancy Bredendick, Rose Marie Burwell, Kirk Curnutt, Albert J. DeFazio III, José Antonio Gurpegui Palacios, Peter Hays, Hilary Justice, J. Gerald Kennedy, Debra Moddelmog, Linda Miller, Linda Wagner Martin, Bill Newmiller, Tod Oliver, Steve Paul, Beatriz Penas Ibáñez, Rena Sanderson, Gail Sinclair, Sandra Spanier, Robert Trogdon, Amy Vondrak, and many others. Carl is indebted to them all. He also wishes to acknowledge Susan Wrynn, Stephen Plotkin, and the John F. Kennedy Library in Boston for assistance with images and research for the conference. Valerie Hemingway, John Hemingway, René Villarreal, Nena Davis, and Paola Dominguín shared fascinating insights into Ernest Hemingway, including their perspectives on the events chronicled in *The Dangerous Summer*, and for this Carl is very grateful. He also wishes to thank Victor Mendes and Muriel Feiner for sharing their extraordinary expertise on the corrida.

For the tremendous hospitality we received from the cities and governments of Málaga and Ronda, Carl will forever be indebted to the mayor of Málaga, D. Francisco de la Torre Prados, and the former mayor of Ronda, D. Antonio María Marín Lara. He also wishes to thank the former director general of La Escuela de Hostelería de Málaga, D. Rafael de la Fuente, and the director general of La Real Meastranza de Caballeria de Ronda, D. Ignacio Herrera de la Muela. Their kindness and assistance were invaluable.

Carl is especially grateful to Mark for agreeing to join this project. He brought his friendship and tremendous energy, knowledge, discipline, organizational ability, good humor, and keen editorial eye to the project when it was most needed. This book wouldn't have been possible without him. One couldn't hope for a better coeditor.

Mark would like to thank all of the friends that he made in Ronda, particularly Mark P. Ott, who has been an unshakeable friend and counselor. He also thanks Carl for all his generosity, including the invitation to join this wonderful project. Mark would also like to acknowledge Eva, the newest Cirino, and her wonderful Galician friends and family.

For their institutional help, we want to thank Appalachian State University, the University of Evansville, the University of South Carolina Beaufort, the University of Idaho, and the United States Air Force Academy. For assistance with research, we want to thank Vito Petruzzelli.

Above all, we want to thank our families for their loving patience and support as we worked long hours on this project for many years. They are simply the best.

Introduction
Imagining Spain

Carl P. Eby and Mark Cirino

In December 1921, a young Ernest Hemingway en route to France with his new bride, Hadley, wrote from aboard the S.S. *Leopoldina* to his old fishing buddy Bill Smith about a brief stopover in the northwestern corner of the Iberian Peninsula: "Vigo, Spain. That's the place for a male. . . . Gaw what a place."

> A harbor almost landlocked about as big as Little Traverse Bay with big, brown, mountains. A male can buy a lateen sailed boat for 5 seeds. Costs a seed a day at the Grand Hotel and the bay swarms with Tuna.
>
> They behave exactly like lainsteins—sardines for shiners—chase them the same way and I saw 3 in the air at once—1 easily 8 feet. The biggest one they've taken this year weighed 850 lbs!
>
> Vigo's about 4 times the size of the Voix and there are three or four little places around the bay to sail to. . . .
>
> Trout streams in the Mts. Tuna in the bay. Green water to swim in and sandy beaches. Vino is 2 peseta a qt. for the 3 year old which can be distinguished by a blue label. Cognac is 4 pesetas a litre.

Little wonder Hemingway promised, "We're going back there" (*Letters* 312).

It wasn't his first taste of Spain—he had spent three days in Gibraltar and Algericas on his way home from World War I in January 1919—but it was his first declaration of love for a country that for him would remain a lifelong passion, and the terms in which he expresses his enthusiasm are worth noting. There is, of course, the love of landscape, fishing, swimming, drinking, and grand hotels that featured so prominently in his life and work—Spain as a paradise for a "male"—but what is perhaps more interesting is that Hemingway somehow imagines Spain in terms of northern Michigan, where he spent all but one of the summers of his youth. The Ria de Vigo is like Petoskey's Little Traverse Bay; Vigo itself is like Charlevoix (although four times bigger); and the tuna are just much bigger versions of Michigan's lake trout (*lainsteins,* a variation on *rainsteins,* or rainbow trout in Ernest's patois[1]). We might speculate that such comparisons were for the benefit of his Michigan pal, yet when, on the slender evidence of his four-hour stay, he wrote a story on Vigo for the *Toronto Star,* he not only describes the tuna fishing but also writes with the authority of a Michigan angler about the fishing in the mountains above Vigo, "where the good fishermen will go when snow drifts along the northern streams and trout lie nose to nose in deep pools under a scum of ice," and the tuna still are imagined in these familiar terms: "Sometimes five and six tuna will be in the air at once in Vigo Bay, shouldering out of the water like porpoises as they herd the sardines, then leaping in a towering jump that is as clean and beautiful as the first leap of a well-hooked rainbow" (*Dateline* 92). Although colored by the romance of the foreign, Vigo, for Hemingway, somehow was home.

Hemingway, of course, is famous for his adopted homes—first Michigan, then Italy, France, Spain, Key West, Kenya, Cuba, and Idaho—and of these, none was more important to his imaginative universe than Spain. Indeed, Spain provides a setting for no fewer than five of his major books—*The Sun Also Rises* (1926), *Death in the Afternoon* (1932), *For Whom the Bell Tolls* (1940), *The Dangerous Summer* (1985), and *The Garden of Eden* (1986)—not to mention the bullfighting vignettes of *In Our Time* (1924); such stories as "Hills Like White Elephants," "The Undefeated," "A Clean Well-Lighted Place," and "The Capital of the World"; his Spanish Civil War journalism; his only full-length play, *The Fifth Column* (1938); and the documentary film on which he collaborated with John Dos Passos and Joris Ivens, *The Spanish Earth* (1937). Though he stayed away from Spain for fifteen years of his adult life, between 1938 and 1953, he called Spain "the country that I loved more than any other except my own" (*DS* 43). His forty-year love affair with the country spanned his career as a writer, and the depth of his engagement with Spain—emotional, psychological, aesthetic, literary, political, military, culinary, and religious—was rich and complex.

Given his affinity for Spain, it is perhaps worth noting that Hemingway never actually resided there for any great length of time. All told, he spent about three years of his life there—typically traveling in Spain for about a month or two annually between 1923 and 1926 (the years leading up to publication of *The Sun Also Rises*), with stays brief enough and breaks between visits long enough to cultivate what Jeffrey Herlihy-Mera calls a perpetual "honeymoon" experience with the country characterized by "euphoria, enchantment, fascination and enthusiasm" (85). During the years leading up to publication of *Death in the Afternoon,* his stays were of longer duration punctuated by longer absences—with visits of three, three, and four months respectively in 1927, 1929, and 1931. After a two-month stay en route to Africa in 1933, Hemingway didn't return until after the outbreak of the Spanish Civil War, when he spent another six months in Spain, in 1937 and 1938, working on *The Spanish Earth* and as a journalist for the North America Newspaper Alliance (NANA). After the war, committed to a self-imposed exile as long as his friends remained in Franco's jails, Hemingway did not return to Spain until 1953, when he stayed for a month, returning again for visits of a month or two in 1954 and 1956. His last long visit to Spain came in the final years of his life, in 1959 and 1960, when he spent seven months in Spain working on *The Dangerous Summer.*[2]

Not that Hemingway lived for any great amount of time in several of his other adopted homes either. He probably spent more time in Spain than he spent in Italy, Kenya, and the mountains of the American West combined. For Hemingway, his adopted homes were often almost as much places of the imagination as places of earth, roots, and stone. As he explained in a passage he deleted from the galleys of *Death in the Afternoon*—a passage he later revised for *A Moveable Feast*—"The artist, like the cabbage . . . , needs transplanting,"[3] and although he believed religiously in assiduous observation, he didn't need to live in Spain to write about it any more than he needed to live in America to write about it. Local color writers, he asserted, might need to live in the place about which they wrote, but any writer who aspires to something more than local color, who "deals with the human heart, with the human mind and with the presence or absence of the human soul" can also "make the country, not merely describe it." And to *make* the country, he builds from his self and his experience, often creating a hybrid country of the imagination, just as the young Ernest in *A Moveable Feast* transports the cold wind whipping past his Parisian café into the story he is writing of Michigan. This means that, for Hemingway, home was often as much the self found elsewhere—partaking of at least an element of projective identification—as it was a mere matter of careful observation, however vital that observation might also be.

The expatriate protagonists of Hemingway's novels have an uncanny ability to fit in or feel at home wherever they roam. Though Americans in Europe, Jake Barnes, Frederic Henry, Robert Jordan, Richard Cantwell, and David Bourne always know the secret handshake of the insider without ever becoming truly one of the natives. When Robert Cohn in *The Sun Also Rises* responds to a banner proclaiming "Hurray for the Foreigners!" by asking, "Where are the foreigners?" he may seem stupid—Bill's reply, "We're the foreigners," certainly makes him seem that way—but marked by his *afición,* Jake doesn't seem like such a foreigner in Spain (158). "Somehow it was taken for granted that an American could not have aficion," he reflects. "He might simulate it or confuse it with excitement, but he could not really have it" (137). And yet Jake *does* have it: so clearly does he have it that Montoya asks him to protect the young bullfighter Romero from foreign predatory women . . . a few pages before Jake introduces Romero to Brett. In *A Farewell to Arms,* Frederic Henry wears the Italian uniform and serves with the Italian army, yet the priest reminds him that he is after all "a foreigner," and the fact that "he speaks Italian with an accent" serves as an easy pretext during the retreat from Caporetto for the battle police to shoot him as a foreign infiltrator (71, 222). In *For Whom the Bell Tolls,* Robert Jordan's accent is of Extremadura, not of his native Montana, but the college Spanish instructor is still told that "it is . . . presumptuous for a foreigner to teach Spanish," and despite becoming a member of the symbolic family in the cave, he remains an outsider, an American *Inglés* (209). These protagonists all straddle the boundary between, or oscillate between, *insider* and *outsider,* occupying a strange liminal geography of the imagination. Hemingway's own position wasn't too different. Even in his boldest attempts to be an "insider" or "go native"—when he fibbed in his youth about having served with the Italian Arditi instead of the American Red Cross, when he established himself as a bullfight aficionado in Spain, or when, on safari in 1954, he shaved his head, dyed his clothes rusty Masai ochre, and began ceremonies (interrupted by his wife) for ritual ear piercing and facial scarification—he was responding to something in these countries and cultures that spoke to the needs of his own imagination, accommodating these countries to himself as much as he altered himself to accommodate the demands of these countries.

And Hemingway knew this. True, in a passage he deleted from galleys to the final chapter of *Death in the Afternoon,* Hemingway warns that Spain "is a strange country . . . and few people have ever gone to it to find it as they expected" (Gal to *DIA* 78). One has to observe both the country and one's own reactions to it carefully and honestly, and one who does this is likely to be surprised. Yet in these same deleted passages he writes that "the heart of a country . . . assuredly does not exist. It is only your own heart, of course. . . ." (Gal to *DIA* 78).

> As an American I know it is very presumptuous of me to write about Spain and I have avoided diagnosing her soul even though, sometimes, in the west of America you are in country that is physically so like Spain that where there

> are no houses you could not tell whether it was Spain or Wyoming. . . . You know, when you find your own country in Spain, how the Spaniards must have felt finding their country in America and you know that you share a common physical knowledge, but I am kept from presuming on this by remembering that none of my ancestors fought at the siege of Zaragoza, nor on the walls at Pamplona, nor in the streets on the Dos de Mayo. . . . (Gal to *DIA* 79)

Hemingway finds his own experience of the Iberian Peninsula to be shaped by his experience of Michigan and Italy, the other two peninsulas that he had "loved like a fool," before they had been spoiled (one by logging and development, and the other by tourism and fascism). Reflecting upon this experience, he writes: "I do not believe any more that if you want to care for anything the best thing to care for is country" (Gal to *DIA* 78). Countries change, and change equals loss. Not that this stopped Hemingway from falling in love with Spain—for "as in all such things you cannot select what you will be fond of. . . ." (Gal to *DIA* 78). But when Hemingway fell in love with Spain, it was because something in the land and the culture spoke to something deep in *him:* "Coming to Spain I found some of the things I believed in being practiced and an opportunity to observe others and in addition I liked the bullfights and the country and some of the people" (Gal to *DIA* 79). Hemingway's ability to feel at home in Spain and in so many other places was rooted at least in part in his ability to find something of *himself* in these places.

This volume gathers an innovative collection of essays that explore how Hemingway imagined Spain, and each of which asks that we imagine Hemingway's relation to Spain in a new way. Although the writers do address Hemingway's canonical fiction, challenging existing critical preconceptions, these essays provide unprecedented focus on his lesser-discussed Spanish works, which will introduce these neglected texts into twenty-first-century considerations of Hemingway and Spain.

María DeGuzmán begins the volume by addressing the "blood and soil" myth to bring multidimensionality to Hemingway's notion of the Spanish earth. DeGuzmán's essay expertly draws from Hemingway's career-long depiction of Spain, showing in particular how his Anglo-American characters experience the fruits of Spain, its culture and natural resources. Lisa Twomey follows by mining periodicals from the 1930s to gauge the Spanish reaction to *Death in the Afternoon,* and she then extends the discussion through the rest of Hemingway's life. Through an incisive reading of these documents, a clearer image emerges of Hemingway's sometimes ambiguous reception in Spain.

Russ Pottle takes on "Hills Like White Elephants," one of Hemingway's most anthologized stories, drawing from aspects of its composition to find a complex allegory of tourism that has not previously been explored. Pottle's assiduous investigation of the geography and culture of northern Spain allows the setting of the short story to emerge as thematically crucial to its meaning.

Ian Grody's focus on Hemingway's American *novillero* friend Sidney Franklin is the most extended treatment in Hemingway studies of this fascinating association and the development and ambiguity of the friendship. Grody argues that the Hemingway–Franklin relationship was reciprocal and mutually beneficial, and charts a detailed trajectory to the biography of this relationship.

Beatriz Penas Ibáñez begins our volume's treatment of *Death in the Afternoon* by pairing it with its sequel, *The Dangerous Summer.* She discusses Hemingway's return to Spain and his attempt to "correct a situation of exclusion" that would allow him to end his exile and return to a country he loved so dearly. Penas Ibáñez's knowledge of the culture and history of Spain finds a dynamic interplay of memory between Hemingway's disquisition on bullfighting in 1932 and its reconsideration in 1960.

Ben Stoltzfus triangulates a discussion of Hemingway's Spain, focusing on the bullfighting as art, the artist as a matador, and both disciplines as dealing with the inevitable specter of death. Stoltzfus expands on these familiar themes through a discussion of the French writer Henry de Montherlant, as well as the notion of Mithraism, an ancient mystery cult that engaged in the slaying of bulls as a rite of initiation. David F. Richter also touches on the violent stakes of Hemingway's bullfighting texts, using the writers Georges Bataille and Federico Garcia Lorca to invoke the *duende,* a spirit particular to Spanish culture that sheds light on the way Hemingway dealt with death and the bullfight. Richter's essay identifies life within death and explores the importance of emotion and death in Spain and in Hemingway's art.

Like Penas Ibáñez, Suzanne del Gizzo finds in Hemingway a disturbing, usually self-defeating trend in which Hemingway returns to "the old front," a scene of success or emotionally potent experience from the past, and attempts to revive that original emotion. To del Gizzo, Hemingway is essentially "disavowing" or rejecting his current age and status and reality, forcing upon himself a problematic "nostalgia in reverse."

James H. Meredith considers 1937 to be the hub of Hemingway's Spanish experiences, and establishes the single year as a key pivot to his entire life and career. Meredith's treatment of Hemingway's crucible experience in the Spanish Civil War, places Hemingway's Spanish works in a broader biographical context. Mark P. Ott continues the examination of this period of Hemingway's life, tackling Hemingway's "The Butterfly and the Tank" by placing the short story in the context of the dissolution of Hemingway's relationship with John Dos Passos.

Hemingway's political leanings are scrutinized in Scott D. Yarbrough's essay, "The Education of Henry: Politics and Context in Hemingway." Yarbrough engages in a reading of politics through an examination of Hemingway's under-discussed Spanish Civil War stories, including "Under the Ridge," "The Denunciation," and "The Butterfly and the Tank." These short stories, most of which have escaped critical attention, are also the topic of Michael Maiwald's analysis. Like Yarbrough, Maiwald focuses on the maligned "Night Before Battle" and "Under the Ridge," showing how a careful reading of those stories yield insights into Hemingway's politics and into their broader historical context.

Lawrence R. Broer's essay ends our volume with an extended meditation on *For Whom the Bell Tolls,* including his own lifelong relationship with the novel. Broer, who published the pioneering study, *Hemingway's Spanish Tragedy* (U of Alabama P 1973) more than forty years ago, reflects on his engagement with Hemingway's notion of Spain, the corrida, and death, paying particular attention to Robert Jordan, the hero of *For Whom the Bell Tolls.*

As Hemingway writes in the famous final chapter of *Death in the Afternoon,* "If [we] could have made this enough of a book it would have had everything in it" (270). It would have had "the Prado, looking like some big American college building. . . . Hadley, with the bull's ear wrapped in a handkerchief. . . . the wooden ring at Alciras where they dragged the dead horses out in the field and you had to pick your way over them. . . . the storks on the houses in Barco de Avila. . . . cider in Bombilla and the road to Pontevedra from Santiago de Campostella" (270–71). It would have had Spain—or at least Hemingway's Spain—in it. But that would be a tall order. Hemingway's engagement with Spain was so complex, so visceral, so rich. Our hope is that by collecting new approaches to Hemingway's classic works and exploring his comparatively neglected texts, this volume can help us to more deeply appreciate this engagement and better understand how Ernest Hemingway imagined Spain.

Notes

1. Many thanks to Robert Trogdon for this clarification.

2. My estimates regarding Hemingway's stays in Spain are extrapolated from Michael Reynolds's *Hemingway: An Annotated Chronology* (Detroit, MI: Omnigraphics, 1991).

3. The passages that I cite from the galleys to *Death in the Afternoon* have been previously published in Susan F. Beegel's *Hemingway's Craft of Omission: Four Manuscript Examples* (Ann Arbor, MI: UMI Research Press, 1988).

Works Cited

Beegel, Susan. *Hemingway's Craft of Omission: Four Manuscript Examples.* Ann Arbor, MI: UMI Research Press, 1988.

Hemingway, Ernest. *The Dangerous Summer.* New York: Scribner, 1985.

———. *Dateline: Toronto.* Ed. William White. New York: Scribner, 1985.

———. *Death in the Afternoon.* New York: Scribner, 1932.

———. *A Farewell to Arms.* New York: Scribner, 1929.

———. *For Whom the Bell Tolls.* New York: Scribner, 1940.

———. Galleys to *Death in the Afternoon.* Book Manuscripts No. 49, Ernest Hemingway Personal Papers. John F. Kennedy Library, Boston.

———. *The Letters of Ernest Hemingway, 1907–1922.* Ed. Sandra Spanier and Robert Trogdon. New York: Cambridge UP, 2011.

———. *A Moveable Feast.* New York: Scribner, 1964.

———. *The Sun Also Rises.* New York: Scribner, 1926.

Hemingway, Mary. *How It Was.* New York: Knopf, 1976.

Herlihy-Mera, Jeffrey. "'He was a Sort of Joke, in Fact': Ernest Hemingway in Spain." *The Hemingway Review* 31.2 (2012): 84–100.

Reynolds, Michael. *Hemingway: An Annotated Chronology.* Detroit, MI: Omnigraphics, 1991.

1

Hemingway in the Dirt of a Blood and Soil Myth

María DeGuzmán

For expatriate U.S. modernists writing and publishing between the early 1920s and the late 1950s, Spain functioned not as a well-charted colony (that was reserved for France) but as a last frontier, a land to be discovered. As I argue in my 2005 book, *Spain's Long Shadow: The Black Legend, Off-Whiteness, and Anglo-American Empire,* twentieth-century writers such as John Dos Passos, Waldo Frank, Gertrude Stein, and Ernest Hemingway, unlike nineteenth-century writers obsessed with racial origins and the physiognomic aspects of race, shifted away from a specifically racial typing of the inhabitants of Spain toward figuring them in relation to their country as land. Dos Passos in *Rosinante to the Road Again* (1922); Waldo Frank in *Virgin Spain: Scenes from the Spiritual Drama of a Great People* (1926; revised in 1942); Stein in *The Autobiography of Alice B. Toklas* (1933) and *Picasso: The Complete Writings* (1934); Hemingway in *The Sun Also Rises* (1926), *Death in the Afternoon* (1932), the script for the film *The Spanish Earth* (1937), and *For Whom the Bell Tolls* (1940); and even Richard Wright in *Pagan Spain* (1957) were primarily interested in Spain as land. Their writings engage with the idea of the Spanish land as a transforming force determining national character, temper, soul, or spirit; as raw material waiting to be transformed (redistributed, fertilized, and tilled); and, most significantly, as a medium helping them to vitalize their work. Spaniards usually figure as peasants, artisans, villagers, laborers, bullfighters, dancers, and guerrilla soldiers—representatives of a primal, "authentic" relationship to the land, if not actual embodiments of both its creative and destructive forces.

To U.S. expatriate modernists, Spain meant land, partly to compensate for their own uprootedness, and Spaniards, as "primitives" or elemental, were supposed to have an implicit connection to it. These modernists saw Spain as sacred terrain for a modern myth of the soil, a myth propagated against modernity's own centrifugal and entropic forces. Spain, however, did not represent just any soil. Historically and symbolically, it was associated with the "discovery"—the conquest and colonization—of the greater part of the Americas by Europeans. Thus, it doubled both as symbol for and destination (if only metaphoric) of the poets, writers, discoverers, and creators of new worlds, of those trying to "make it new." Spain became for these writers both a figurative and a very literal ground of experience upon which to constitute their art practices and their own identities as expatriate Americans or Americans abroad "mak[ing] it new" again. In a world already old and mapped and increasingly mediated by the mechanisms of finance and technology, these modernists went to Spain on a simultaneously nostalgic/retrospective and future-oriented/prospective voyage toward a new frontier, a "last good country," to use Hemingway's phrase.

For Hemingway, this paradoxical project took the form of a reenactment of Anglo-American frontier values such as rugged individualism, courageous deeds, ritualized battles with nature (through bullfighting, hunting, and fishing) and with the "natives" (in the Spanish Civil War), camaraderie with male companions (the gang in *The Sun Also Rises,* guerrilla soldiers in *For Whom the Bell Tolls*), and what is coded as an authentic relationship with the soil (ingesting, like a peasant, the fruits of the earth; being baptized in bulls' blood; getting covered with Spanish sand and dust; baking, like clay, in the Spanish sun). The land(s) of Spain and Spaniards became for Hemingway what the earth was for Antaeus, the giant who wrestled with Hercules and whose strength derived from his physical connection with his mother Earth. Hemingway's Spanish venture partook of a visionary colonialism. Without staying and becoming permanently involved with the country and the people about whom he wrote, he used Spain as raw material for his retrospective liberalism. In a sense, he took the goods and ran: he went to Spain, mined it for its possibilities, and left its continuing problems for its inhabitants to handle. Ezra Pound once observed that Spain was "an emotional luxury to a gang of sap-headed dilettantes" (quoted in Cunard 27). The statement is harshly hyperbolic, but with a measure of truth in it. For all of their demonstrable experience of Spain, Hemingway's "Spanish" novels—*The Sun Also Rises* and *For Whom the Bell Tolls*—can be centrally located within the parameters of Anglo-American imperial ideology.[1] Hemingway's passion for the Spanish earth and the mythic identification of his Anglo-American heroes with that dirt were steeped in a blood and soil myth dependent on Heideggerian notions of authenticity. This myth, moreover, contained resonances of the blood and soil myth of fascist ideologies developing throughout the 1920s and early 1930s, ideologies that came to their horrific fruition in the later 1930s. Emmanuel Levinas writes of the "obsessive grip" of myths (*Entre Nous* 31) and of a desire to liberate humanity from the barbarism accompanying the resurgence of these myths that sacrifice human lives in the process of transmuting uniqueness, difference, and Otherness into a totalitarian Sameness.

As I argue in *Spain's Long Shadow, The Sun Also Rises* and *For Whom the Bell Tolls* form two different stages of Hemingway's mythic identification with Spain through the dramatized interaction between the man and Spain as earth or, more precisely, soil. *The Sun Also Rises* represents the first stage of the myth and *For Whom the Bell Tolls,* the second. *The Sun Also Rises* is all about choosing one's "last good country," and I mean this in an ideologically, geopolitically loaded way, not merely in the universalizing sense that Hemingway identifies, for example, in a letter to his editor, Maxwell Perkins, written 19 November 1926: "The point of the book [*The Sun Also Rises*] to me was that the earth abideth forever—having a great deal of fondness and admiration for the earth and not a hell of a lot for my generation. . . . I didn't mean the book to be a hollow or bitter satire but a damn tragedy with the earth abiding for ever [sic] as the hero" (*SL* 229). Despite this universalizing moral, the contents of *The Sun Also Rises* are particularizing. The earth that is most revered is not just any earth, but the Spanish earth. Jake Barnes chooses Spain in contrast to his foil, the anti-Semitically debased Jew Robert Cohn. In the terms defined by language theorist and psychoanalyst Julia Kristeva, Cohn is the *abject,* the embodiment of all that is opposed to and inassimilable by the *I* (1)—an I embodied in *The Sun Also Rises* by Jake, the narrator. Finding himself in France, Cohn dreams of escaping to an idealized South America, yet never chooses to go there. In fact, Cohn seems incapable of commitment to either countries or women, or they to him. If *The Sun Also Rises* concerns choosing one's "last good country," *For Whom the Bell Tolls* is about "being there"—the choice already having been made—and about Robert Jordan, the Anglo-American hero with the promised-land last name, lying on his belly "on the brown, pine-needled floor of the [Spanish] forest" (*FWTBT* 1). Much can be said about Jake Barnes and Robert Cohn as foils, and about the significance of Cohn's various attributes: his desire to go to South America, his book-knowledge, and his abjection as a kept man and as a man whom women leave. These attributes are closely contrasted to those of Jake: his choice of Spain, his alternation between correspondence (story writing, letter-writing, and telegrams) and physical activity, and the somewhat mysterious injury that keeps Jake from being physically intimate, beyond an exchange of embraces or kisses, with anyone. Although it is Jake whom his friend Bill accuses of having "fake European standards" (*SAR* 115), it is to Robert Cohn that Hemingway attributes such inauthenticity. One might even add "fake expatriate U.S. modernist standards." Expatriation seems to have generated in Hemingway a degree of private guilt, shading into public shame. In other words, Hemingway imagines Robert Cohn and deploys all the scenarios involving him both to allow Jake a relatively guilt-free experience of discovery and to grant the narrator an authentic relationship to the Spanish earth/soil, thus giving the narrative authenticity. "In *Being and Time* (1927), Martin Heidegger defines 'authenticity' as the condition of those who reflect on the identity they acquired at birth so as to critically assess the values and goals of that identity and 'choose' their own identity. . . . [furthermore,] for Heidegger, 'being there' passively is never enough" (DeGuzmán 217–18). One has to think and act to prove one's authenticity. Hemingway seems to have constructed Jake Barnes under the weight of this injunction.

Levinas (who once began work on a book on Heidegger but abandoned it when Heidegger became involved with the Nazi Party) points out in his dialogic essay "Philosophy, Justice, and Love" that Heidegger's writings were preoccupied with a particular setting for the demonstration of this authenticity: "Whatever the case may be, he [Heidegger] has a very great sense for everything that is part of the landscape; not the artistic landscape, but the place in which man is enrooted. It is absolutely not a philosophy of the émigré[.] I would even say that it is not a philosophy of the emigrant" (117). The Heideggerian hero is the enrooted man or the man who enroots himself, commits himself to a place. And, as Levinas also observes, that place is converted into a ground of being that becomes as important as, if not more important than, any particular human being. Heideggerian thought too easily accommodates itself to the dismissal or, perhaps more worrisome, to the dehumanization of the emigrant, the displaced person.

In offering up Robert Cohn as a foil to authenticity in *The Sun Also Rises,* Hemingway conceives him in disturbingly anti-Semitic terms that echo Heidegger's. Published only a year after *The Sun Also Rises, Being and Time* suggests a broader context for concerns about authenticity and culture in the late 1920s and 1930s. *The Sun Also Rises* represents Hemingway's expression of a broader concern with questions of authenticity among expatriate U.S. modernists and, moreover, of concern over these issues within an even wider European and Euro-American framework.

Anti-Semitism (or an enactment of it which is quite nearly indistinguishable from the complex itself) not only forms the backdrop of *The Sun Also Rises* and its presentation of an authentic relation to "country"—in which Cohn's position as foil to Jake is constantly underscored by the anti-Semitism he endures—but also runs like a troublesome seam (not a mere thread) throughout the narrative from Jake's observation in the book's opening line—"Robert Cohn was once middleweight boxing champion of Princeton" (3)—to Brett's statement summing up the bullfighter Pedro Romero's personal effect on her: "I'm all right again. He's wiped out that damned Cohn" (243). Add to that Jake's reply approving Cohn's erasure—"Good" (243)—and the story leaves readers and critics with precious little room for indulging in apologetics about the anti-Semitism, the continual Jew-baiting, in *The Sun Also Rises.* However, I do not call attention to this to take Hemingway to task; not only does such an exercise seem rather futile to me more than eighty-five years after the book's publication, but also many other critics have already voiced such responses. In his 2006 article on Hemingway's anti-Semitism and the representation of Robert Cohn, Jeremy Kaye documents much of this scholarship, as well as the scholarship that actually takes Cohn to task for not more adequately embodying a white, heterosexual masculine ideal. The critical contribution of Kaye's article is his argument that Cohn's role in the book is not entirely contained in and certainly not marginalized by anti-Semitic stereotype, but exceeds the supposed predictability of stereotype as a fetish entirely necessary and central to Jake's sense of himself as the white, male hero. "Cohn's presence—" Kaye writes, "indeed, his penis [the fact that he has one, unlike, everyone assumes, Jake]—allows Jake to deny his own castration (symbolic and literal) and project that lack onto Cohn's Jewishness. In order for this denial to function, however, Jake must first identify with Cohn, because Cohn has the penis he needs, before he can reject him as a Jew, thereby disavowing Cohn's importance in the making of his manhood" (53). I agree with much of the content of Kaye's careful and illuminating analysis of the intersection of anti-Semitism and fictions of masculinity, but I differ from him on the relationship between stereotype and fetish. Unlike Kaye, I do not see stereotype in flat, predictable terms. The unsettling power of stereotypes lies in their dynamism, in their multidimensionality (which entails their functioning as fetish, if the occasion calls for it), and in their involvement or complicity with master narratives, with myths.

The Sun Also Rises participates in this blood and soil myth by denying Cohn's full humanity. He is reduced to something to be wiped out—a stain or a residue—rather than functioning as a character with subjectivity such as

Jake's or even Brett's. If represented as a person at all, he is typecast—defined by the role of the Other whose otherness does not (is not permitted to) elicit respect and responsibility for the Other on the part of the self (in, for instance, a Levinasian formulation).[2] The narrative relegates Cohn to persecution or, at best, hostile indifference. He is expendable for the sake of the cause, the blood and soil myth. Though Jake and Brett would hardly seem to qualify as the proper protagonists for the blood and soil myth—being, as they are, obviously deracinated expatriates and imperfect specimens of humanity by the standards of those sorts of myths (Jake is an emasculated drunk and Brett is a consummately unfaithful woman who wanders from man to man)—their disqualification pales in comparison to Cohn's, or that is how the story scripts the encounter between Cohn, Brett, and Jake. Cohn's proximity inspires nothing but contempt. Cohn, dehumanized by the end of the narrative into "the human punching-bag" (*SAR* 199) (though the phrase is originally imputed to Jake), is not treated as a brother-in-arms. Jake and Brett reserve that treatment for each other. Beyond what might be construed as the mutual exclusivity of the couple (hardly exclusive in the case of Brett), the narrative as a whole excludes Cohn. If, as Levinas has argued, "the foundation of consciousness is justice" and "consciousness is born as the presence of the third party in the proximity of the one for the other," *The Sun Also Rises* refuses to be (re)cognizant of Cohn in this way or to extend him justice ("Peace and Proximity," 169). Instead, it traps itself in a closed-circuit and not very happy reciprocity between Jake and Brett, the not-quite-almost-sometimes couple who ride down the Gran Via in a taxi cab memorializing Madrid and their own relationship simultaneously.

What I mean by this double "memorializing" is that, after Jake drinks multiple bottles of *rioja* wine at lunch, he and Brett take a cab ride to "see Madrid" (*SAR* 246) and savor the "damned good time" (247) they could have had together—in other words, their relationship that was and was not. Feminist critic and philosopher Avital Ronell, in her 1992 book *Crack Wars: Literature Addiction Mania,* writes at length on the use of alcohol and other drugs by writers and in literature. According to her analysis, alcohol is deployed as part of a logic of preservationist, "resurrectionist memory": "At one point Baudelaire seems to ask: whom are you preserving in alcohol? This logic called for a resurrectionist memory, the supreme lucidity of intoxication, which arises when you have something in you that must be encrypted. Hence the ambivalent structure stimulant/tranquilizer" (Ronell 5). The last scene of *The Sun Also Rises* encapsulates precisely this complex dynamic. Indeed, both Jake and Brett have plenty to encrypt, to encode in the sense of both burying and preserving—for example, all the things about which they cannot and do not speak directly, including their unresolved relationship to each other and their questionable relationship, as wandering expatriates, to any given place. But, as the title of the novel constantly reminds readers, "the sun also rises." What is buried and preserved will reemerge, will quite literally "rise" resurrected for us to behold, through the alchemical transfiguration of art (and, for Hemingway and for his protagonists, of alcohol coursing in the blood), casting a long shadow: that of the scapegoated figure of Robert Cohn.

The last actions of the novel are of the cab turning "out onto the Gran Via" (*SAR* 247), Brett remarking on the "damned good time" they could have had together, and a "mounted policeman in khaki directing traffic" and raising his baton, causing the cab to slow down suddenly and Brett to press against Jake in the back seat (247). Numerous readers and critics have read the scene as one more iteration of a phallic wish for sexual potency (the raised baton) that never materializes for Jake. Moreover, the scene affords an opportunity to inscribe Jake in a memorialization of Madrid and, by extension, Spain. The cab turns onto the Gran Via (literally, "the Great Road"), a main thoroughfare of Madrid graced by elegant nineteenth-century and turn-of-the-century buildings, hotels, movie theaters, and shops, and, to the west, leading down to the Plaza España, the plaza of Spain. In their preoccupation over Jake's supposedly emasculating wound, critics have paid scant attention to the fact that the more corporeal coupling or connection occurs between Jake and the Spanish earth, the very dust of it. From this coupling Cohn is likewise excluded—in fact, he is depicted as far too bookish (9–12) and preppy-clean (45), capable only of second-hand or vicarious living.

I highlight the involvement of *The Sun Also Rises* in the blood and soil myth to explore what might otherwise appear to be an uncomplicated sensualist's celebration of the Spanish earth through numerous descriptions of Spain's landscape and earth and through the relationship that the narrative elaborates between Jake and, quite literally, the very dust of the Spanish earth. Dust is mentioned at the very first crossing from France into Spain. At the Spanish frontier, for example, "the guard spat in the dust" (92). The white road into Spain is a "dusty" one (93). Jake's coat is "gray with dust" (96) by the time he and Bill arrive in Pamplona. The references to dust are scattered throughout the Spanish sections (105).

Valerie Hemingway—secretary to Ernest Hemingway, wife to Hemingway's youngest son, Gregory, and a writer herself—remarks that Hemingway admired painters, especially the work of the French postimpressionists and their landscapes as well as that of the cubists:

> Ernest drew our attention to his favorites and in particular to one Cézanne that had influenced his early work. He said then, as I had heard him say before, that he always tried to write as good as the best picture that was ever painted. (78)
>
> . . .
>
> Again, Ernest told me that if he had not been a writer, he would have liked to have become a painter, and that his objective as a writer was to invent with words a world as real and innovative as that a painter conjured up with his brush. (138)

Certainly, a number of the descriptions of Spanish earth in *The Sun Also Rises* read like landscape paintings turned into words, a type of *ekphrasis* or *ut pictura poesis.* Some of the descriptions closely conform to pastoral landscape conventions, particularly as structured by postimpressionist techniques into distinct planes or color fields. For example: "We came down out of the mountains and through an oak forest, and there were white cattle grazing in the forest. Down below there were grassy plains and clear streams, and then we crossed a stream and . . ." (*SAR* 93).

But the narrative is not content to propel itself forward on these verbal landscapes. Instead, it must ritualize the relationship between Jake and the earth through a proliferating set of references to the very dust or dried soil of the earth and through Jake's consumption and incorporation of its animals, crops, and fruits. Already in this 1926 novel Hemingway was attempting to find a solution to the voracious hunger for Spain and its land later articulated by the character Catherine Bourne in his posthumously published novel *The Garden of Eden:* "I never wanted to be a painter nor a writer until I came to this country [Spain]. Now it's just like being hungry all the time and there's nothing you can ever do about it" (53). Catherine makes this remark shortly after her husband, David, has stated: "They [the Spaniards] never did have landscape painters" (52), and she replies, "It's terrible to have such a wonderful country and no good painters ever paint it" (52). Such passages from *The Garden of Eden* quite nakedly disclose Hemingway's proprietary attitude toward Spain and the Spanish earth, "the last good country." In *The Sun Also Rises,* Hemingway attains this country not only by painting with words, but through Jake ingesting—eating—Spain; in *For Whom the Bell Tolls,* he does so by having the Spanish earth incorporate his hero, Robert Jordan. Jake's and Robert's actions foreshadow those of Catherine and David Bourne in *The Garden of Eden:* while they converse about Spanish painting and wanting to paint the

Spanish earth, they are continuously eating and drinking the products of that earth—gazpacho soup and Valdepeñas wine.

Edible incorporation is one of the defining features of the second half of the mythic identification of Hemingway with Spain via his heroes, a feature that characterizes *For Whom the Bell Tolls,* published fourteen years after *The Sun Also Rises.* Carl Eby, who has written extensively about fetishism in Hemingway, follows the representation in *For Whom the Bell Tolls* of edible, erotic, and eroticized incorporation of food and people, and of people metaphorized into food through the lenses of Freudian psychoanalytic paradigms. In his highly incisive essay on the perversely sexualized pet name "little rabbit" given by Robert Jordan, the protagonist of *For Whom the Bell Tolls,* to his love interest, Maria, Eby convincingly argues that the scenes of edible incorporation in this novel and other works by Hemingway are designed to ward off the fear of castration (210–11). I would add, in a more Lacanian vein, that these scenes are designed to ward off the fear of (or suspicion of) inadequacy and ineffectualness more generally—not only the personal inadequacy in author and protagonist (Hemingway and Robert Jordan) as men whose masculinity must be shored up, but also as U.S. men abroad who must ward off fears or charges of cultural inauthenticity as expatriates. These anxieties are likewise evident in *The Sun Also Rises.* Their manifestations are numerous, but one significant scene of anxiety implying that Jake may be as inadequate as he imagines Cohn to be unfolds in a conversation between these two characters about going to another country to live life more fully rather than waiting for death to catch them unawares. Cohn says that he wants to go to South America and Jake replies, "Listen, Robert, going to another country doesn't make any difference. I've tried all that. You can't get away from yourself by moving from one place to another" (*SAR* 11). Evidently, while Jake seems to be doing the same thing that he disparages Cohn for doing—going from one country to another (i.e., from the United States to France to Spain)—readers are not supposed to see Jake in this light. The narrative works to associate Jake's itinerancy with seasoned experience and wisdom rather than with foolishness and vanity. Such passages underscore how far *The Sun Also Rises* is from an uncomplicated sensualist's celebration of the Spanish earth. In this novel, the fabric of the mythic telluric identification of Hemingway with Spain is dependent from start to finish on an obsessive counter-myth: the myth of the abjected wandering Jew. This counter-myth is given concrete expression in the bespectacled though muscled personage of Robert Cohn, who is described first at Princeton, New Jersey, followed by Carmel, California; Provincetown, Massachusetts; and France; then back in New York City; back in Paris wishing he were in South America; followed by San Sebastian, Spain; Bayonne, France; and finally Pamplona, Spain, where he descends into slapstick violence.

A central irony of the characterization of Robert Cohn is that movement from one country to another typified the lives and work of many expatriate U.S. modernists and, specifically, of Hemingway himself, who engaged with more countries than wives: Italy, France, Spain, Kenya, Cuba, and the United States. Thus, who is the "Cohn"—or the con-artist, if you will—in this scenario? The vehemence with which Robert Cohn must be continually abjected in *The Sun Also Rises,* so that Jake can be authenticized or validated in his choice of "the last good country," reveals the instability of the first stage of Hemingway's mythic identification with Spain: the choosing of the "last good country" and the association of the novel's Anglo-American hero with Spain. By instability, I mean that the myth of choice and genuine association is haunted and shaken by that which has been constructed as opposed to it, by the *abject*—that which Kristeva defines as having the sole quality of "being opposed to I" (1). The "I"—or, in the case of *The Sun Also Rises,* the Jake-narrator—cannot abide the abject, cannot recognize it for fear not only of contamination, but of annihilation. The abject is the inassimilable and unacceptable part of the "I," or of the narrator. As Kristeva observes of the functioning of the abject (consider Cohn cast as the "wrong kind of expatriate," the "failed writer," the "fake," and so forth), "from its place of banishment, the abject does not cease challenging its master" (2) and threatening that master with annihilation of, among other things, his self-congratulatory narcissistic image of himself.

One way of viewing *For Whom the Bell Tolls* in the overall context of Hemingway's engagement with Spain is as an attempt to complete the mythic/legendary identification of Hemingway with Spain through his Anglo-American heroes. The narrative endeavors to close the gap or the unstable relation between hero and earth/soil that can be detected in *The Sun Also Rises.* This view of *For Whom the Bell Tolls* as completing the mythic identification with Spain first expressed in *The Sun Also Rises* may not be initially apparent because they are quite different sorts of narratives. For example, *The Sun Also Rises* is written in the first person and moves from the recent past to the present, where it stays, flowing in a forward direction without much sense of a future or a far-distant past beyond Cohn's college days or Jake's involvement in World War I, where he received his defining wound. Simple dialogues and pared down descriptions of people, places, and actions characterize its narrative. The longest descriptions are of the Spanish land, of the Fiesta of San Fermín in Pamplona, and of the bullfights. *For Whom the Bell Tolls,* on the other hand, is written in the third person, from the perspective of a selective-omniscient narrator whose line of sight is most closely aligned with the consciousness and actions of the Anglo-American hero, Robert Jordan. It is more than double the length of *The Sun Also Rises.* Moreover, the narrative moves backward and forward in much larger swathes of time than in *The Sun Also Rises,* as well as in much smaller increments (for instance, the famous "now" and "nowhere" passage of chapter 13). While the present action largely concerns waiting for the right hour to blow up a bridge, to accompany an attack on Segovia by the Loyalist forces fighting against Francisco Franco's Nationalists, the spatiotemporal range of the novel is far more disparate and complex than that of *The Sun Also Rises.* In terms of present time, the novel deals with a mere four days until, as the Russian Comrade General Golz explains, "a stated hour based on the time set for the attack" (5). However, accounts are nested within accounts that weave together historical fact, fiction, and interpretation to portray and comment on many aspects of the Spanish Civil War (particularly brutality in the name of ideals that betrays these very ideals beyond recognition). Other aspects represented include the involvement in the Spanish Civil War of Russia, Italy, the United States, and other countries, and the more global struggle between fascism and other forms of political ideology and organization, such as communism. The novel also concerns itself with the relationship between the local and the national in Spain and Spanish culture as Hemingway conceived of these. In addition, readers find extensive representations of endgame ethical dilemmas involving allegiances and killing in war, hunting, and blood sports such as bullfighting. Finally, the novel offers a significantly lengthy meditation on language(s) and consciousness (318). Like a Russian novel, *For Whom the Bell Tolls* is monumental in scale.

Yet, despite these major differences between the two novels, together they form the two stages of Hemingway's mythic identification with the Spanish soil. By offering readers Robert Jordan, a committed, revitalized, nonimpotent version of Jake, *For Whom the Bell Tolls* is plotted to overcome the inauthenticity that Cohn represents for Jake as the foil who follows him wherever he goes. Jordan performs several of the same actions that Jake does in the earlier novel. He ingests the food of Spain even more avidly than Jake; and given the scarcity of food during the Spanish Civil War, its presence in *For Whom the Bell Tolls* cannot be taken for granted, and thus its ingestion is raised to a kind of sacrament, shadowed by the very symbolic cannibalism that Eby mentions in his 1998 essay "Rabbit Stew and Blowing Dorothy's Bridges: Love, Aggression, and Fetishism in *For Whom the Bell Tolls*": the ingestion of more than food, of human flesh (215). As I point out in my book, "Some of the other guerrilla fighters [Jordan's *compañeros*] are portrayed as cold cuts: 'Robert Jordan looked carefully at the other three men at the table. One had a large flat face, flat and brown as a Serrano ham'" (DeGuzmán 219). Jordan, like Jake, has physical contact with the Spanish soil, only in Jordan's case it is not confined to dust and trout fishing. *For Whom the Bell Tolls* enacts nothing less than the bodily incorporation of its Anglo-American hero, Robert Jordan, into the Spanish earth both metaphorically and literally. Metaphorically, the fusion of his body with the Spanish earth/soil is accomplished through his romance with Maria, the young Spanish woman with whom he falls in love at first sight. Jordan addresses her in terms of one of the totem animals of Spain—a rabbit; *Hispania* signifies "land of rabbits," after all. Maria and Jordan's relationship with her are also figured in terms of land. When they make love, Jordan feels the earth move. Maria's body is described in terms of land, earth: "her breasts like two small hills that rise out of the long plain where there is a well, and the far country beyond the hills was the valley of her throat where his lips were" (*FWTBT* 341). The land described as part of a John Donne–like blazon of her body (one thinks here of Donne's poem "To His Mistress Going to Bed") corresponds to the description of the Spanish earth in *For Whom the Bell Tolls* and other works by Hemingway: hills, plains, valleys, the far country, and certain colors, such as tawny gold and red-gold. And this country (the obvious pun hardly needs to be indicated) lies there for him to claim, to merge with: "the valley of her throat where his lips were." Which valley, whether of the throat or the delta of Venus, does not matter. The point is that Maria's body is yet another site of signification for the desired Heideggerian integration of hero with place, for the enrooting of Robert Jordan.

Jordan's bodily fusion with the Spanish earth also occurs literally in that he sleeps and dies on it. Hemingway often deploys a representation of sleep or sleeping as a prefigurement of death; he certainly does so in both *The Sun Also Rises* and *For Whom the Bell Tolls*. In the latter, the robe that Robert Jordan spreads on "the forest floor" and on which he and Maria sleep in chapter 7 foreshadows his final position in chapter 43 at the novel's conclusion: "He was completely integrated now and he took a good long look at everything. . . . He was waiting until the officer reached the sunlit place where the first trees of the pine forest joined the green slope of the meadow. He could feel his heart beating against the pine needle floor of the forest" (471). Now as Jordan lies on the robe spread out on the forest floor, it is not Maria that he awaits but rather the fascist officer: as Jordan, fighting unconsciousness, shoots him, the officer will join him in death. The last image is of Robert Jordan's "heart beating against the pine needle floor of the forest" (471). He is so close to the Spanish earth that his heart is beating on it. And not only that: he is hemorrhaging internally from a broken leg, his blood pooling to merge with the earth, and it is highly likely that he will die of this injury where he lies. Even higher is the probability that he will be found and killed by the fascist forces moving through the forest, who will leave his body where it lies.

Death is a virtual certainty, an outcome that suits Hemingway's purpose of stabilizing the claim to an authentic ground of being for this Anglo-American hero through Jordan's coalescence with the Spanish earth. Commenting on Heidegger's concept of authenticity in the face of the mediocrity or, at the very least, the pressure of the group's thoughts, Levinas focuses on death or the willingness to die as the Heideggerian litmus test of consciousness against the domination of the self-compromising presence of "they" in that consciousness. According to Levinas, the departure from this "they" is, for Heidegger, "brought about by a resolved and free determination made by *being-there* which is thus *being-for-death,* anticipating death in the courage of anxiety. In the courage of anxiety, not in the fear and evasions of the everyday! Perfect authenticity!" ("Philosophy, Justice, and Love" 214). Significantly, in the concluding scene of *For Whom the Bell Tolls,* Robert Jordan is alone. He has told his comrades to move on without him, since his mortal wound has made him a liability to them, and he refuses to be the occasion of their capture or death. Not only does he refuse to allow his needs to compromise their lives but, furthermore, he does not want his care of and fear for them to compromise the actions that he feels he must take to combat the fascist forces. For example, to Maria, who does not want to abandon him in his terribly damaged state, he says: "What I do now I do alone. I could not do it well with thee" (*FWTBT* 463). And so he sends her away, too—although, aside from his decision to die at the hands of the enemy, his decision to do so is the most painful he must make.

He rejects several choices: he does not hide or shoot himself or have one of his comrades shoot him to evade the more than unpleasant contingencies of capture—probably torture and/or eventual execution if he were to survive the wounds he has already received. Instead, he waits "until the [fascist] officer reached the sunlit place where the first trees of the pine forest joined the green slope of the meadow" (471). The reader is left with the definite impression that Jordan will shoot that officer, when, ironically, he reaches his place in the sun, so to speak. And the shooting of the officer most certainly will draw down enemy fire on Jordan. The detail of Jordan's beating heart viscerally reminds readers of the intensity of anguish and anxiety anyone in Jordan's situation would be experiencing. The narrative deliberately aligns readers' sensibilities with that wrackingly fragile yet persistent heart "beating against the pine needle floor of the forest" (471). The last lingering impression is that a sacrifice is about to take place. Jordan's heart (in every sense of the word) has been laid upon the sacrificial altar of the Spanish earth.

For Whom the Bell Tolls revisits the logic of the scapegoat and reverses the formula of *The Sun Also Rises.* A scapegoat is an animal or person on whose head the sins of the people are symbolically or metaphorically placed, after which the animal or person is ostracized from the community and made to wander (and die) in the wilderness. The scapegoat bears the blame for others and is generally the object of an irrational hostility. Robert Cohn is made to play this role in *The Sun Also Rises* and the narrative extends him no sympathy for it. He truly is a scapegoat both intranarratively and metanarratively. The characterization and portrayal of Robert Jordan in *For Whom the Bell Tolls* inverts the Cohn model, however. Cohn is the scapegoat for all the U.S. expatriates who do not have an authentic relationship with the Spanish land/earth/soil. Ultimately, he is symbolically ejected from what is represented as the very heart of Spanish culture—the world of bullfighting. In Brett's eyes, Pedro Romero cancels him out. Robert Jordan, on the other hand, becomes the perfect animal sacrifice for the cause of the Republic and for the good of the Spanish earth. His foil is Pablo, the head of the guerrilla band, who is losing belief in the cause if it means his death. The contrast between Robert Jordan and Pablo is much more stable, less unambiguously drawn, than the one between Jake Barnes and Robert Cohn, in which Cohn functions like Jake's disavowed shadow, or Shadow in the Jungian sense. Worth noting is that Cohn is presented as a boxer, so it is entirely appropriate to imagine a shadow-boxing relationship between Jake and Cohn.

Even though the contrast between Pablo and Robert Jordan is more stable, however, Pablo is no small foil. Jordan's first words about him are that he has heard that he is an "excellent guerilla [sic] leader," "loyal to the republic," that he proves his "loyalty through . . . acts," and that he is "a man both serious and valiant" (*FWTBT* 10). Yet over the course of the narrative, Pablo is depicted as territorial, distrusting, cynical, cruel, and a drunkard, unable to share power when he should, treacherously capable of deserting or selling out from a gloomy disillusionment with the cause (128), and, worst of all, afraid to die and superstitious on account of this fear (250). Anselmo, the old man and the cicerone of the guerrilla band, delivers the most damning description of Pablo in three short sentences: "But since a long time he is *muy flojo* . . . He is very flaccid. He is very much afraid to die" (26). The insult to Pablo's masculinity is evident in that adjective *flaccid.* He is presented as the failed site of phallic power. Ultimately, *For Whom the Bell Tolls* equates this fear of death with the opposite of being a "good man," a "very serious man" (46). Pablo is rendered not man enough to willingly sacrifice himself. Robert Jordan, on account of his death and imminent thanatopic[3] merger with the soil of Spain, proves that he is a worthy hero and as true a "patriot" of this "last good country" as can be found.

For Whom the Bell Tolls did seal the mythic identification of Hemingway with Spain. The alchemical fusion of Robert Jordan and Maria, the Spanish woman, whose body was brown like the earth and golden like the fields of grain, as well as the powerful opening and closing descriptions of Robert Jordan's visceral contact with "the brown, pine-needled floor of the forest" (1), did, in fact, do the trick. Expatriate U.S. modernist Hemingway and his Anglo-American heroes were, by and large, accepted in the United States, in Spain itself, and elsewhere as legitimate insiders rather than merely as tourists, informants, or visionary colonialists (part of Pound's "gang of sap-headed dilettantes" [quoted in Cunard 27]). In *For Whom the Bell Tolls*, the desire for this insider status flashes across Jordan's mind as when he tells Pilar, "That I am a foreigner is not my fault. I would rather have been born here" (15). Jordan labors to be accepted as an insider. He does so through his actions as lover and brother-in-arms. Jordan's willing death for the cause of the Republic but even more this merger of man with the last good country seals and sealed the deal.

This does not mean that this mythic identification with Spain and the Spanish earth did not prompt critical reactions. In some cases, as I mention in *Spain's Long Shadow*, the dirt of Spain clung too well to Hemingway and the protagonists that functioned as his surrogates, drawing down on him criticism and jokes, including the charge that he was a "primitive" man, a cave-dweller (his character Robert Jordan spends most of his time in a cave), a bellowing bull, or (in Wyndham Lewis's phrase) a "dumb ox"—a beast with four hooves in the dust (DeGuzmán 223–24). For the most part, however, the myth has been wildly successful. The legend lives on, and to this day generates many a Hemingway-inspired pilgrimage to Pamplona, San Sebastian, Madrid, and the town of Ronda, cradle of the telluric art of the bullfight.

I have presented the two progressive stages of the myth of the identification of the Hemingway hero and Hemingway with Spain, with the second stage completing what was initiated in the first. But, one might well wonder if the success of Hemingway's mythic identification with Spain did not and does not still require both steps equally: is the jaded expatriate Jake as crucial to the redeemer/redeemed Jordan as Jordan is to fulfilling the longing for connection with Spain that Jake expresses by his gesture of running his fishing rod case through the Spanish dust? Of course, since Jake and Jordan are only characters on the pages of two separate novels, they know nothing of one another. So this question is directed at readers and those who have participated in some way in the Hemingway myth of identification with Spain. This participation takes any number of forms. For instance, there are those who have read *The Sun Also Rises* and felt a subsequent urge to attend San Fermín or visit Pamplona. Others have sought to link Hemingway's descriptions of places and events of the Spanish Civil War to physical locations outside Madrid. And there are those scholars who have attended conferences on Hemingway's work and found themselves mimicking the itineraries and habits of the expatriates in Spain, as described by Hemingway. As John W. Aldridge has pointed out, for example, "F. Scott Fitzgerald dubbed Ernest Hemingway's [*The Sun Also Rises*] 'a romance and a guidebook'" (123). Allyson Nadia Field expands on these recessed observations in her essay "Expatriate Lifestyle as Tourist Destination: *The Sun Also Rises* and Experiential Travelogue of the Twenties": "Hemingway was reputedly disdainful of tourists, yet . . . repetition of place names [in *The Sun Also Rises*] is organized into itineraries similar to those of travel guides contemporaneous to the novel. While not explicitly a guidebook, [the novel] can be considered as part of the tradition of travelogues . . . that offer experiential guides to a lifestyle, rather than to monuments or museums" (29–30). Field's article focuses on Hemingway's commodification of Paris and the codification of his experience that would allow legions of readers to easily reproduce it. A similar argument can be made about the rendition of experiences of Spain in *The Sun Also Rises,* despite its preoccupation with *afición* and authenticity.

The fact of the matter is that the jaded character of Jake, who narrowly saves himself from being just another dilettantish expatriate by demonstrating a visceral attachment to the Spanish dust and to the art of bullfighting—by showing, in other words, some *afición* and thus authenticity—is also the Jake who likes to eat, drink, and take in the sights. Jake of *afición* is also Jake the tourist, very much the tourist, though the novel attempts in many ways to attribute more gravitas to him than to the other expatriates. Readers follow and even imitate Jake the tourist and Jake the hedonist. Precious few would want to step into his shoes otherwise—into the shoes of the war-wounded, emasculated Jake who pines after a Brett always somewhat out of reach and certainly beyond keeps. For the most part, readers have not followed and would rather not follow in the footsteps of Robert Jordan, whose trajectory is far more dire than Jake's—who must live his life "all the way up" (*SAR* 10) in four short days and then die among the pines of Spain. Though many readers may have fantasized about being a hero as Robert Jordan is, most readers have not wanted to share his fate, or his fatal wound. Thus the appeal of *For Whom the Bell Tolls* as a tourist or lifestyle guidebook is limited, although it did manage to become a kind of alternative "history book" on the Spanish Civil War.

While within the framework of the Hemingway narrative Jake is not the ideal hero through which to achieve integration with the Spanish earth (and Robert Jordan is), beyond that framework—beyond the covers of the books—Jake is indispensable to the creation and maintenance of the Hemingway-inspired tourist industry. Jake's experiences provide the less daunting, more easily reproducible template for pleasurable or business contact with Spain. Unlike Robert Jordan, Jake stays in hotels, goes fishing, swimming, and hiking, and attends bullfights. He eats hearty meals free from fear or the anticipation of enemy fire. He travels around from San Sebastian to Burguete to Pamplona to Madrid. Hemingway provides a great deal of detail about where Jake and his friends reside, eat, and drink, exactly what they consume, and their modes of transportation. Though the novel is obsessed with distinguishing the real from the fake, the original from the copy, and in achieving authenticity, it codifies its rituals and makes them eminently reproducible. Readers have not hesitated to reproduce the experiences described in *The Sun Also Rises.* The novel rails against the practice of getting ideas out of books, but it accommodates itself to just such a practice at every turn. Its success as a guidebook or tourist travelogue can be demonstrated by the number of places in Spain with placards referring to Hemingway's historical presence at one time or another in particular locations.

The mythic identification with Spain by both Hemingway and his heroes needed the cynical half-hedonistic, half-stoic Jake at least as much as it needed the committed hero Robert Jordan. And along with Jake comes Cohn because, unlike Jordan's relation to Pablo, from whom he is clearly distinguished by the end of the novel and who forms no part of the Robert Jordan–Maria couple, Cohn—that much disliked and yet somewhat envied wealthy cosmopolitan—is with Brett and Jake in their imaginations to the end of *The Sun Also Rises.* On the final five pages of the novel, as Jeremy Kaye has remarked (53–54), they are still preoccupied with Cohn and whatever failures and abjections he represents in the face of their own rather conventional desires for fulfillment and authenticity. Hence, Brett may claim, "I'm all right again. He's [the bullfighter Pedro Romero] wiped out that damn Cohn" (*SAR* 243), but actually the Cohn specter remains, or no such exorcising statement would be necessary. What does the specter of Cohn represent to Jake and to Brett? To Jake, Cohn seems to represent failed manhood and yet also masculinity that might, or perhaps even has, usurped his. After all, despite various failings, Cohn did have an affair with Brett, against which Jake's highly ambiguous relationship with her stands in painful contrast. For Brett, Cohn represents failed romance. He fell in love with her and "his tennis game went all to pieces" (45). She never fell in love with him. His existence in her life underscores her penchant for not loving the men she can have and who she permits to keep her with their money until she discards them—Count Mippipopolous (53), Mike Campbell, Cohn himself—and for falling in love with men she knows from the outset that she cannot have or will not retain: Jake and Pedro Romero.[4] For Brett, Cohn attests to her banal compromises with life, her weary worldliness, her inability to choose what she really desires, perhaps even her inability to wholeheartedly *want* her desire in the way that Pedro Romero displays his profound *afición*, his passion.

Notes

This essay is dedicated to my friend and colleague Linda Wagner-Martin for her suggestion that I attend and present at the 12th International Hemingway Conference in Malaga and Ronda, Spain, June 25–30, 2006. I thank her and the people I met there for a memorable time. As the title indicates, I wish this essay to serve as a continuation of and companion piece to the section on Hemingway in the chapter "Sacred Bulls of Modernism" from my book *Spain's Long Shadow: The Black Legend, Off-Whiteness, and Anglo-American Empire.*

1. For a detailed explanation of this, see *Spain's Long Shadow.*

2. I maintain that "typecast" or "stereotype" and the psychocultural emotional ambivalence to which one is subject as someone else's fetish are not mutually exclusive roles and can work in tandem with one another.

3. Here I allude to William Cullen Bryant's poem "Thanatopsis."

4. Whether Brett has ever fallen in love with Jake remains unclear throughout the narrative. Despite all her affairs, she clearly feels some kind of passion for him and she returns to him intermittently. Early on in the story, she says to Jake, "Love you? I simply turn all to jelly when you touch me" (*SAR* 26).

Works Cited

Aldridge, John W. "Afterthoughts on the Twenties and *The Sun Also Rises.*" In *New Essays on* The Sun Also Rises. Ed. Linda Wagner-Martin. Cambridge, UK: Cambridge UP, 1987. 109–29.

Cunard, Nancy, ed. "Authors Take Sides on the Spanish War." Pamphlet. London: Left Review, 1937. 1–30.

DeGuzmán, María. *Spain's Long Shadow: The Black Legend, Off-Whiteness, and Anglo-American Empire.* Minneapolis: U of Minnesota P, 2005.

Eby, Carl P. "Rabbit Stew and Blowing Dorothy's Bridges: Love, Aggression, and Fetishism in *For Whom the Bell Tolls.*" *Twentieth Century Literature* 44.2 (1998): 204–18.

Field, Allyson Nadia. "Expatriate Lifestyle as Tourist Destinations: *The Sun Also Rises* and Experiential Travelogues of the Twenties." *Hemingway Review* 25. 2 (2006): 29–43.

Hemingway, Ernest. *Ernest Hemingway: Selected Letters, 1917–1961.* Ed. Carlos Baker. New York: Charles Scribner's Sons, 1981.

———. *For Whom the Bell Tolls.* 1940. New York: Macmillan, 1987.

———. *The Garden of Eden.* 1986. New York: Simon and Schuster, 1995.

———. *The Sun Also Rises.* 1926. New York: Macmillan, 1986.

Hemingway, Valerie. *Running with the Bulls.* New York: Ballantine Books, 2004.

Kaye, Jeremy. "The 'Whine' of Jewish Manhood: Re-Reading Hemingway's Anti-Semitism, Reimagining Robert Cohn." *Hemingway Review* 25.2 (2006): 44–60.

Kristeva, Julia. *Powers of Horror: An Essay on Abjection.* Trans. Leon S. Roudiez. New York: Columbia UP, 1982.

Levinas, Emmanuel. "Peace and Proximity." In his *Basic Philosophical Writings.* Ed. Adriaan T. Peperzak, Simon Critchley, and Robert Bernasconi. Bloomington: Indiana UP, 1996. 161–69.

———. "Philosophy, Justice, and Love." In his *Entre Nous: On Thinking-of-the-Other.* Trans. Michael B. Smith and Barbara Harshav. New York: Columbia UP, 1998. 104–21.

Ronell, Avital. *Crack Wars: Literature Addiction Mania.* Urbana: U of Illinois P, 2004.

2

Ernest Hemingway—¿Amigo de España?

Lisa Twomey

In 1953, after his first trip to Spain since the end of the civil war, Ernest Hemingway wrote to his friend Bernard Berenson that the trip had gone very well. Although the border crossing had been a bit "spooky," he told his friend that the Spanish people actually "seemed rather proud and pleased that one had the cojones to come." He went on to describe the places he had taken his wife Mary, but lamented that "she could have had all Spain, and freely, if she had not the taint of being married to me" (*SL* 823).

Although he said no more about this in his letter, Hemingway was undoubtedly referring to the ghost of his Spanish Civil War past which somehow tainted his present travels in Franco's Spain. After having shown his support for the Republican cause through newspaper articles, public speeches, and fiction, it is not surprising that Hemingway felt uneasy when he first returned to Spain. This trip could not have been that bad, though, for he returned again in 1954, 1956, 1959, and 1960, and he was planning another trip when he died in July 1961. It would seem, then, that Hemingway became fairly comfortable with traveling around Spain during the 1950s, despite Franco's dictatorship. What became of that feeling of being tainted by his past? Did the regime simply put up with Hemingway, like an uncomfortable but tolerable guest? Did Spain's government and people truly bear no hard feelings toward Hemingway about his participation in or writings on their civil war? What did the Spanish people really think of having Hemingway back in their country?

This paper tries to answer these questions by reviewing a series of articles on Hemingway that appeared in the Spanish press, particularly during the

Franco years (1939–75) but also in the decades preceding his dictatorship. The Spain of the 1920s and 1930s was drastically different from postwar Spain, and Hemingway's relationship with the country had to adapt to the changing times and politics. Analyzing the words and images of Spanish journalists and critics allows us to define more accurately the author's relationship with the country throughout these years. Although Hemingway learned a great deal about Spain's language, people, history, and culture during his travels there in the 1920s and 1930s, his focus during these trips was above all on the bullfight. The writer was known in taurine circles and his face was familiar to those attending the corridas, but his literary reputation in the country was practically nonexistent. No Spanish publishing company chose to translate any of Hemingway's early works during these years (not even those set in Spain),[1] and Spanish critics paid little attention to his growing international literary fame. The author belonged, it seemed, to the world of matadors and muletas.

It is therefore not surprising that, in 1933, it was Hemingway's treatise on the bullfight, *Death in the Afternoon* (published a year earlier in the United States) that finally stirred up some interest in his publications. Although this book would not be published in Spain until 1968 (LaPrade 151), several bullfighting critics in Spain had read the treatise and praised it in articles appearing, for the most part, in newspapers and bullfighting journals. In September 1933, for example, Rafael Hernández published the article "Míster Ernest Hemingway, el amigo de España" in the newspaper *La libertad.* The commentary does not say much about Hemingway's recent book, but rather focuses on his success as a writer and his great love for Spain and the bullfight. Regarding *Death in the Afternoon,* the journalist declares: "The Spanish people are indebted to him. The work he has undertaken to combat the errors and legends invented about the bullfight outside of Spain is more than enough reason for us to be grateful to him" (7). Another critic, Tomás Orts-Ramos, declared in an April 1933 article that *Death in the Afternoon* was "admirable . . . the best book [on bullfighting] written by a foreigner that I have ever read" (4). An anonymous critic from the daily paper *El Sol* praised the profound meaning inherent in the treatise and also affirmed Hemingway's expertise on bullfighting: "Hemingway knows all there is to know about bullfighting, and he adores Spain and describes her passionately" ("*Death in the Afternoon*" 2).

It is clear, given these statements, that before the Spanish Civil War Hemingway was indeed considered "el amigo de España" (the friend of Spain) that Hernández declared him to be, at least in the bullfighting world: here his treatise was applauded and his love for Spain appreciated and praised. However, the general silence of literary critics and publishers indicates that, although Hemingway had made a name for himself among aficionados of the bullfight, others in Spain were not as eager to get to know his works.[2] The lack of attention given to his novels and short stories was very likely a reaction to his almost exclusive interest in the bullfight when visiting Spain and his apparent ignorance of or indifference to the turmoil in the country in the years leading up to the civil war.

When war did break out, however, Hemingway soon demonstrated his concern for the suffering republic and for the well-being of the Spanish people. His loyalty to the Second Spanish Republic was not overlooked by the news media, as is evident in José Delgado's article "Dos camaradas de América: Hemmingway [sic] y John Dos Passos," which appeared in the daily paper *Ahora* in April 1937. This commentary illustrates how Hemingway was portrayed by the press (and therefore perceived by the Spanish people) in the middle of the war.

Without even reading Delgado's article, several things stand out. First, the pictures that the editors selected sharply contrast the two men: a fierce-looking Hemingway stares defiantly at the reader, while in another photo Dos Passos looks civilized and amiable in a suit and tie. By choosing a "tough guy" picture of Hemingway, the editors evidently preferred to highlight this legendary aspect of the writer's persona: this is the Hemingway that hunts lions and survives severe injuries in war, not the Hemingway that spends hours bent over sheaves of paper in an effort to write one true sentence. Second, Hemingway's last name is spelled incorrectly throughout the piece, and in the caption under his picture he is even referred to as "John Hemmingway." Such errors illustrate how little he was known in Spanish literary circles at this time: nobody was reading Hemingway and nobody was writing about him either; he was known for the adventures he led and because his name was repeated in bullfighting circles, but not because his works had made an impact on the Spanish literary scene. The headline of the article is also revealing, as it states "Two American Comrades." The author is again depicted as a comrade and friend of Spain: in 1933 he was seen as a friend of bullfighting aficionados; by 1937, he is considered a friend and ally of Republican Spain. Throughout the article Delgado describes what he calls Hemingway's "great and unselfish love" for the country (8).

Two years later the Republican army had been defeated and Franco was ruling the country. The censorship begun during the war continued in the postwar period, and the new government soon published a list of authors whose works were prohibited in Spain. Not surprisingly (especially considering his image as a Republican comrade in 1937), Hemingway's name appeared on the list (Villanueva 10).

This ban on his books was not very serious, however, for just a few years later, in 1946 and 1948, respectively, *The Torrents of Spring* and *The Sun Also*

Rises appeared in Spanish bookshops.[3] While it is unclear why these two books were chosen for publication at this time, it is worth noting that they were published in the same years in which Franco's government began making efforts to befriend Western countries after the end of World War II. The dictator was acutely aware of Spain's need for affluent allies and financial aid to make it through the difficult postwar years, and in an attempt to appear more open and democratic to foreign governments—thus attracting their support—the regime relaxed some of its oppressive practices, including censorship. As Douglas LaPrade states in his book *La censura de Hemingway en España,* "Spain's desire to attract tourism and foreign investors allowed censors to be more indulgent" (8). LaPrade goes further, linking the 1948 Spanish publication of *The Sun Also Rises* to Franco's plan to improve his image with the U.S. government: "Recognizing that many North Americans depended on Hemingway's writings for their impressions of Spain, the Spanish government realized that if they were receptive to Hemingway's works they would be indicating to the United States that they were allowing more freedom of information" (9). While this assertion is difficult to prove, it may have been a factor in allowing Hemingway's novels and short stories to be published in postwar Spain. Regardless of the government's motives in allowing the publication of Hemingway's early works in Spain, these publications had almost no impact on the contemporary literary scene, and the little they had was quite negative. A 1952 book of "moral criticism" (published by a Catholic priest) classified *The Torrents of Spring* as "harmful" and advised readers that it "should not be read" (González Ruíz 53). While *The Sun Also Rises* was not mentioned in that book of criticism, it did garner criticism from others in the Spanish press that was anything but positive. One anonymous critic did recommend that Spaniards read the book, if only to see "how great Hemingway's lack of knowledge of Spain" really was ("Cuatro títulos . . ." 27).

Nonetheless, these early Spanish publications of Hemingway's works indicate that, although the literary world was not yet open to his writings, things were starting to change for the author and his relationship with Spain: in just a few years he had gone from being banned by the Franco regime to having two books—one on Spain (and not exactly the most morally sound book by conservative Catholic standards)—published there, practically without censorship.[4]

Hemingway's image in the Spanish press would also change quickly, as the following examples illustrate. On 16 May 1953, a picture of Hemingway and a brief commentary appeared in the daily newspaper *Pueblo,* which was run by the Syndicated Organization of the regime. It was published the day after a large military parade commemorating Franco's victory over the Republican army and about a month and a half before Hemingway returned to Spain for the first time. The headline reads "Sobre las campanas" ("Regarding the Bells"), and below it is a photograph of a shirtless Hemingway, navigating his boat *Pilar* through Caribbean waters. The paragraph below the picture states the following:

> This sea lion is really not more than an apprentice sailor. His name is Ernest Hemingway and he wrote a famous book about Spain called *For Whom the Bell Tolls.* The bells tolled—according to Hemingway—for the Spanish people, drunk with blood, dust and hate. Seeing this photo of the writer and remembering his book, we have contrasted the tragic red picture that he so relentlessly painted of us with the picture full of sunshine from the *Paseo de la Castellana* yesterday morning; our best troops, in the midst of a packed, enthusiastic and applauding crowd. Victory was born of that tremendous fight under tolling funeral bells that we solemnized yesterday. ("Sobre las campanas" 3)

The editor of *Pueblo* thus takes advantage of this picture of a cold and distant-looking Hemingway and the public's general knowledge of *For Whom the Bell Tolls* to exalt Franco's triumph and the sacrifice that it entailed. This gratuitous stab at Hemingway, published in a newspaper that was close to the regime, is clearly a piece of propaganda in favor of Franco's victory. Gone is Hemingway, the "amigo de España" of 1933; Hemingway the "comrade" of Republican Spain is remembered, although not fondly, by those who had fought on the opposite side during the civil war.

This negative feeling toward Hemingway disappeared soon after. In July of that same year Hemingway returned to Spain and attended the San Fermín festival in Pamplona. While there, a reporter, Octavio Aparicio, asked permission to interview and photograph him for the journal *El Español.* Octavio's brother Juan was the head of the National Delegation of Press and Propaganda, and the journal *El Español* was founded by this delegation. Octavio Aparicio was therefore close to the regime and certainly aware of the power of the press, yet he depicts Hemingway with surprising warmth and praise, calling him a "famous novelist" and describing him in almost legendary terms. Aparicio deals openly with the subject of Hemingway's controversial writings about Spain, stating: "He has been to Spain many other times, although in his writings he has not always known how to depict us. . . . But that depends on how one looks at things" (62). With this brief commentary, Aparicio shows compassion and understanding regarding *For Whom the Bell Tolls,* suggesting that although Spaniards might not agree with the American author, Hemingway, like anyone else, simply had his own perspective on the war, and any controversy was unwarranted. Aparicio welcomed the author to Spain and had a friendly conversation with him.

Aparicio's attitude, which stands in contrast to the one portrayed in *Pueblo* just a month and a half earlier, presages the regime's acceptance of Hemingway in Spain from 1953 onward. That year, 1953, was a turning point not only in Spain's attitude toward Hemingway, but also in the political relationship between Spain and the United States. This was the year that the United States and Spain signed the Pact of Madrid, a military and economic agreement that formalized the renewed friendship between the governments of the two nations. At the same time, American products and culture, particularly in the areas of beverages, fashion, movies, and literature, were becoming more prevalent in Spanish society. Most Spanish citizens probably regarded Hemingway's return to their country as a part of this recent influx of "made-in-USA" products. The social and political situation of the country in the 1950s thus fostered the positive reception of Hemingway's works.

Another significant event of 1953 for Hemingway was the publication of a Spanish edition of *The Old Man and the Sea,* an event that would finally inspire interest there in the author's long-ignored literary works. The novel had first appeared in *Life* magazine in 1952, followed by its publication in book form the same year. It first appeared in Spain in March 1953, in the Spanish edition of *Life,* but this publication was probably insignificant since the Spanish *Life* was a relatively new magazine on Spanish newsstands.[5] This was followed, however, by the much more significant eighteen-part serialization of the book in November and December 1953 by the daily newpaper *El Alcázar,* which also printed a glowing review. The fact that any newspaper wanted to dedicate so much time and space to Hemingway is remarkable, but far more so is that it happened in this particular daily, since *El Alcázar* was an extremely conservative, Catholic paper of the far right that shared the Franco Regime's ideals. Its publication of *The Old Man and the Sea* confirms what Octavio Aparicio's July article already seemed to indicate: official sectors of Spain were anxious to welcome Hemingway and his works to the country.

The Old Man and the Sea was the perfect novel for doing just that. Santiago, the title character, is a model of honor, dignity, and hard work, someone readers will admire regardless of their varying political, religious, or ideological points of view. His story of suffering and losing—yet without being defeated—was perfect for battle-weary Spain, which had also suffered many hardships and losses but remained proudly standing. Moreover, the Christian symbolism that Hemingway used to depict Santiago appealed to the more Catholic sector of the regime that had been so critical of *Torrents of Spring*. The government censors could not object to its publication, and critics both far from and close to the regime could only praise this book, immensely enhancing Hemingway's literary reputation in Spain.

Hemingway's 1954 Nobel Prize was covered extensively in the Spanish press and literary journals, which likewise improved his image in the country.[6] Nevertheless, some in Spain still disapproved of Hemingway's civil war past—not so much his participation in the war as his fictitious depiction of it in *For Whom the Bell Tolls*.[7] Although in 1954 Spanish readers still scarcely knew Hemingway's novels and short stories, many had heard unfavorable rumors of this book. Critics reacted differently to the Spanish Civil War novel: while some accepted it without problems and a few even praised it, others needed to express their discontent before they were able to accept other Hemingway works. For example, in 1954, the critic Alberto Clavería wrote an article full of praise for *The Old Man and the Sea*, yet in alluding to *For Whom the Bell Tolls*, he added, "Let's forget [*For Whom the Bell Tolls*], fellow Spaniards. For if we don't, we will not be able to speak well of Hemingway" (1).

Critic Víctor de la Serna took a similar approach in a 1954 article. Although he devoted most of the piece to *The Old Man and the Sea*, before praising this novel, de la Serna considered *For Whom the Bell Tolls*: "We forgive him for everything in the book, for the 'democratic' vulgarity, the historic falseness, now let's forget about it. (And he, if he hasn't already forgotten, would like to forget *For Whom the Bell Tolls*, 'a book I would not write if I had to do it over again,' as Hemingway said last spring . . . when he was in Madrid)" (23). While it is doubtful if Hemingway said these exact words, de la Serna's inclusion of this quote in his article is telling. Hard feelings concerning Hemingway's writings on the war evidently still existed among Spaniards, but they were still willing (even eager) to forgive and forget. This willingness was most likely spurred by Hemingway's friendly visits to Spain in recent months, as well as by admiration for *The Old Man and the Sea*, an admiration so profound that it broke down the Spanish animosity for his work created by *For Whom the Bell Tolls*.[8]

These articles (and many not mentioned here, as more than twenty commentaries on Hemingway were published in Spain in 1953 and 1954) show that by the early 1950s both the author and his works were starting to win acceptance—and even celebration—in Spain, the country that had taken so long to publish any of his fiction.[9] These reactions appeared more frequently in periodicals close to the regime, and much less frequently in the newspapers and journals that were trying to function more independently, despite the government's incessant censorship. Hemingway has led his readers to think that he felt somewhat uncomfortable or uneasy about Spain's government during his visits to the country in the 1950s, uncertain of how he was perceived because of his allegiance to the Republic during the civil war. This idea exists not only in the United States but also in Spain. In his 2002 memoirs, for example, journalist and author Marino Gómez-Santos recalls Hemingway's supposed need to hide while traveling through Spain: "The fact that Hemingway lived in El Escorial had to do with his interest in camouflaging himself; he didn't want problems with people from the Regime because he had been in Spain during the civil war, with the International Brigades, and although the Nobel Prize gave him some kind of immunity, he did not feel safe. . . . At no time during those 1950s trips did he appear at literary acts, nor did he hold press conferences. He did not have contact with 'official' writers, nor did he want to be received by any academic institutions" (182).

Although Gómez-Santos is a reputable writer and biographer who had been close to Hemingway during his final trips to Spain (particularly in 1959), this statement reveals several misconceptions about the author in Francoist Spain. First, while it is true that Hemingway stayed in a hotel in El Escorial, outside of Madrid, in 1956, that was the only time he did so, and his reason was that both he and his wife Mary were ill at that time and preferred the fresh mountain air to the busy streets of Madrid, just an hour away. Second, Hemingway's refusal to hold press conferences in Spain should surprise no one; they were something he avoided all over the world, including the United States. He did grant many personal interviews while traveling through Spain, and journalists often commented on how friendly and humble he was, often asking if he had given them enough material for their articles. Third, Hemingway was in contact with several writers while in Spain, including the "official" writer Rafael García Serrano, who was a friend of Hemingway's as well as an active member of the Falange.[10]

Of most interest for the purposes of this essay, though, is Gómez-Santos's statement that Hemingway "did not feel safe" while visiting Spain and felt he had to hide from the government. Could this be true? A 1956 interview with Hemingway that appeared in the daily newspaper *Arriba* shows how far from the truth this supposition is. *Arriba* was the official newspaper of the Falange, the political party that supported the 1936 coup that began Spain's civil war and resulted in Franco's rise to power. *Arriba*'s two-page article on Hemingway included several photographs of the American author with Rodrigo Royo, the interviewer, at the bar and terrace of Hemingway's El Escorial hotel, where the two drank whiskey and spoke pleasantly of everything from literature to bullfighting and the war. As Octavio Aparicio did in his 1953 interview of

Hemingway, Royo showed a remarkable degree of openness and understanding when speaking of topics that could have been touchy for Hemingway. The American writer, for his part, showed no fear when talking about his participation in the war:

> "It's curious," Hemingway says, "when you were fighting against the Russians, on the German side, I was fighting too, but on the other side, and now here we are drinking whiskey and talking about literature."
>
> "Yes, things do change."
>
> "And the important thing—the *Maestro* interrupts me—is literature. War never brings about anything good, but when you fight nobly, as the two of us did, we at least have the compensation of not having any hard feelings . . ."

This conversation demonstrates that the topic of alliances or allegiances in war was not taboo for Hemingway, nor was the subject of his writings on the Spanish conflict. Royo not only mentioned *For Whom the Bell Tolls,* he even asked the American author to write a story about the young men from *The Sun Also Rises* that went on to fight in the civil war. Hemingway replied that he already had done that, as one of the *requetés* in Sordo's group was created in homage for the young men from Pamplona that had fought in the war.[11] He goes on to make the shocking declaration that he would not even have written the novel if he had read Benito Pérez Galdós first.[12] Had Hemingway read this author's books earlier, he stated, he would not have written his own war novel for "it would not have been necessary." While this is clearly not an apology for his novel on the war, Hemingway does imply with this statement that he never intended to write a politically charged novel on the 1936–39 war, but rather the story of the Spanish people's epic fight for something they believed in, and of their character when facing that fight. Had he known Galdós had already done that, he would not have needed to, for that great literary undertaking had already been accomplished. Later in the interview, Hemingway praised the Spanish novel *The Cypresses Believe in God* by José María Gironella. His admiration is surprising given that Gironella wrote this novel (the first book in a trilogy on the Spanish Civil War) in response to *For Whom the Bell Tolls,* for he wanted to correct the errors he felt Hemingway had made in his book.[13]

What kind of image was Hemingway projecting to the Spanish public through this interview in the *falangista* newspaper *Arriba?* He made statements more to the liking of those sympathetic to the regime (the more probable reading audience of *Arriba*) than to those hoping for an end to the dictatorship. His humility when speaking of his own novels and his sincere praise of a

Spanish author who had openly criticized *For Whom the Bell Tolls* (even though Hemingway was almost certainly unaware of that criticism) cast him in a new light that must have been favorably received by Franco's government. Royo's conclusion in the article was decisive: "Hemingway clearly understands Spain and the Spanish people." The message *Arriba* sends is also clear: Spaniards need not hold a grudge against Hemingway, for he was a great friend of all of Spain.

It is thus evident that, despite what Gómez-Santos perceived and many Hemingway readers believe even today, if Hemingway needed to hide from anyone in Spain in the 1950s, it was not from members of the Franco regime. Hemingway's declarations in the *Arriba* article were more likely to upset those wishing to bring back the Republic than Franco's supporters, especially since Hemingway had so fiercely defended the Republic in articles and speeches just twenty years earlier. Throughout the 1950s, Hemingway moved about Spain freely, and his whereabouts during those years were of great interest to the Spanish public.

Hemingway's notoriety was again evident when he visited the deathbed of the great Spanish author Pío Baroja in October 1956.[14] The media carried this story, and newspapers affiliated with the regime were among those that exalted Hemingway's humility at Baroja's side. *El Alcázar,* the conservative newspaper that published *The Old Man and the Sea* in 1954, published an article and a photo of Hemingway (at a bullfight, not at Baroja's bedside), praising the American author as a "humble and superior man." The article carried no title but rather quoted Hemingway's words to Baroja in big bold print: "Allow me to pay this simple homage to you, the man who taught so much to those of us who, when we were young, wanted to become writers" ("Permítame" 11). A few weeks later, this same newspaper ran an article on Baroja's funeral as its lead, with a front-page picture portraying Baroja's casket as it exited his home. In front of the casket in the foreground of the photograph is Hemingway's large and unmistakable profile. The sincere attention and respect that the American writer paid the old and ailing Spanish author was almost bigger news than that of Baroja's illness and death.

After his 1956 visit, Hemingway did not return to Spain until 1959, when the Spanish press again spotlighted his visits. This was the year Hemingway describes in *The Dangerous Summer,* and a few newspapers closely followed Hemingway's travels. *Pueblo,* especially, gave all the details on the writer's bill clip being robbed in the Murcia bullring, and helped turn this rather trivial incident into the short-lived Premio Hemingway de Periodismo, the Hemingway Award for Journalism. *El Alcázar* likewise followed Hemingway's movements around Spain, almost to the point of being ridiculous. One paparazzi-style article, for example, included five photographs of Hemingway on one evening in different parts of Madrid, with the headline "Hemingway said goodnight to Ordóñez, then he drank tequila, and afterwards he had dinner in private" ("Hemingway se despidió" last page).

In August 1959, Hemingway witnessed a young girl being hit by a car in the small town of Aranjuez. The swift and caring way Hemingway tended to the girl prompted considerable comment in the newspapers, as well as some more extensive reflection. The writer Daniel Sueiro, for example, published a full-page commentary on this incident in the Catholic and monarchic newspaper *ABC*. The title of his article, "Hemingway, or Solidarity," is telling. Sueiro praises the writer's humility and humanity as he stooped to pick up the hurt girl, and depicted his simple and instinctive gesture as representative of Hemingway's life and works, with their profound meaning. After reflecting on these things, Sueiro concludes that in both Hemingway's fiction and his life "the value of human solidarity and human love will live on" (5). A few years earlier it would have been impossible to find this kind of statement about Hemingway or his fiction in the Spanish press. Sueiro's reflections, however, are based on the Hemingway of *The Old Man and the Sea*, the more recent Hemingway that Spain had again adopted as a close friend.

Spain's renewed openness to Hemingway in the 1950s, however suffered a setback after the Spanish publication of *The Dangerous Summer* in the fall of 1960, a book that provoked a fierce response in the Spanish press. Virtually no Spanish journalist or critic defended Hemingway's unfavorable comments about the matador Manolete and the tricks that he supposedly performed, although some did urge the public not to make such a big deal out of a foreigner's viewpoint on something so Spanish as the bullfight. As critic Mariano Tudela stated, Hemingway was "head-over-heels in love with everything Spanish" and, blinded by his love, he sometimes made mistakes when writing. But, Tudela concludes, "he made mistakes always with and for the sake of love, which is a beautiful way to be mistaken" (7). Tudela's opinion was not shared by all, however; many writers published articles describing what bullfighting critic Juan León called "the unjustified and unjust" way Hemingway viewed Manolete and *toreo* in general (23).[15]

The shock of Hemingway's death in July 1961, less than a year later, in some ways reconciled those upset about his assertions in *The Dangerous Summer*. Newspapers, magazines, and taurine and literary journals all published commentaries, reflections, photos, and critiques of the author's life and works. Some headlines pointed to how close the Spanish people felt to Hemingway at this time. *Arriba*, the daily paper of the Falange, for example, ran a story entitled "An admirer of Spain has died" ("Ha muerto . . ." 9). Another conservative newspaper, *ABC,* declared in bold print that readers should remember Hemingway "moved by how much he loved Spain and the Spanish people" (Massip 39). The author's relationship with the country had become something to be proud of, and the numerous articles that appeared immediately after his death and in the following months attest to reciprocal Spanish affection and respect for Hemingway.[16]

One article even used Hemingway's sincere love for Spain as propaganda. On 15 July 1961, the newspaper *ABC* published a front-page article on Hemingway, written by the priest Padre Félix García, entitled "País para vivir" ("A country to live in"). García took this title from a statement Hemingway had made the year before after having been falsely reported dead at the Málaga bullring. After the confusion had been cleared up, the author declared that he would not die in Spain, for Spain was "a country to live in." Padre García takes advantage of this clever comment not to praise Hemingway so much as to criticize the Spanish writers and intellectuals who were always complaining about the country and its problems, claiming it unfit for living. Hemingway's comment, says García, "stems from a personal feeling, a lived experience. For it is possible that it was in Spain that he felt the most passion and joy for life. And thus he proclaimed it out loud, like a challenge to so many 'anguished' and resentful Spaniards who claim over and over again that Spain is a disgusting country where they cannot live because they lack air and have an abundance of impertinence." (1). Speaking further of these discontented Spaniards who envy the freedom and "well-being" of people living in other countries, García ironically contrasts them to all the foreign writers and intellectuals, Hemingway among them, who come to Spain because they are "tired of their 'well-being' and of their mechanized lives and of their useless freedom . . . and they discover that Spain has large reserves of joy, of spirit, of something untainted and undeniable" (1). That something undeniable, asserts García, is a simple life of faith, for people never live better than when they know they will have a "decent death." Hemingway's earlier statement is thus used to exalt the religiosity of Franco's Spain. While some considered the regime's close ties to the Catholic Church to be a limitation of freedom, García uses Hemingway's words to support his contention that this is actually the way to freedom. It is curious that just eight years earlier, in 1953, *Pueblo* had used Hemingway's picture to disparage the writer in a propagandistic piece in favor of the regime. Now, in 1961, the author is again being used as propaganda, but this time by celebrating Hemingway's love of Spain and using it to support Franco's Spain. As Royo said to Hemingway in his 1956 interview, "things do change."

What all of these articles illustrate is an incredible change in how Hemingway was perceived in Spain over the years and by whom he was praised or condemned. Portions of the Spanish press nearly always portrayed him as a friend of Spain—but different portions of the press at different times portrayed him as a friend of different sectors or even "sides" of Spain. In the 1930s, given the almost complete lack of attention given to his works, he was primarily seen as a friend of bullfighting aficionados but not of the literary world. During the Spanish Civil War, he was seen as a comrade and friend of the Republic and its supporters. As a result, in the early years of the Franco dictatorship, Hemingway was viewed as a potential enemy of the regime, a perception that caused his books to be banned and his person to be mocked or criticized in the press. In the late forties, though, Spain began to change politically and open itself to the outside world. As a result, Hemingway returned to the country and, from 1953 until his death in 1961, the writer again came to be considered by the press as an admirer of Spain and a friend to all, especially those close to the government.

The fact that in less than fifteen years perceptions of Hemingway shifted from his being regarded as an ally of the Republic to his being celebrated as a champion of Spain, at least by some periodicals closest to the Franco regime, is perhaps not all that surprising. The American author realized that Spain had changed, and by accepting the country for what it had come to be, he gained the freedom to visit its cities and travel the countryside he so loved. Hemingway never spoke out against Franco's dictatorship, nor did he ally himself with exiled Republicans still hoping to bring about a return to democracy. Franco's regime, for its part, recognized that simply by visiting Spain Hemingway had the power to improve Spain's image both at home and abroad, as pictures of him and news of his travels spread the word that the country was open to tourists and worth visiting. The articles that appeared in the Spanish press, particularly in those periodicals favoring the regime, did much more than tolerate Hemingway's presence; they reveled in it.

The question remains: Did members or representatives of the Franco regime consciously decide to use Hemingway's visits as propaganda? It seems unlikely. The extensive coverage of the writer in the Spanish press was part of a general effort by Spain to open itself to Western countries after World War II and to welcome foreign culture, music, food, and people. Hemingway made it easy for the dictatorship by happily granting personal interviews at bullfights and bars, always smiling when a camera was pointed at him, and never speaking out against the regime or remembering unpleasant events from the war. It is evident that the more Hemingway praised Spain, the more the media close to the government wanted to cover his visits.

Thus, while Hemingway's return to Spain in 1953 probably was quite "spooky" for him at first, it is clear that very little of his past "tainted" his experiences in Spain from 1953 to his death in 1961. On the contrary, he was welcomed by almost all as a friend to Spain, and his past was either understood or forgiven—even forgotten—by those who could have taken offense from his novels or actions in the civil war. The author's silence with respect to the continuing dictatorship of Francisco Franco could even have been perceived of as approval, a fact that certainly delighted the regime and alienated those still working, in exile or in secret, to bring democracy back to Spain.

Notes

1. There is one exception, however. José Janés published *The Torrents of Spring* in the Catalan language in 1937, in the midst of the Spanish Civil War. It certainly had a small reading public, limited to Catalan speakers living in Barcelona. For more on this publication, see Douglas LaPrade's *La censura de Hemingway en España.*

2. One critic did write on Hemingway in the literary journal *Revista de Occidente,* but his article was a review of a single work, *Death in the Afternoon.* See Lino Novas Calvo, "Dos escritores norteamericanos," *Revista de Occidente.*

3. *The Torrents of Spring* was published in one volume with "The Undefeated." The inclusion of this short story, which takes place in Spain, is curious, as it has nothing to do with the novel.

4. The censor recommended only one deletion on one page in the novel, but since the text is not in the archive it is unclear what the recommendation was. It also is not clear whether or not the publisher followed the censor's directions to delete the line(s).

5. *Life* magazine initiated publication of a Spanish edition only in January 1953, and Hemingway's novel appeared in the issue of 30 March.

6. Although his Nobel Prize incited an enormous number of articles about Hemingway and his works, it was above all *The Old Man and the Sea* that prompted Spanish critics to recognize and accept Hemingway's literary talent. Already in 1953, before the Nobel Prize was announced, critics were starting to pay attention to Hemingway, always praising his most recent novel.

7. At this time in Spain, little to no mention was made of his war dispatches and they seemed to be unknown by all. This was certainly to Hemingway's benefit.

8. For more information on the reception of *For Whom the Bell Tolls* in postwar Spain, see Twomey, "Taboo."

9. In countries such as France, Germany, Norway, and Sweden, readers were able to find Hemingway's stories and novels in translation as early as the late 1920s.

10. Another mistake made by Gómez-Santos is his assertion that Hemingway was in Spain as a part of the International Brigades when in reality he was a war correspondent. It is possible that in conversation Hemingway led Gómez-Santos to believe he had fought in the war, as the two knew each other rather well in the late 1950s. Hemingway himself may also have given Gómez-Santos the idea that he was being watched by Franco's regime, or that he needed to be careful while traveling through Spain.

11. Hemingway misspoke when referring to the *requeté.* A *requeté* was a Carlist volunteer from Navarra on the Nationalist side of the war (not the Loyalist), and El Sordo's group was for the Republic. The mistake is not important, as Hemingway was simply speaking casually in a friendly interview. In mentioning a *requeté,* Hemingway could have been referring to the cavalryman that rode into camp and was shot by Jordan (*FWTBT* 302).

12. He is referring to the nineteenth-century Spanish author's *Episodios Nacionales,* which is a collection of forty-six historical novels on Spain.

13. In a 1952 article, José María Gironella stated that he wrote his novels on the war in response not only to Hemingway's novel but also to those of Malraux, Koestler, and Bernanos. See the author's comments in the 1 October 1952 issue of *Correo Literario.* As this article was published in a little-known Spanish literary journal a year before Hemingway returned to Spain, it is not likely that he was aware of Gironella's statement. *The Cypresses Believe in God* was an international success, and Hemingway could have read the book in Spanish or in the 1955 English translation published by Alfred A. Knopf (New York). According to Brasch and Sigman, Hemingway did own a copy of this book (145).

14. Rodrigo Royo's interview with Hemingway appeared in *Arriba* on 5 October 1956, and commentaries on Hemingway's visit to Baroja appeared in the press on and around 13 October of that year.

15. Journalists', aficionados', and critics' reaction to Hemingway's story was enormous, so much so that it is impossible to review in this article. For more details on the reception of *The Dangerous Summer* in Spain, see Lisa A. Twomey's book *Hemingway en la crítica y ficción españolas de posguerra.*

16. Around sixty articles appeared in the Spanish media in the weeks and months following Hemingway's death.

Works Cited

Aparicio López, Octavio. "¡Corre, que te cogen!" *El Español* 19–25 July 1953: 60–63.

Brasch, James D., and Joseph Sigman. *Hemingway's Library: A Composite Record.* New York: Garland, 1981.

Clavería, Alberto. "Arte y artesanía en Hemingway." *Correo Literario* 1 Feb. 1954: 1, 14.

"Cuatro títulos, cuatro autores . . . Hemingway." *Triunfo* 6 Oct. 1948: 27.

"*Death in the Afternoon.*" *El Sol* 30 Mar. 1933: 2.

Delgado, José. "Dos camaradas de América: Hemmingway y John Dos Passos." *Ahora* 25 Apr. 1937: 11, 8.

García, Padre Félix. "País para vivir." *ABC* 15 July 1961: 1.

Gómez-Santos, Marino. *La memoria cruel.* Madrid: Espasa-Calpe, S.A., 2002.

González Ruíz, Nicolás. *6.000 novelas: Crítica moral y literaria.* Madrid: Acción Católica, 1952.

"Ha muerto un admirador de España." *Arriba* 4 July 1961: 9.

Hemingway, Ernest. *Ernest Hemingway: Selected Letters, 1917–1961.* Ed. Carlos Baker. New York: Charles Scribner's Sons, 1981.

"Hemingway se despidió de Ordóñez. . . ." *El Alcázar* 18 May 1959: last page.

Hernández, Rafael. "Míster Ernest Hemingway, el amigo de España." *La Libertad* 24 Sept. 1933: 7.

LaPrade, Douglas. *La Censura de Hemingway en España.* Salamanca: Ediciones de la Universidad de Salamanca, 1991.

León, Juan. "Sin salir del burladero." *Arriba* 10 Nov. 1960: 23.

Massip, José María. "A Hemingway le tendremos que recordarlo conmovidos por lo que amó a España y a los españoles." *ABC* 4 July 1961: 39.

Novas Calvo, Lino. "Dos escritores norteamericanos (Hemingway y Faulkner)." Review of *Death in the Afternoon* by Ernest Hemingway. *Revista de Occidente* Jan. 1933: 92 –103.

Orts-Ramos, Tomás. "Ernest Hemingway: *Death in the Afternoon.*" Review. *La Fiesta Brava* 7 Apr. 1933: 3–4.

"Permítame que le rinda este sencillo homenaje a usted. . . ." *El Alcázar* 13 Oct. 1956: 11.

Royo, Rodrigo. "Las pequeñas confesiones de Hemingway." *Arriba* 5 Oct. 1956.

Serna, Víctor de la. "'Papa' no volvería a escribir *Por quién doblan las campanas.*" *Ateneo* 15 Nov. 1954: 22–23.

"Sobre las campanas." *Pueblo* 16 May 1953: 3.

Sueiro, Daniel. "Hemingway o la solidaridad." *ABC* 19 Aug. 1959: 5.

Twomey, Lisa A. *Hemingway en la crítica y en la ficción de la España de postguerra.* Valencia: Universitat de València, 2012.

———. "Taboo or Tolerable? Hemingway's *For Whom the Bell Tolls* in Postwar Spain." *Hemingway Review* 30.2 (2011): 54–72.

Villanueva, Darío. *'El Jarama' de Sánchez Ferlosio: su estructura y significado.* Santiago de Compostela: Universidad de Santiago de Compostela, 1993.

3

Allegories of Travel and Tourism in "Hills Like White Elephants"

Russ Pottle

The title simile for Ernest Hemingway's short story "Hills Like White Elephants" originates in an untitled ink manuscript in which Hemingway recorded scenes from Spain in the summer of 1925. Written on the fly shortly after Hemingway and his first wife, Hadley Richardson, left the festival of San Fermín in the northern city of Pamplona, the manuscript describes rail travel through a station near the "mud built town" of Caseta. The train arrives to the narrator's boorish exclamation, "Look at those god-dam white mountains"; full beers are swept to the ground by an errant curtain during a short stopover; and as the train departs the station, the narrator spies a young boy sitting beside two priests and surreptitiously reading a cheap novel titled "More Man Than Curate" (UM f472).

During the spring and early summer of 1925, the Hemingways and their circle of friends lurched from one social disaster to the next (Reynolds, *Paris Years* 286–305), and according to Paul Smith, the slapstick qualities of Hemingway's untitled manuscript reveal the extent of "the relief Ernest and Hadley felt at leaving Pamplona on their own after . . . the intrigues and arguments that troubled the . . . fiesta" (205). Good cheer was not enough to sustain a plot line, however: shortly after the train leaves Caseta, the narrative peters out, and Hemingway evidently shoved the manuscript aside. It wasn't until 1927, two years later, that he took it up again, gutting the text of all but some descriptive lines from its opening pages and some time cues from the stopover, and refashioning it into a portrait of a young couple trying not to argue over whether Jig, the woman, should have an abortion.[1]

"Hills" is widely anthologized for its display of Hemingway's iceberg aesthetic, its groundbreaking use of dialogue to convey action and meaning, and its daring subject matter (Lamb 468–73; Reynolds, "Ernest Hemingway" 30; Smith 207). Within Hemingway studies, however, the story is regularly turned back on the author's personal life. The abortion alluded to by Jig and her companion, the American, for instance, is often read in reference to biographical themes rather than as the point of the story itself. From this perspective, for example, Hilary Justice argues that Hemingway wrote "Hills" partly as a private revelation to his second wife, Pauline Pfeiffer, about a separation that the two endured in 1926, during Hemingway's divorce from Hadley Richardson. This time apart, requested by Hadley as a condition for agreeing to the divorce, was notoriously difficult. Hemingway was despondent and possibly suicidal without Pauline, his mood deeply affected by the separation, which began on 24 September and was to have lasted one hundred days. Hadley relented halfway through, but by that time a terrified loneliness had taken hold in Hemingway. For her part, Pauline felt pressured to abandon her still-married paramour for the sake of her personal reputation and in fidelity to her family's Catholic morals. Even with Hadley's request off the table by mid-November, the couple, at Pauline's choice, did not reunite until early January 1927, with Ernest in limbo the entire time. According to Justice, Hemingway transfigured these desperate months in a "cross-gendered" autobiographical allegory, in which he becomes the pregnant girl of "Hills," willing to desert her present lifestyle for a more rewarding future, while Pauline figures as the American, uncertain of what to do in the face of a complex decision but eventually joining his companion in affirming the product of their love (31; 39–54).

In a reverse construction of this allegory, David Wyche identifies Hemingway as the American and expands the reference to abortion in Hemingway's life to cover not just the rugged early period in his relationship with Pauline, but also "aborted relationships with [Hemingway's] friends and mentors and, most important, the failure of the author's marriage to Hadley" (72). In this reading, Jig is everyone in Hemingway's life whom he had left, or would leave, behind as his writing drove him on. The abortion signifies Hemingway's knowledge that he had, and probably would again, let important personal and professional relationships die "before [they] had time to grow into . . . complex and meaningful life" (72). Where Justice sees Hemingway as documenting the time when his relationship with Pauline hung on a knife's edge, Wyche sees him as warning Pauline that Hadley's marital fate might one day be her own.

It may be useful to read "Hills Like White Elephants" as an allegory of another sort, however: as an allegory of the differences between the traveler and the tourist. Such a reading creates its own series of associations with Hemingway's work and life. Discussing "Hills" through the lens of travel writing may seem counterintuitive. First, its main characters go nowhere during the story. They move solely within the confines of a small railway station, and even their dialogue feels claustrophobic. Second, the story's geographic location is described only vaguely in the opening sentence: "The hills across the valley of the Ebro were long and white" (69). By contrast, the original untitled manuscript from which "Hills" was recast creates motion in its descriptions of arrival and departure and provides a solid sense of place for the stopover. Equally important, it identifies Pamplona as the point of departure for the day's travel. All these attributes disappear in the text published as "Hills Like White Elephants," first in August 1927 in the literary magazine *transition* and again later that year in Hemingway's short-story collection *Men Without Women* (Smith 205–6). Yet the fact that Hemingway denuded "Hills" of larger movements and identifying place names does little to detract from the significance of travel in the story, nor does it obscure the importance of seeing travel as a value expressed in the narrative and its characters.

To the informed reader, a sweltering station in a valley near the Ebro River and the choice of traveling to Madrid or Barcelona would add up to only one sum: Jig and the American have come from Pamplona, sometime during or after the San Fermínes. An experienced traveler, familiar with Hemingway's tastes and habits, would suspect this without the benefit of details from the 1925 manuscript. The third leg of a junction along the valley of the Ebro, with the other two legs pointing toward Madrid and Barcelona, could only point to Pamplona. Now, with the festival behind them and the heat ratcheting toward its August height, the two are traveling along the railway that descends southwest from Pamplona to Castejón and then drops southeast along the Ebro toward Zaragoza. The town that Hemingway spells "Caseta" in the untitled manuscript is Casetas (Flora 43), located northwest of Zaragoza, which Hemingway spells "Saragossa" in the manuscript.[2]

From Casetas, Hemingway knew that Jig and the American could depart west toward the interior, for Madrid, or east toward the Mediterranean coast, for Barcelona, on an express train that runs between the two cities. While the vague opening of "Hills" might locate the story in a number of places, including the area around Castejón, which lies on the Ebro, surrounded by arid hills, Hemingway's experience in 1925 would have told him that the express between Barcelona and Madrid did not stop at Castejón. At roughly thirty-two miles northwest of Casetas, it is too far off the express line to qualify as a possible location. Given Hemingway's use of the name Caseta in the untitled manuscript and the physical layout of the Spanish railway system, Casetas is the only option for the story's setting.

The untitled 1925 sketch indicates that the narrator and his companion, Hadley, are waiting in the station at Casetas for the express, although the narrator comments that "it seemed . . . much better sense" to rest down the line in Zaragoza and "go on to Madrid the next day" (UM f472: 3). If the travel were as slow as Hemingway suggests in the untitled manuscript, where a train takes about thirty minutes to cover the nine miles from Casetas to Zaragoza, Jig and the American would have been on the rails most of the day, since Pamplona is about sixty-five miles from Casetas, with extra time for stops. The drop in elevation between the cooler hills around Pamplona and the hotter valley outside Zaragoza is considerable, and in July the daytime temperature between the two can differ by as much as fifteen to twenty degrees Fahrenheit. In a letter dated 15 July 1925, a day after he and Hadley had left the fiesta, Hemingway wrote that the San Fermínes had seen "no bad hot weather" that year (*SL* 167). Reliable estimates show that daytime temperatures indeed sat in a comfortable range during almost all of the Hemingways' thirteen-day stay in Pamplona, in keeping with regular temperature patterns of the upper elevations. On only one day could the weather have been considered warm. Even hours after Ernest and Hadley had left Pamplona, the mercury reached only the low seventies.[3]

In the untitled manuscript, however, the narrator explains that "it had been a long hot trip from Pamplona" (UM f472: 3). Hemingway may have forgotten the relative cool of the hills, in keeping with what his biographer Michael Reynolds calls a period of "bent memories and loose facts, iron filings on a white page that any magnet can rearrange" (Reynolds, *Paris Years* 299). He simply may have remembered the trip as hot because he was drunk for part of it. The 15 July letter reports that "a kid whose father raised wine near Tafalla" was generous with his samples, to the point where a soused Hemingway "either lost or gave away [his and Hadley's rail] tickets" (*SL* 167). Or he might already have been shading his material, edging into fiction during the sketch with a short sentence that expressed how he and Hadley had felt once they found the eighty-five-degree heat outside Zaragoza on 14 July.

Still, heat spikes in Pamplona are not unknown. Three days after the Hemingways departed the fiesta, the temperature jumped into sweaty territory. The afternoon before they arrived had likewise been hot. Later, the month closed out with daytime highs hovering around or above ninety degrees. An experienced traveler would know that Pamplona could be at the apex of a spike on any day in July, with the result that Jig and the American might have begun their three or four train-bound hours in discomfort, in addition to whatever conditions their layovers might have presented. At the very least, that traveler would know the valley outside Zaragoza would be hot in mid- to late July. To an informed observer, heat on the train ride from Pamplona and during the layover in the station near Casetas could have fueled the couple's pressure-cooker dialogue.

The story's final version conceals these details about place and season below the waterline, in the depths of Hemingway's iceberg. But a reader with Hemingway's knowledge of Spain's geography and climate and culture would see that pause taken by Jig and the American in the railway station as part of a larger picture. The two have "discovered Pamplona," in the louche sense Reynolds gives that phrase (*1930s* 15), but the unsettling surprise of Jig's pregnancy has complicated any further plans. The abandon of carnival occurs in a short, almost hermitically sealed time span (Bakhtin, *Problems* 175–76; Bakhtin, *Rabelais* 10), something Hemingway acknowledges in *The Sun Also Rises,* published the year before he began final work on "Hills": "The things that happened could only have happened during a fiesta. Everything became quite unreal finally and it seemed as though nothing could have any consequences" (158). The revelation of Jig's condition—made perhaps during the festival, perhaps during one or two hungover days the couple might have spent in Pamplona afterward, or perhaps during the train ride itself[4]—has closed the door between carnival time and "real" time more firmly still. Now the American wants to go Madrid, where he believes he can find someone willing to perform an abortion. Jig wants to go in the opposite direction, away from the destination that signifies the end of her pregnancy (O'Brien 22–23). Knowing from where Jig and the American have come and what they have seen, the informed reader would realize that the couple unexpectedly face the themes of life, death, and renewal portrayed in the dizzying pageants of the San Fermínes.[5] This reader would understand that where Jig and the American go next marks a decision about how to absorb the sudden impact of these themes in their own lives. Quite clearly, the next stage of travel will produce lasting effects.

Even to the general reader, the very starkness of the setting—a station between two lines of rails in the sun—would emphasize the importance of travel in the lives of the main characters. Justice writes that the different tracks "presumably [represent] two directions of travel" (42), but the nature of the station and the things that occur within it intensify "presumably" to "definitively." Detached from an easily identifiable locale, the place exists only to launch passengers in one direction or another. To reinforce this function, signs of travel stand out in the couple's baggage and the story's timetable. The bags sit out in the open, festooned with "labels" that indicate an ongoing tour (76). In the story's first paragraph, the narrative explains that a train will arrive in forty minutes and remain at the station for precisely two minutes ("Hills" 69). Thirty-five minutes into the text's narrative time, the reader is reminded twice that the train will appear in five minutes (76–77).

Details in the text supply any knowledge the general reader lacks about the valley and climate outside Zaragoza. In the first paragraph, the narrator states flatly that the weather "was very hot," and the American echoes this observation three sentences later (69). Soon after, the reader is told that the hills were "white in the sun and the country was brown and dry" (70). This environment reflects the couple's relationship: increasingly uncomfortable, increasingly desiccated. Unaware of Zaragoza and its hotels thirty minutes away, a general reader sees no option for staying and arguing further about terminating Jig's pregnancy. The barroom is the only facility in the station, and the server from the bar seems more concerned with reminding people when they are to leave than she is with selling drinks. Whichever way the decision about Jig's pregnancy falls,[6] it is made under pressure, with only minutes to spare.

The story's setting is no existential plain where characters wait like Vladimir and Estragon in Beckett's *Waiting for Godot.* The ready bags, the text's ticking clock, and the story's tense atmosphere show that travel in one direction or another is imminent. From these clues, the general reader can draw the same conclusion as the informed reader: the decision as to where Jig and the American go next will produce lasting effects. Assuming that both the informed and the general reader catch the drift of the couple's conversation,[7] the story presents itself tied as tightly to questions about travel as it does to questions about people and relationships.

In fact, "Hills Like White Elephants" may be tied to questions about people and relationships *through* questions of travel. It was written on the heels of Hemingway's first great travel-based success, *The Sun Also Rises,* in which the kind of traveler one is gives great insight into one's character. As H. R. Stoneback demonstrates, the way in which Robert Cohn, early in that novel, proposes a tour of South America marks him as a shallow jerk, while the way in which Jake Barnes adheres to his "annual summer pilgrimage to Spain" marks him as a complex, moral person (22–26). In *The Sun Also Rises,* how and why a character travels, just as much as where he or she might go, are measures of that character's depth.[8] This distinction extends into "Hills Like White Elephants," where the dialogue between Jig and the American can be read not only as an allegory of Hemingway's personal life but also as an allegory of the differences between the traveler and the tourist. This distinction between travel and tourism is a central concern of travel writing studies, and applying it, as it is found in travel writing criticism, to the main characters of "Hills" provides further insight into the story and expands the allegorical connections between Hemingway's life and his early works, influenced by his travels in Spain.

Today, the boundary between travel and tourism grows ever narrower, as undiscovered or undocumented regions shrink and packaged tours proliferate. Lawrence Mintz's argument that tourism should not be "particularly suspect or socially problematic," because it "is simply another example of artistic expression, of our rendering the world as we see it and/or want it to be" (48), shows more than the capacity of postmodern theory to make meaning from destinations like Walt Disney World's Epcot Center: it demonstrates also the leveling effects of modern commercial and industrial development on many types of travel. As Alison Russell observes, those who would call themselves travelers now resort to increasingly eccentric itineraries or arduous methods to distinguish themselves from tourists, for whom even the heights of Everest lie within reach of commercial packaging (8–10). John Urry goes so far as to as to identify today's informed traveler as the "post-tourist," who understands that "tourism is a game, or rather a whole series of games with multiple texts and no single, authentic touristic experience" (qtd. in Russell 7). In the face of these collapsing categories, the travel writing scholar Paul Fussell writes that any contemporary discussion of travel sounds like "a threnody" (*Abroad* 37).

In Hemingway's time, however, the line between travel and tourism seemed broader, as articulated in Fussell's distinction between exploration, travel, and tourism in Anglo-American writing from the 1920s and 1930s. Fussell writes that the explorer, traveler, and tourist "all . . . make journeys, but the explorer seeks the undiscovered, the traveler that which has been discovered by the mind working in history, the tourist that which has been discovered by entrepreneurship and prepared for him by the arts of mass publicity" (*Abroad* 39). Each experience, Fussell explains, lies along a diminishing scale: "If the explorer moves toward the risks of the formless and the unknown, the tourist moves toward the security of pure cliché. It is between these two poles that the traveler mediates, retaining all he can of the excitement of the unpredictable attaching to exploration, and fusing that with the pleasure of 'knowing where one is' belonging to tourism" (*Abroad* 39). Fussell's definitions resonate in "Hills," as the story elevates the explorer and traveler through the perceptions of Jig and takes tourism to task through the words and actions of the American. Jig is open to what Fussell calls the more authentic experience of the explorer or traveler. After her first round of verbal fencing with the American, which begins with her observation about the hills looking like white elephants, segues awkwardly into references to the abortion, and ends inconclusively with his saying, "I don't want you to do it if you feel that way," Jig looks to the "fields of grain and trees along the banks of the Ebro," watches the "shadow of a cloud" slip across that landscape, and tells the American, "we could have all this" ("Hills" 74). Like an explorer, she is drawn to the formless and the unknown, signified by the trackless fertile side of the valley. If Jig begins the story as young and inexperienced as some interpretations suggest (e.g., Renner 28–29), then her transition to womanhood, signified by her defense of pregnancy and prospective childbirth, is a metaphor for the explorer's plunge into undiscovered territory.

But her desire is not all a wild-eyed rush off to the woods. Like a traveler also, she works out a context for what she finds. When the American says, "I've known lots of people that have done it," and the girl replies with irony, "So have I. . . . And afterward they were all so happy" (73), she reveals a deeper awareness of time, event, and causal relation, the constituent parts of history. As she moves from her statement that that the hills dominating the valley "look like white elephants" (70), to her judgment that their "coloring" is "lovely" (71), and finally toward her appeal to the life and fertility present on one side of the railway station, Jig discerns in the landscape a metaphor for the possibilities that lie in bringing her pregnancy to term. This is the intellect at play in history, rendering the raw material of exploration into an image that forges a link between the physical and the metaphysical.

A number of critical studies describe Jig's mental process during this part of the story as "imaginative" or "poetic" (e.g., Hashmi 75). More strikingly, however, her thinking parallels the workings of travel writing. Fussell asserts that, in general, travel writing "mediates between two poles: the individual physical things it describes, on the one hand, and the larger theme that it is 'about' on the other" (*Travel* 16). As Casey Blanton explains, "What travel books are 'about' is the interplay between observer and observed, between a traveler's own philosophical biases and preconceptions and the tests those ideas and prejudices endure as a result of the journey" (5). Thus, James Jubak calls travel writing "a journey of an individual perceiving mind" and argues that travel texts show "the creation of a pattern that is but a reflection of that single observing mind" (128). Even rigorously composed travel writings suffer such patterning. Eric Leed reports that, with regard to Euro-American scientific explorations, "Four hundred years of scientific travel and disciplined observation produced a history of nature that was clearly a product . . . marked by the traveler's motives and tendencies" (210). He concludes that "the observing traveler, while in passage, . . . connects all that is discrete and rooted, selecting and removing examples of rarity and beauty and placing them within an artificial world of knowledge, a world in which the relations of things to one another are precisely stated and fixed" (212).

In processing the landscape from raw material to metaphor, Jig reveals herself, with apologies to Ralph Waldo Emerson, as girl perceiving. The pattern she creates from the verdant side of the hills is the reflection of her own mind, shaped for communicating to her unreflective companion a world he cannot or will not imagine—quite in keeping with William Spengemann's description of travel writing as "portraying the world as the cause and symbol of the traveler's response to it, rather than as an independent reality which precedes and dictates his perceptions" (qtd. in Blanton 19).[9] Blanton, Jubak, Fussell, and Leed describe travel as a way of seeing, and Jig shows this way of seeing in her dialogue. If Jig ultimately concedes to aborting her pregnancy, then the terms of travel writing criticism add force to Frederick Busch's assertion that Jig "buries her way of seeing as she will bury her child" (762).

For his part, the American is surely a tourist. Systematically, he calls up Fussell's description of the tourist as consumer. He manages all the commercial transactions described in the narrative, including the one in which he is subtly talked into an up-sell, a tactic employed by the hospitality industry in which a server suggests to patrons a more expensive version of what they've ordered. In this case, the American orders two beers and quickly is talked into two "big ones" ("Hills" 69). And like a seasoned customer, he readily identifies a commercial sign—an advertisement for the liquor Anis del Toro—painted on the beaded curtain separating the bar from the railway platform. For Jig, the paint on the curtain is only "something," an indeterminate sign. For the American, however, it is immediately the sign of a commercial product: "Anis del Toro. It's a drink" (70). Paul Rankin argues that Jig's inability to identify the advertisement is feigned, part of an elaborate strategy by which Jig "outwits her boorish American *inamorato* and manipulates both the conversation and the man at each turn to control the shared destiny of her and the unborn child" (234, 236). Indeed, in Pamplona she might have seen the liquor advertised among the drink sellers, as Jake Barnes did the day before the San Fermínes began (*SAR* 150). Yet too much in "Hills" argues for Jig's ignorance on this score. She does not understand Spanish—the American has to translate twice for her ("Hills" 70–71, 76–77)—and she calls her experience with the liquor "new" (71). In fact, her unmediated experience lends weight to the moment. Like so many commercial products, the drink promises to be different but turns out to be the same, in the comforting way that tourism, according to Fussell, allows the tourist to know exactly where he or she is, because no commercially prepared experience is truly different or meaningful. Jig may indeed have the upper hand in dialogue, but her disappointment in the *anis* is palpable: "'It tastes like licorice,' the girl said and put the glass down. 'That's the way with everything' [the American responds]" (71).

Who better to know than the tourist? A growing number of critical interrogations of tourist identity question any easy divisions between tourists and residents, as well as the received wisdom that tourism "tarnishes all it touches, destroying 'authentic cultures' and polluting earthy paradises" (Abram and Waldren 1). Fussell, however, entertains no troublesome negotiations. "The resemblance between the tourist and the client of a massage parlor," he states, "is closer than it would be polite to emphasize" (*Abroad* 42). From Fussell's perspective, tourism is structured as a series of prearranged encounters or experiences that, while they may provide a certain level of pleasure, offer absolutely no surprises and therefore no revelations. The tourist/client knows in advance what to expect and when to expect it. Most of Fussell's polemic is directed at contemporary tourist culture, with its homogenized airports and day tours that rely more on impressing clients with modes of transportation than with actual contact with places or people (*Abroad* 42–45). Still, the American's knowledge of "everything" connected to drinking anise-flavored liquors resonates with Fussell's main argument that tourism flattens all experience into a regulated sameness.

Then there is the American's concern with timetables and luggage, one difficulty that Fussell says tourists face in adhering to their prearranged timetables (the other is fending off would-be tour guides) (*Abroad* 45–47). Alerted by the bartender, the American checks to see if the train is coming. He alone handles the bags, labeled with the names of "all the hotels where [the couple has] spent nights" (76). Justice shows that in drafting the story, Hemingway originally used the word *stopped* to describe the couple's hotel behavior, but later he sharpened the image to "spent nights" (47). In its final form, the phrase strikes the ear with the empty ring of coins falling, an echo of the tourist's commercial passage.

Then, too, there is the attitude the American takes toward sexual matters. A primary motive for tourism, according to Fussell, is "to realize fantasies of erotic freedom" (*Abroad* 42), a motive that lies inside the American's argument for the abortion. Of course, authentic travel carries its own erotic charge. As Fussell notes, "Making love in novel environments, free from the censorship and inhibitions of the familiar, is one of the headiest experiences travel promises" (*Abroad* 113). In his 1932 disquisition on bullfighting, *Death in the Afternoon,* Hemingway himself would include "sexual intercourse" in a list of things the traveler should experience (62). Even when sex is not on offer or at issue, a charged eroticism haunts the most sterile-seeming travel activities. For instance, of the famed nineteenth-century evolutionary scientist and traveler Alfred Russel Wallace, Leed writes that "on more than one occasion Wallace recognized something libidinous" in his globe-trotting quest for rare insects (211). The tourist, however, "is best defined as a fantasist equipped temporarily with unaccustomed power" in both commercial and sexual senses (Fussell, *Abroad* 42). Because it is only fantastical, this power ends at a tour's terminus, when the tourist returns to his or her regular social status in the home culture. Unlike the traveler, for whom erotic experience is considered a rite of passage and, in some cases, a path to attaining self knowledge,[10] the tourist does not integrate new sexual understanding or behavior into a developing life. This definition echoes in Stanley Renner's assertion that "readers [of "Hills"] surely . . . recognize that it is the unencumbered sexual playhouse the American has been enjoying that he stubbornly tries to preserve throughout the struggle over the abortion decision" (33).

A final point of identification is the American's narrow language, what Pamela Smiley calls his "repetition of key words and phrases" (9). Among these repeated or variant words are "'simple . . . not really . . . wouldn't mind . . . we'll be fine,'" and so forth ("Hills" 72–76 *passim*). The physical ease they communicate stands in contrast to significations from the vocabulary of authentic travel. Fussell writes that "travel is work. Etymologically a traveler is one who suffers *travail*, a word deriving in its turn from *tripalium*, a torture instrument consisting of three stakes designed to rack the body" (*Abroad* 39). For Leed, travel appears in the earliest Western literature in "an ostensibly negative sense," as its effect is to "strip, reduce, and waste the passenger" (6), while Helen Carr shows that writers in Hemingway's time were keenly aware of the degree to which hardship buttressed a traveler's credibility (78–83). Although Hemingway contemporaries like Evelyn Waugh and Peter Fleming questioned the need for, or even the current availability of, hazards endured by earlier travelers (Carr 78, 82–83), bodily danger was nevertheless a possible consequence of travel. Hemingway's notorious war wound, sustained in 1918 at Fossalta di Piave, in Italy, is an early entry on a lifetime list of travel injuries, and the memory of it shaped *The Sun Also Rises* and *A Farewell to Arms*, the novels that bookend "Hills."

In rejecting the ease the American offers her, arguing against the abortion, Jig draws out an unexpected valence in the word *traveler*, since its root, *travail*, is also associated with the rigors of labor and childbirth. With delivery still a chancy thing in the 1920s, an element of real physical risk lies in Jig's carrying her pregnancy through. Reynolds shows that Hemingway was especially sensitive to this level of danger. The son of a doctor and a woman "who continued bearing children until she was forty-three and he was fifteen," Hemingway witnessed once more the harrowing difficulties of childbirth in 1922, while covering the end of the Greco-Turkish War, and those experiences haunted his stories and novels (Reynolds, *Paris Years* 77). Brian Burnes adds that during the time Hemingway spent recovering from his leg wound, he read through "his father's copies of the American Medical Association journal," which contained "articles on stillbirth, birth trauma, nitrous oxide anesthesia for childbirth and hemorrhage as a cause of maternal death." Hemingway missed the birth of his first son in 1923 (Reynolds, *Paris Years* 149), but he wrote about excruciating labor and delivery in the short story "Indian Camp," published just six months later. At no point before composing "Hills" was Hemingway far from reminders of women's *travail.* Given Hemingway's close and continuing knowledge of obstetrical peril, Jig's comment on the tourist's shallow, comfortable sensibility is all the more scathing: "That's all we do, isn't it—look at things and try new drinks?" ("Hills" 71).

The couple's debate echoes off even the station's rails. These tracks are central to Justice's cross-gendered allegory, for which set the American chooses will determine whether he accepts "the weighty commitment of parenthood" (49). But the tension between travel and tourism resonates in them also. Rail had been part of the tourist industry since 1841, when Thomas Cook and Son first sold Continental excursions to the English middle class (Blanton 19–20; Buzzard 48; Fussell, *Abroad* 38; Hulme and Youngs 7). These early tour packages involved boats and trains, immediately setting siege to sea and rail lines. According to Fussell, authentic sea voyages held out until the 1950s for trans-Atlantic travel and until the 1970s for trans-Pacific travel. Each eventually became "a victim of the jet plane and the cost of oil and the cost of skilled labor" (*Abroad* 37; see also Blanton 23). Rail was more vulnerable. Always more a mode of delivery than of travel thanks to its origins in cargo and military transport, rail lent itself too easily to packaging, despite what Fussell documents as British travelers' unbridled enthusiasm for the train during a short period in the nineteenth and twentieth centuries (*Abroad* 63–64, 75, 132–33).

Hemingway understood rail's vulnerability to tourism by the time he began writing "Hills." Ted Wayland argues that regular ski trips to the Alps during the early 1920s alerted Hemingway to the increasingly close relationship between trains and tourists. Describing a winter sports world in which rail travel was essential to skiers' ascents of mountain slopes, but was also so extensive that lazy people could dispense with any climb to reach the head of a run, Wayland explains:

> The journalism and fiction Hemingway wrote in the 1920s and 1930s reveals an interesting pattern: when it comes to describing the cycle of up and down movement inherent in skiing, his earliest writing is more explicitly engaged

> with the modern technology of the rail networks built to move tourists up the mountains. Hemingway's stories written just a few years later efface this technology and emphasize exclusively the labor of climbing up the hill under one's own power. This shift signifies an increasing concern with the commodification of winter sport and a corresponding desire to imagine a more autonomous sporting experience. (4)

Wayland identifies the point of transition from more to less inclusion of rail in the experience of authentic sport as appearing in Hemingway's short story "An Alpine Idyll" (6), which was published in the same collection as "Hills Like White Elephants."

In the 1920s and 1930s, rail as a mode of travel was alive but under duress, and Hemingway's awareness of the encroachments by tourism and its sensibilities on the authenticity of train travel pervades "Hills." As with other elements in the story, the tracks could go either way: not simply to Madrid or to Barcelona, but, metaphorically, toward the authentic experience of the traveler or toward the inauthentic experience of the tourist.

In its main conflict, and even in the nuances of its setting, "Hills Like White Elephants" presents an allegorical struggle for survival between the authentic and the plastic. Fussell refers in passing to *The Sun Also Rises* and *Death in the Afternoon*—both of which prominently introduced Spanish geography and culture to a Stateside audience—as "guide book" writing, in the sense that the "guide book is addressed to those who plan to follow the traveler, doing what he has done, but more selectively" (*Abroad* 203).[11] Although composed during the same time and drawing on some of the same experiences that informed those works, "Hills" is certainly not guide book fiction. One cannot imagine wanting to follow Jig and the American and do what they did, even selectively, if the end result might be that conversation on the railway platform. Instead, "Hills" is an allegorical meditation on the explorer's, traveler's, and tourist's different ways of seeing, with the knowledge that from seeing extends choice, action, and lasting effects.

Fussell asserts that "the terms *exploration, travel,* and *tourism* are slippery" (*Abroad* 38), and despite an urge drawn from *The Sun Also Rises* to count characters firmly among travelers or tourists, that fluidity shows in "Hills." For example, the confidence exhibited by the tourist, demonstrated in the American's repeated assertion that he "knows" things, is surprisingly present in Jig's discourse, at exactly the moment she thinks like a travel writer. How does she *know* that the couple "could have all this?" She doesn't know the land, and the text insists on the land's inscrutability. According to various interpretations, the shadow of the cloud slipping over the landscape could represent either life or death or both (Justice 25–26; Wyche 58–59). So when Jig looks out over the mysterious fields, sees the ambiguous shadow, peers through the trees, and makes a positive pronouncement, can she be trusted? Or is her appropriation of the landscape simply an example of touristic consumption? Her longing, even in the abstract, can be read as a transactional gesture, abetted by ignorance about the landscape. What makes her so sure, other than her own convictions—the "knowledge" she impresses on the hills themselves—that the land holds redemption or promises life? Jig says confidently that people who take the path to Madrid end up unhappy, but she does not say that people who take the path to Barcelona end up happy.[12] She offers only her uninformed perception of the landscape and her easy transformation of it into an overdetermined sign. David Grant, likening Jig to Milly Theale in Henry James's *Wings of the Dove,* suggests that she views the "scene" of the story as an "object of desire" and attempts possess it as a source of pleasure (270). As the earlier discussion of interplay in travel texts demonstrates, this is a trap into which travel writers often fall, and it should signal difficulty for the contemporary reader in sorting the story's characters into easy moral categories.

Miriam Mandel shows that other characters from Hemingway's fiction display conflicted behavior around purity in travel. Having welded a cosmopolitan attitude onto the "See America First" ethic of the early twentieth century, Hemingway regularly created travelers who seem unusually fixed on "consumer comfort":

> Robert Jordan takes pride in his top-of-the-line sleeping bag, which provides cozy, homey warmth and privacy in a rough, mountainous outdoor setting. This self-indulgent . . . consumerism is so firmly entrenched in the Hemingway Text that it intrudes even into the Depression-era *To Have and Have Not,* where Harry Morgan owns incongruously expensive equipment—his fishing rod boasts a Hardy reel and his boat has at least one fast, sporty "hundred horse Kermath" engine—even as financial distress leads him to the illegal activities which eventually cost him his life. (Mandel 99)

In company with his creations, Hemingway stood on a troubled spot among exploration, travel, and tourism. Stuart McIver writes that Hemingway famously hated "tourism and its inevitable end-product, tourists" (90), and Kevin Maier describes "tensions and problems" that Hemingway encountered in differentiating his own travel from mass tourism in his *Esquire* letters (66). These feelings became sharply visible in the 1930s, when Hemingway moved to Key West and became a tourist attraction himself (McIver 61–62; Reynolds, *1930s* 200; Shiflet and Curnutt); in 1933–34, during his first African safari, when he sought "to distinguish his experiences by avoiding both fellow travelers and their haunts" (Wittman 49); and in 1953–54, during another safari, when it became clear that "the leisure and comfort" planned for the African outlands by luxury hotel developers would "create . . . an impediment to a real, authentic experience of Africa" (Del Gizzo 13). But Hemingway's own position as a traveler underwent an odd development during the decade that produced "Hills." Reynolds notes that when the Hemingways arrived in Paris in 1921, Hemingway privately bought and used "a general guide to the city's historic past" to counter any impression that he was a neophyte: "Absorbing all for his own, Ernest would use it as first-hand knowledge in his writing or in the presence of less experienced tourists. He himself could not bear to be taken for a tourist, a person who learned French, as his wife had, by studying it in a book" (Reynolds, *Paris Years* 9)—even though he appears to have learned *about* the French in exactly that way.

If exploration and travel are journeys in search of the authentic and tourism is a journey in search of the inauthentic, then Hemingway's nearly frantic pursuit of the explorer's and the traveler's ways of seeing would place his sympathies with Jig, lending weight to Justice's assertion that the pregnant girl is a version of Hemingway himself. Mandel writes that, for Hemingway, travel is "focused on the recovery or construction of a better self. . . . There are dangers, but the psychological rewards of finding a spiritual home are great" (101). This construction of travel certainly resonates with Jig's impression of the hills around Casetas and her desire for Barcelona.

However, if Wyche is correct that the American is more Hemingway's self-reflecting image, then the question of whether "Hills" was intended as a warning to Pauline might be expanded to ask to what degree the portrait of the American reflects Hemingway's self-loathing. Reynolds writes that in *The Sun Also Rises,* the "narrator tells us that Robert Cohn got his ideas out of books, as if books were an untrustworthy source," with the conclusion that Cohn's behavior is Hemingway's "joke on himself" (*Paris Years* 9–10).

But Reynolds shows also that Hemingway displayed a darker pattern of self-consciousness in the years before composing "Hills." Writing about Hemingway's having seen his father only twice between 1921 and 1928, Reynolds muses, "Perhaps it was not only his parents but his entire early life in Oak Park that he wanted forever buried. . . . The new Ernest Hemingway—courageous war veteran, experimental writer, veteran newsman, skilled sportsman and European traveler—was his own creation, a persona whose early roots would not bear close examination" (*Paris Years* 134). Yet in 1925, when Hemingway began acidly to outline the Paris arts community for *The Sun Also Rises,* his new persona became subject to uncomfortable self-scrutiny. "It was different now," Reynolds relates, "for he had become a part of the [Latin] Quarter, one of its local heroes. Some of the contempt of which he wrote so convincingly was self-contempt" (*Paris Years* 309). Hemingway longed to be an authentic explorer or traveler, but on some level he seems to acknowledge an underlying plastic—a trace of the American—in his self-presentation.

Mandel writes that Hemingway ultimately "practiced . . . a kind of anti-tourism, in which the traveler 'passes' as a native in the settings he visits, changing himself from outsider to insider" (93–94). Yet Fussell insists that "the anti-tourist is not to be confused with the traveler: his motive is not inquiry but self-protection and vanity" (*Abroad* 47). Fussell's dissection of the anti-tourist recalls Hemingway's motive for reading the Paris guidebook, and Reynolds's report of Hemingway's using information gleaned from that text echoes in Fussell's further elaboration of the anti-tourist's dilemma: "The anti-tourist's persuasion that he is really a traveler instead of a tourist is both a symptom and a cause of what the British journalist Alan Brien has designated *tourist angst,* defined as 'a gnawing suspicion that after all . . . you are still a tourist like every other tourist'" (*Abroad* 49).

Even in Hemingway's best-intended moments, tourist angst does seem to color the traveler's sensibility. Reynolds writes, for instance, that the American journalist Guy Hickok, a pal of Hemingway's uninitiated into the rituals and actions of the corrida, "with Hemingway beside him . . . was able to write with shrewd, inside knowledge while seeing his first bullfights [in 1929]. . . . There were stunning moments in the ring when Felix Rodríguez danced too close with his bull as he slipped the sword into the killing spot, and with Ernest's help, Hickok saw it" (*1930s* 15).[13] Reynolds' description brings out the care Hemingway took with the corrida and his friends, but it also conjures the image of Hemingway as tour guide and Hickok as tourist, or of Hemingway in the grip of tourist angst, using what local knowledge he had accumulated to shore up his reputation as an aficionado. If Hickok did write with a sharper insight, thanks to Hemingway, whose insight was it really—the one leading the tour or the one being led? And if Hemingway did help Hickok see things he would have missed, who was really seeing those things—the one who knew what he was seeing or the one being told what he was seeing? And which self benefits from the exchange—the one seeking new experience or the one protecting its vanity by proudly showing off its knowledge?

Discussing the relationship between *The Sun Also Rises* and *Death in the Afternoon,* Stoneback writes that food and wine can be seen in both novels as "part of a values scheme that one 'can get to know'" (105). Travel, too, can be read as part of a values scheme in Hemingway's work, particularly in the earlier work inspired by Spain. However, this scheme should be examined warily. The values expressed in travel may appear more clearly defined in *The Sun Also Rises,* where most characters line up behind Cohn the jerk tourist or Barnes the moral traveler. But they are less clear, and therefore more interesting, in "Hills Like White Elephants," in which the dialogue between main characters and the discords of Hemingway's own life resonate with differing and sometimes contradictory attitudes.

As a meditation on travel and tourism, on which is better or more attractive, on which is in danger or on the rise, "Hills Like White Elephants" helps mark the centrality of travel in Hemingway's writing in the late 1920s and early 1930s. Despite its differences from other works written by Hemingway during the same period, "Hills," through its travel/tourism allegory, revisits the concerns of character expressed in *The Sun Also Rises,* while the argument between Jig and the American presages the dissections of bravery and cowardice, of different styles of bullfighting, of art and sport, and of many other things in *Death in the Afternoon.* In fact, the allegorical nature of "Hills" offers a prototype for the extended comparisons between matadors and writers as artists that Reynolds identifies in *Death in the Afternoon* (*1930s* 79), a work that arguably marks a turning point in Hemingway's career and his approach to literature. "Hills" may be read as singular and topical, as Justice and Wyche argue. But, through the lens of travel studies, it also should be read more broadly, encompassing more meanings and extending further into the heart of Hemingway's work and life than is apparent at first, or even third, look.

Notes

1. For authoritative statements on, or summaries of, textual and personal sources and possible influences for, "Hills," including the germ of the story that would eventually orient the plot, see Flora (42), Koloze (117–20), Smith (204–7), and Fleming.

2. Hemingway was careful about place names, and no doubt his spelling of *Casetas* would have been corrected had he chosen to name the town in "Hills," although Flora notes that the town is or was listed as "Caseta on some maps" (43). *Saragossa* was the received Anglicization of *Zaragoza* in Hemingway's time and would have appeared in contemporary English-language descriptions of the area or on maps of Spain. As late as 1963, two years after Hemingway's death, *The Columbia Encyclopedia,* 3rd edition, acknowledged the spelling *Zaragoza* but entered the descriptive entry for the city under *Saragossa.* Hemingway uses the Anglicized spelling in both the untitled manuscript and his personal correspondence (UM f472: 3; *SL* 169).

3. Temperature and precipitation data for the month of July 1925 in Pamplona and Zaragoza are provided by Russell Vose, of the National Oceanic and Atmospheric Administration, and Enric Aguilar, of the University Rovira i Virgili de Tarragona. Methods used to determine these data are described in Brunet, et al. The original temperature measurements are rendered in tenths of degrees Centigrade (Vose). For American ease in reading, I have converted these measurements to degrees Fahrenheit and rounded to the nearest whole number. Any resulting inaccuracies, no matter how small, are mine, as are subsequent judgments about temperature and relative comfort. Comfortable daytime temperatures are between the mid-60s and mid-70s Fahrenheit· Warm is around 80 degrees. Uncomfortable is 85 degrees and higher.

4. Jig's assertion that "every day we make it more impossible" ("Hills" 74) implies that the couple have discussed pregnancy and abortion for at least a day or two, making it unlikely that Jig has just revealed her pregnancy during their train journey to Casetas. However, if this outburst indicates that Jig suddenly understands that her life with the American has never promised a real future and that she is better off without him (Lamb, Kozikowski, Renner), the third option gains more currency.

5. Bakhtin identifies these themes in the medieval carnival from which the Pamplona festival descends (*Problems* 101–32, 155–76, *Rabelais* 4–20). Stoneback discusses them as they appear in specific rituals of the San Fermínes and illuminates their meaning to Hemingway's protagonist Jake Barnes in *The Sun Also Rises* (240–67).

6. Koloze reviews opinions about whether Jig agrees to the abortion and whether she remains in a relationship with the American (120–24). Working from a spatial analysis of the railway station, Justice argues that the American accepts Jig's vision of a life together with a child (39–50). From the perspective of early twentieth-century parenting mores, Gillette writes that the story "can produce a happy ending" only if Jig and the American remain a couple and have the baby (57–58).

7. Hollander notes that Virginia Woolf apparently believed "the operation in question [to be] a tonsillectomy" (216).

8. See also Baker's discussion of travel and character in *The Sun Also Rises* in his *The Writer as Artist* (83–85).

9. Spengemann applies this description to travel writing by the American Romantics. Blanton, however, demonstrates that its terms extend internationally to the modernists, as exemplified by Hemingway's contemporary Graham Greene (59–70), and that those terms implicitly include both the Romantics and the modernists in what Blanton describes as "the heyday of travel writing," the period "between 1850 and 1930" (19).

10. This view is only one perspective. Pratt, for instance, shows that the eroticism of travel, in whatever context, is often as problematic as it is helpful or affirming (86–107).

11. Baker calls *Death in the Afternoon* "a history, a guide, a report, and a descriptive analysis" (146)—all terms that apply to Fussell's definition of guidebook travel writing.

12. Herman emphasizes the ultimately speculative nature of Jig's assertions in this part of the dialogue.

13. Herlihy-Mera's essay on Spaniards' perceptions of Hemingway indicates that, while Hemingway's knowledge of bullfighting was certainly superior to Hickok's, describing it as "shrewd" and "inside" probably is overstating the case.

Works Cited

Abram, Simone, and Jacqueline Waldren. Introduction. *Tourists and Tourism: Identifying People and Places.* Ed. Simone Abram, Jacqueline Waldren, and Donald Macleod. New York: Berg, 1997. 1–11. Berg Ethnicity and Identity Series.

Baker, Carlos. *Hemingway: The Writer as Artist.* 4th ed. Princeton: Princeton UP, 1972.

Bakhtin, Mikhail. *Problems of Dostoevsky's Poetics.* Ed. and trans. Caryl Emerson. Minneapolis: U of Minnesota P, 1984. Theory and History of Literature 8.

———. *Rabelais and His World.* Trans. Hélène Iswolsky. Bloomington: Indiana UP, 1984.

Blanton, Casey. *Travel Writing: The Self and the World.* 1995. New York: Routledge, 2002. Genres in Context.

Brunet, Manola, Oscar Saladié, Phil Jones, Javier Sigró, Enric Aguilar, Anders Moberg, David Lister, Alexander Walther, Diego Lopez, and Carlos Almarza. "The Development of a New Dataset of Spanish Daily Adjusted Temperature Series (SDATS) (1850–2003)." *International Journal of Climatology* 26 (2006): 1777–1802.

Burnes, Brian. "Two Births in 1928 KC: A Son and a Novel Insight." *Kansas City Star* 27 June 1999. Web. 19 Oct. 2007.

Busch, Frederick. "On 'Hills Like White Elephants.'" *Norton Anthology of Short Fiction.* 6th ed. Ed. R. V. Cassill, et al. New York: Norton, 2000. 761–62.

Buzzard, James. "The Grand Tour and After (1660–1840)." In *The Cambridge Companion to Travel Writing.* Ed. Peter Hulme and Tim Youngs. Cambridge, UK: Cambridge UP, 2002. 37–52.

Carr, Helen. "Modernism and Travel." In *The Cambridge Companion to Travel Writing.* Ed. Peter Hulme and Tim Youngs. Cambridge, UK: Cambridge UP, 2002. 70–86.

Del Gizzo, Suzanne. "'Glow in the Dark Authors:' Hemingway's Celebrity and Legacy in *Under Kilimanjaro.*" *Hemingway Review* 29.2 (2010): 7–27.

Fleming, Robert. "An Early Manuscript of Hemingway's 'Hills Like White Elephants.'" *Notes on Modern American Literature* 7.1 (1983): item 3.

Flora, Joseph. *Reading Hemingway's* Men Without Women*: Glossary and Commentary.* Kent: Kent State UP, 2008. Reading Hemingway Series 2.

Fussell, Paul. *Abroad: British Literary Traveling Between the Wars.* Oxford: Oxford UP, 1980.

———, ed. *The Norton Book of Travel.* New York: Norton, 1987.

Gillette, Meg. "Making Modern Parents in Ernest Hemingway's 'Hills Like White Elephants' and Viña Delmar's *Bad Girl.*" *Modern Fiction Studies* 53 (2007): 50–69.

Grant, David. "Hemingway's 'Hills Like White Elephants' and the Tradition of the American in Europe." *Studies in Short Fiction* 35.3 (1998): 267–76.

Hashmi, Nilofer. "'Hills Like White Elephants': The Jilting of Jig." *Hemingway Review* 23.1 (2003): 72–83.

Hemingway, Ernest. *Death in the Afternoon.* New York: Scribner, 1932.

———. *Ernest Hemingway: Selected Letters, 1917–1961.* Ed. Carlos Baker. New York: Charles Scribner's Sons, 1981.

———. "Hills Like White Elephants." In *Men Without Women.* New York: Scribner, 1927. 69–77.

———. *The Sun Also Rises.* New York: Scribner, 1926.

———. Untitled Manuscript. File 472. Hemingway Collection. John F. Kennedy Library, Boston.

Herman, David. "Narrative Theory and the Intentional Stance." *Partial Answers: A Journal of Literature and the History of Ideas* 6.2 (2008): 233–60.

Herlihy-Mera, Jeffrey. "'He Was Sort of a Joke, In Fact': Ernest Hemingway in Spain." *The Hemingway Review* 31.2 (Spring 2012): 84–100.

Hollander, John. "Hemingway's Extraordinary Reality." In *Modern Critical Views: Ernest Hemingway.* Ed. Harold Bloom. New York: Chelsea, 1985. 211–16.

Hulme, Peter, and Tim Youngs. Introduction. *The Cambridge Companion to Travel Writing.* Ed. Peter Hulme and Tim Youngs. Cambridge, UK: Cambridge UP, 2002. 1–13.

Jubak, James. "The Influence of Travel Narrative on Melville's *Mardi.*" *Genre* 9 (1976): 121–33.

Justice, Hilary. *The Bones of the Others: The Hemingway Text from the Lost Manuscripts to the Posthumous Novels.* Kent: Kent State UP, 2006.

Koloze, Jeff. *An Ethical Analysis of the Portrayal of Abortion in American Fiction: Dreiser, Hemingway, Faulkner, Dos Passos, Brautigan, and Irving.* Lewiston, NY: Edwin Mellen, 2005. Studies in American Literature 78.

Kozikowski, Stanley. "Hemingway's 'Hills Like White Elephants.'" *Explicator* 52.2 (1994): 107–9.

Lamb, Robert Paul. "Hemingway and the Creation of Twentieth-Century Dialogue." *Twentieth Century Literature* 42.4 (1996): 453–80.

Leed, Eric. *The Mind of the Traveler: From Gilgamesh to Global Tourism.* New York: Basic Books, 1991.

Maier, Kevin. "'A Trick Men Learn in Paris': Hemingway, *Esquire,* and Mass Tourism." *Hemingway Review* 31.2 (2012): 65–83.

Mandel, Miriam. "Configuring There as Here: Hemingway's Travels and the 'See American First' Movement." *Hemingway Review* 19.1 (1999): 93–105.

McIver, Stuart B. *Hemingway's Key West.* Sarasota: Pineapple Press, 1993.

Mintz, Lawrence. "Simulated Tourism at Busch Gardens: The Old Country and Disney's World Showcase, Epcot Center." *Journal of Popular Culture* 32.3 (1998): 47–58.

O'Brien, Timothy. "Allusion, Word-Play, and the Central Conflict in Hemingway's 'Hills Like White Elephants.'" *Hemingway Review* 12.1 (1992): 19–25.

Pratt, Mary Louise. *Imperial Eyes: Travel Writing and Transculturation.* New York: Routledge, 1992.

Rankin, Paul. "Hemingway's 'Hills Like White Elephants.'" *Explicator* 63.4 (2005): 234–37.

Reynolds, Michael. "Ernest Hemingway, 1899–1961: A Brief Biography." In *A Historical Guide to Ernest Hemingway.* Ed. Linda Wagner Martin. New York: Oxford UP, 2000. 15–50.

———. *Hemingway: The 1930s.* New York: Norton, 1997.

———. *Hemingway: The Paris Years.* New York: Norton, 1989.

Renner, Stanley. "Moving to the Girl's Side of 'Hills Like White Elephants.'" *Hemingway Review* 15.1 (1995): 27–42.

Russell, Alison. *Crossing Boundaries: Postmodern Travel Literature.* New York: Palgrave, 2000.

Shiflet, E. Stone, and Kirk Curnutt. "Letters and Literary Tourism: Hemingway as Your Key West Correspondent in 'The Sights of Whitehead Street.'" In *Key West Hemingway: A Reassessment.* Eds. Kirk Curnutt and Gail D. Sinclair. Gainesville: UP of Florida, 2009. 220–40.

Smiley, Pamela. "Gender-Linked Miscommunication in 'Hills Like White Elephants.'" *Hemingway Review* 8.1 (1988): 2–12.

Smith, Paul. *A Reader's Guide to the Short Stories of Ernest Hemingway.* Boston: G. K. Hall, 1989.

Spengemann, William C. The Adventurous Muse: The Poetics of American Fiction, 1789–1900. New Haven: Yale UP, 1977.

Stoneback, H. R. *Reading Hemingway's* The Sun Also Rises: *Glossary and Commentary.* Kent: Kent State UP, 2007. Reading Hemingway Series 1.

Vose, Russell. "More data." Message to the Author. 30 Aug. 2007. E-mail.

Wayland, Ted. "Hemingway's Alpine Idylls." Ernest Hemingway Society and Foundation and the Society for American Travel Writing. American Literature Association 18th Annual Conference on American Literature. Westin Copley Place, Boston, MA. 26 May 2007. Conference Paper.

Wittman, Emily O. "A Circuit of Ordeals: Nostalgia and the Romance of Hardship in Graham Greene's *Journey Without Maps* and Ernest Hemingway's *Green Hills of Africa.*" *Prose Studies* 33.1 (2011): 44–61.

Wyche, David. "Letting the Air into a Relationship: Metaphorical Abortion in 'Hills Like White Elephants.'" *Hemingway Review* 22.1 (2002): 58–73.

4

Hemingway and Franklin

Men Without Women

Ian Grody

August 1929. Ernest Hemingway wires Guy Hickock, "Will write something for you if I meet him but not under my name. You see I could sell an interview with him by me (signed) for a thousand seeds" (Mellow 388). Hickock is a correspondent for the *Brooklyn Daily Eagle* and the *him* to whom Hemingway refers in his wire is Sidney Franklin, the Jewish, Brooklyn-born *novillero,* whose recent successes in the bullrings of Spain echo through expatriate cafés and critics' circles.

Two months earlier, Franklin debuted at the *plaza de toros* in Seville, displaying what one Spanish critic called "unequalled art"—and word of Franklin's impressive capework and "phlegmatic serenity" was soon relayed overseas (Ribalow and Ribalow 379). The *New York Times* reported of Franklin's 9 June debut: "The spectators gave him a tremendous ovation, carrying him on their shoulders out of the bull ring and shouting, 'Viva el Americano'" ("Brooklyn Matador" 1). Weeks later, Hemingway wrote Hickock that he had heard Franklin "had been 'carried out on the shoulders, again,' this time in San Sebastián" (Mellow 388). Testaments to Franklin's accomplishments, inside and outside of the bullring, would later be refuted by a list of critics, including Vicente Vega and Tony Brand in the magazine *Toros* and John McCormick in *Bullfighting: Art, Technique and Spanish Society* (McCormick 157). To this day, debate rages regarding the validity of Franklin's talent, at least among bullfighting scholars who have not forgotten "El Niño de la Sinagoga."

September, 1929. Hemingway and the Yankee torero meet at Café Gran Via in Madrid following one of Franklin's fights. Franklin agrees to an interview with Hemingway, and what begins as a benign question-and-answer session becomes something bigger and more significant in the lives of both men.[1] Their meeting sparks an intimate friendship, a complex partnership that spans the 1930s. Franklin, dubbed the Bullfighter from Brooklyn and El Yanqui Flamenco, would be of great help to Hemingway during the writing of *Death in the Afternoon,* and Franklin's image and manner of speech (a coarse "Brooklynese") can be identified in a number of Hemingway's works, particularly the short story "The Mother of a Queen" and the passage of *Death in the Afternoon* referred to in its manuscript version as "Portrait of Three or the Paella" (Mellow 412). Of course there is "A Short Estimate of the American, Sidney Franklin, as a Matador," the portion of *Death in the Afternoon* devoted solely to the Brooklyn torero. There, Hemingway not only praises Franklin's expertise in the bullring ("he is a great and fine artist and no history of bullfighting that is ever written can be complete unless it gives him the space he is entitled to"), but also extols Franklin's character ("he is a charming companion, one of the best story tellers I have ever heard") (*DIA* 475–76). As James Mellow writes, "Franklin was intimately connected to Hemingway's sketch of the idyllic masculine rites that were an inescapable feature of his view of life and literature" (407).

After the publication of *Death in the Afternoon* in 1932, Hemingway and Franklin collaborated on the translation of *Shadows of the Sun,* a "trashy" bullfighting novel (Smith 232). They then worked together on a motion picture treatment for *Death in the Afternoon* and, together, attempted to introduce bullfighting to the population of Cuba (Leff 181). Eventually, Franklin would accompany Hemingway as an assistant correspondent during the Spanish Civil War.

In 1934, Franklin visited Hemingway's Key West home. Hemingway's friend Arnold Samuelson, who was present, observed that "[Franklin] seemed to be the one man [Hemingway] completely admired . . . [Samuelson] had never seen E. H., so pleased to see anyone" (Samuelson 120). The feeling was reciprocated; Franklin described his admiration for the author and bullfighting aficionado in his gossipy autobiography, *Bullfighter from Brooklyn.* "Little by little he amazed me," Franklin wrote. "There didn't seem to be a thing he didn't know about nature and sports" (*Bullfighter* 178).

Hemingway and Franklin were two men linked by love of tauromaquia, but the celebration of bullfighting was only one aspect of the idea of masculinity that bound them. To them, masculinity—life as men without women—required the suppression of the feminine in their respective persons, an end toward which both Hemingway and Franklin strove until the ends of their lives. This is not to assert that either man focused his life on this single end, nor to say that Hemingway and Franklin were unable to embrace the complexities of gender; however, it was this fear of their own feminine components that, to a great degree, connected these men, a fact that is all the more compelling when one considers that Franklin spent his life as a closeted homosexual.[2] Given Hemingway's popular reputation as a masculine giant and the new scholarship investigating and questioning the dimensions of that masculinity, the relationship between the author and the American torero assumes particular significance today.

July 11, 1903. Sidney Franklin is born. Originally named Sidney Frumpkin, he is the fifth of nine children. In a three-part 1949 interview with Lillian Ross of *The New Yorker,* "El Único Matador," Maestro Franklin described his difficult childhood. "I didn't fit in," Franklin said. The smallest of his male classmates, Franklin was excluded from athletics, so the future bull killer took up alternative activities. He joined *The Brooklyn Daily Eagle*'s Aunt Jean's Humane Club, which promoted animal rights. The young Franklin, who would later be idolized by American male icon James Dean and lionized in letters by man's man Ernest Hemingway, belonged to "the old *New York Globe's* Bedtime Story Club, an organization devoted to the glorification of Peter Rabbit." As a teenager, Franklin fell in love with the stage and took a job at a local theater, performing between-act song-and-dance numbers with two teenage girls. To prevent his father from finding out, he used the (stage) name Sidney Franklin—selecting "Franklin" after Ben Franklin,[3] whose biography Sidney was reading at the time. "To my father, the theatre was sacrilege. He detested it," Franklin said. As an adult Franklin would adopt this view himself, arguing that the theater "was too feministic . . . Of course, it's up to a man to assert himself, but that I had to learn later on" (Ross 169). Despite Franklin's adult reappraisal of the theater, he had no qualms about the cinema, appearing as an extra in *The Black Pirate,* Douglas Fairbanks's 1926 swashbuckling adventure, and portraying himself in Eddie Cantor's 1932 comedy, *The Kid from Spain.*

Franklin's parents were working-class Russian immigrants. Sidney's mother, Lübba, was an affectionate homemaker, who supported the young Sidney's interest in the arts and his efforts at sketching and acting, which Sidney's father, Abram, most likely considered "too feministic." In 1929, Lübba loaned Sidney the money he needed to go to Spain, purchase new swords and uniforms, and pursue a career as a Spanish matador (Franklin, *Bullfighter* 121). She concealed this from Abram, who considered all of Sidney's aspirations equally ridiculous. According to Franklin, Abram, a bullish patrolman with a volatile temper, "never showed any affection for his children" (Ross 168). Sidney's physical description of Pa Frumpkin in his autobiography is reminiscent of "Papa" Hemingway: "Pa," as Sidney called him, was a "strong, broad-shouldered man" with a moustache. "We were always at war," he added (Franklin, *Bullfighter* 4).

June 7, 1922. Abram administers a particularly brutal beating to a nineteen-year-old Sidney, knocking him unconscious. According to Sidney, he had spent the weekend away from home and had failed to check in with his parents. The next day, Sidney, fed up with his father, boards the S.S. *Monterey* for Mexico where he witnesses his first bullfight, convinces the matador Gaona to train him, and starts on the path that would eventually lead him to a Sunday evening encounter with a certain writer from Oak Park, Illinois (Franklin, *Bullfighter* 5). However, the man Hemingway would meet was Sidney *Franklin,* the reinvented version of Sidney Frumpkin—a self-proclaimed superman who had severed ties to his father's name and to his own "too feministic" history.

As Robert E. Gajdusek observes in "Sacrifice and Redemption: The Meaning of the Boy/Son and Man/Father Dialectic in the Work of Ernest Hemingway," many Hemingway heroes take typical first names in place of typical surnames (Robert Jordan, Nick Adams, Frederic Henry), eradicating "the father through the lost patronymic, . . . abrogating the surname and in so doing disdaining parental inheritance." Here, as Gajdusek notes, "the individual seems to be trying to make a whole person of himself without recourse to parental inheritance" (97–98). It is interesting to consider the theory of the lost or changed patronymic in relation to Sidney Frumpkin/Franklin, whose reinvention included a comparable name-change. However, the adult transition from Frumpkin to Franklin probably had less to do with dissociation from Abram than it did with shedding an ethnic identity—something many celebrities still do today. That said, the source of Franklin's *desire* for celebrity—his acutely felt hunger for adulation—may very well have been a longing for the praise and approval he did not receive from Pa.

Hemingway's well-documented upbringing can be considered a negative image of Franklin's, in which domestic dynamics were practically, if not absolutely, converse. Whereas Abram Frumkin dominated in Sidney's home, in Hemingway's family, it was his mother, Grace Hall Hemingway, who ruled. Ernest's father, Clarence, was subservient and consequently unmanned, or so it seemed to Ernest. This left a lasting impression on the young writer. As Gajdusek notes, "Hemingway's perception of his own father, Clarence Hemingway's inadequacy as man and father [is reflected in] . . . stories like 'Indian Camp' and 'The Doctor and the Doctor's Wife'" (103). In Hemingway's work, father figures consistently fall short of authentic manhood; this is quite literally so in "My Old Man," in which the protagonist's father is cast as a jockey (although, factually speaking, "My Old Man" is not one of Hemingway's more autobiographical short stories). Yet it was only with Clarence that Ernest could physically express his masculinity:

hunt, fish, and wear straw hats and Huck Finn-style overalls. With Grace, Ernest was dressed as the pseudo-twin of his older sister, Marcelline, sometimes as boys and sometimes as girls, an "illusion (or delusion) of twinhood" she perpetuated "through kindergarten age and beyond" (Mellow 11). Thus, Hemingway's earliest idea of masculinity already involved distance from women.[4]

As an adolescent Hemingway would find support for this philosophy in the works of his favorite male authors. In *Hemingway's Quarrel with Androgyny,* Mark Spilka cites Kipling and Thomas Hughes as the most influential of these authors. Kipling's work, Spilka writes, "helped to shape [Hemingway's] definitions of male independence and his emerging attitudes toward women as they served or threatened that independence" (92). Spilka also asserts that "Thomas Hughes's precedent, that manliness is achieved though separation from women, would be followed by Ernest Hemingway in the century ahead" (21). From these authors and others, Hemingway would forge an idea of masculinity characterized by, in Robert Moss's phrase, "uncomplaining toil, devotion to duty, fearlessness in battle, constant stoicism" (qtd. in Spilka 107).[5] Later in his life, Hemingway came to see bullfighters as the embodiment of these masculine traits—bullfighters like Cayetano Ordóñez, Nicanor Villalta, and certainly Sidney Franklin. In *Death in the Afternoon,* Hemingway identifies these traits as they applied specifically to Franklin, describing him as " brave with a cold, serene, and intelligent valor" (473). This begs the question: Did Hemingway chose Franklin as a companion *because* he possessed these ideals or was Hemingway—the mythmaker—actively *creating* Franklin in the image of an idealized fictional hero? The answer may be both.

For Hemingway, bullfighting also represented the triumph of man over death. Hemingway's own fear of death and lifelong obsession with the subject has filled books: those he has written and those written about him. As Hemingway very clearly states of the bullfight in *Death in the Afternoon,* "I feel very fine while it is going on and have a feeling of life and death and mortality and immortality" (4). Like Hemingway, Jake Barnes of *The Sun Also Rises* overcomes *his* fear of death only through "the bullfighter's triumph over it and feeling of immortality" (Capellan 153). Hemingway's close association with Franklin only enhanced the proximity of this feeling, this triumph. It probably was Franklin's death-defying lifestyle that made him, as Arnold Samuelson observed, "the man [Hemingway] most admired."

For Franklin, like Hemingway, bullfighting was a masculine trial. To label Franklin's bulls Pa Frumpkin (as Ross notes, in the slang of the day, Franklin's father, as a policeman, "would have been referred to as a bull" [168]) or the ghost of Sidney Frumpkin seems too easy, but it is obvious that by fighting bulls Franklin wished to validate his own masculine virtues. According to Franklin, "there can be no crooked work in the bullring, because you can't talk to the bull. You can't tell him to lie down, and you will divide the purse. You either get him or he gets you" (quoted in Ribalow and Ribalow 377). This masculine trial culminates in the kill. "The matador is committed to the kill by rules and professional honor, and if he be brave or cowardly this is where it will show . . . Courage or its lack can not be concealed" ("Yanqui Torero" 120). The notion of the *rules* of masculinity may very well have been an inheritance from Franklin's father—a list that in time was revised and expanded by Hemingway himself.

But bullfighting provided more than masculine affirmation for Franklin. Just as Hemingway used bullfighting to conquer his fear of death, Franklin used bullfighting as a sex substitute, an alternative to sex. Because, as a young man, he could not or would not act on his desires,[6] Franklin discharged his pent-up sexual energy in the *plaza de toros.* "Facing a bull as big as a cathedral gives me a deep feeling, a terribly vital emotion," Franklin is quoted as saying in *True* magazine. "I have trouble breathing, that's how overwhelmed I am. I tingle" ("Yanqui Torero" 120). Author and one-time bullfighting student Patrick Cunningham may have witnessed Franklin experiencing such bullfighting-inspired stimulation. In *A River of Lions,* a semi-fictionalized account of his experience with Franklin, Cunningham describes a scene in which the narrator (a thinly veiled Cunningham) watches Stanley Philips (an equally thinly veiled Sidney Franklin) perform cape work. "During his slow pivot," Cunningham writes, "he faced me and I saw the bulge in his crotch, straining beneath the tight fitting corto pants; so carried away in his own fantasy he had produced an erection" (10–11). Since *A River of Lions* is a novel, this scene does not confirm that Cunningham actually witnessed such an erection in Franklin, but even Hemingway spoke of bullfighting as an aphrodisiac in the "Some Reactions" section of *Death in the Afternoon,* which lends some plausibility to the tale.[7]

During the 1929 bullfighting season, Hemingway accompanied Franklin on his tour of Spain. There, they could be men without women. Hemingway's wife Pauline was at home in Key West, and Franklin, who claimed to have learned from his teacher, Gaona, that women deprive toreros of their vital strength, easily resisted the charms of his female admirers (Franklin, *Bullfighter* 109). Who needed women when there were bulls? According to Franklin, he and Hemingway often became so rapt in bull talk that Franklin had Hemingway's "bed or cot moved into his room, and . . . they shared the double bed when nothing else was available" (Mellow 389). Like many of Franklin's claims, this one cannot be confirmed, but photographs taken by Madrid's Manzanares

River in July 1931 reflect a comparable degree of intimacy between Franklin and Hemingway. In one particular photo, a smiling, shirtless Hemingway rests an easy elbow on a nude Franklin's shoulder. Franklin's genitals are obscured by a Spanish periodical. As James Mellow writes in his Hemingway biography, these "photographs deny Hemingway's later claim that he never liked the touch of other men" (40–48). Such exhibitions of male intimacy seem to violate the rules of masculinity that bound Franklin and Hemingway, but more likely they are evidence of a bond so strong that its rules could comfortably be bent.

On the banks of the Manzanares, Franklin, recovering from a leg injury, would aid Hemingway as Hemingway completed the manuscript of *Death in the Afternoon.* In his autobiography, Franklin writes, "All I was interested in was to see that he captured the underlying causes and effects as well as interpreted the subject clearly and fairly in all its aspects, bad as well as good. And he most certainly did" *(Bullfighter* 205). As a result of his regular presence and contributions, Franklin would become, as Jeffrey Meyers notes, "a minor hero of the book" (230). Among the photographs that Hemingway included in *Death in the Afternoon,* only two are of Franklin; however, these two are used to illustrate a proper kill and artful cape-work. By juxtaposing these images with images of the matador Cagancho, Hemingway suggests that Franklin, an American, is the superior of his Spanish peer—a blasphemous notion to many Spanish critics (Brand 181).

Yet *Death in the Afternoon* says far more about Hemingway than it does about Franklin or any kind of bull or bullfighter. On one level, it is an important example of Hemingway's experimental writing and a deeply researched bullfighting treatise, but it is also, as John Raeburn comments in *Fame Became of Him,* "a portrait of the author as he wished to appear" (38). According to Raeburn, *Death in the Afternoon,* "allowed Hemingway to flaunt his hard-boiled view of life and death, and suggested a perhaps inordinate fascination with courage. For Hemingway squeamishness was opposed to manliness" (39). If Raeburn is right, if Hemingway did believe that squeamishness was a feminine attribute, then this could, at least in part, explain the collapse of his friendship with Franklin during the Spanish Civil War.

February, 1937. Hemingway and Franklin leave New York on the S.S. *Paris.* From Paris, Hemingway continues to Madrid, where he covers the Spanish Civil War for the North American Newspaper Alliance. After much difficulty obtaining the appropriate paperwork,[8] Franklin joins Hemingway as Hemingway's assistant, sleeping in room 109 of the Hotel Florida, which connects to Hemingway's room, 108 (Koch 125).[9] In Madrid, Franklin cooks breakfast, types dispatches, and is exceptionally helpful to Hemingway during the filming of

Joris Ivens's documentary, *The Spanish Earth.* Over the course of subsequent months, however, Franklin finds the experience of war too difficult to endure. He is shaken by an explosion at the Hotel Florida and traumatized by his experience at the Guadalajara front. Perhaps, as Meyers supposes, "Franklin became jealous of Hemingway's attachment to Martha Gellhorn," with whom Hemingway was having an affair (231). "Martha detested Sidney from minute one. She saw [Franklin as a] simpleton, . . . a hostile witness, loyal to Pauline," and steered Hemingway away from him (Koch 76). Also, with Gellhorn around, Hemingway and Franklin were no longer men without women. To Franklin, this must have been a violation of contract.

To Hemingway, Franklin's squeamishness in the wartime environment likewise must have been a violation of the idea of masculinity by which he and Franklin abided. It is probable that it was Franklin's timidity, and not, as Meyers proposes, the revelation that Franklin was "a secret homosexual . . . and a child molester" (231), that alienated Hemingway.[10] Hemingway may have reacted to Franklin's failure to cope with human atrocity as he had once reacted to the failure by his former friend Robert McAlmon to look at the rotting carcass of a dead dog, delivering a lecture on the importance of facing up to "grim reality" (McAlmon and Boyle 160). Whatever the catalyst, Franklin's departure from Spain during the middle of the war marked the end of his nine years of intimate association with Hemingway (Mellow 236–37).

In later years, Hemingway would claim that he had never accompanied Franklin during the 1929 bullfighting season, stating "'I never traveled with Franklin's bullfighting troupe . . . That is all ballroom bananas'" (qtd. in Delaplane 13). Firing back, Franklin gossiped to friends that Hemingway suffered from an undersized "sexual organ . . . like that of a little boy" (Brian 64–65). Mud-slinging and false accusations by both men polluted the history of what had once been a formidable partnership. It is no surprise that Hemingway and Franklin reacted to the end of their friendship in this fashion—and few or none of the accusations exchanged should be believed. Hemingway, for one, was a horrible liar. As Carl Eby points out, Hemingway "was frequently less than diligent when it came to distinguishing between fantasy and reality in his own life" (Eby 156), a sentiment echoed by the author himself in *Under Kilimanjaro:* "All a writer of fiction is really is a congenital liar who invents from his own knowledge or that of other men. I am a writer of fiction and so I am a liar too and invent from what I know and what I've heard. I'm a liar" (*UK* 113).

Needless to say, Franklin also had a penchant for make-believe; as Barnaby Conrad commented in his review of Franklin's autobiography, "As long as there's a Sidney Franklin there will be Sidney Franklin stories" (7). Elsewhere he observed that "just about every other third page" of *A Bullfighter from Brooklyn* was "true" (quoted in Denis 64). What is more, Franklin was historically sensitive to criticism and verbal attacks. In 1934, Franklin sued Columbia Pictures for $300,000 for referring to him as a "bull-thrower" in one of their newsreels, although eventually the case was dropped ("Franklin, in Court" 29). Years later, when author Lyn Sherwood wrote a parody of Franklin in the bullfighting magazine *Clarin*, Franklin sent two thugs to Sherwood's home, demanding that Sherwood "lay off the old man" (Sherwood 1). No doubt both Franklin and Hemingway valued their time spent together and were to some degree disappointed by the friendship's collapse. Naturally, the lies were spawned from this disappointment.

Despite the bad blood that developed between the two men, Hemingway never denied Franklin's talent as a matador. In a 1948 letter to Lillian Ross, Hemingway wrote, I "never reneged on Sidney because really saw him good and it would be a crime to deny it" (*SL* 646). Franklin likewise retained his respect for Hemingway as a bullfighting expert. In 1949, Franklin told Lillian Ross, "I may disagree with Ernest, but I'll always give him the benefit of the doubt, because he is a genius" (qtd. in Ross 150). The bullfighter and the author could exchange personal blows, but professionally they were forever linked. *Death in the Afternoon* was proof. To deny Franklin's skill as a matador, Hemingway would have had to deny his own bullfighting expertise. To deny Hemingway's bullfighting expertise, Franklin would have had to discredit the praise Hemingway bestowed on him in "A Brief Estimate." Bullfighting was a central source of masculine pride for both Hemingway and Franklin, and neither man wished to jeopardize his claim to it. In this respect, Hemingway and Franklin needed one another more than ever *after* their friendship had ended—to honor the masculine contract that had once joined them, to preserve their masculine integrities. Thus Hemingway retained his manhood on account of Franklin, and vice versa.

Notes

1. In his autobiography, Franklin offers a self-aggrandizing description of his first encounter with Hemingway. According to Franklin, Hemingway's disheveled appearance led him to mistake the writer for a beggar. Franklin then claims that when he invited Hemingway to join his caravan, Hemingway practically burst into tears. Though Hemingway was known to dress in tattered shirts and bedroom slippers and it is possible that Franklin *did* mistake him for a beggar, the idea of Hemingway coming near tears is less believable.

2. Franklin's sexuality is discussed at great length in Patrick Cunningham's *A River Of Lions*. Cunningham's Stanley Philips ("The Torero from Texas"), a thinly veiled version of an aging Sidney Franklin (The Bullfighter from Brooklyn), wines, dines, and beds several teenage boys. "The King of American Bullfighters," Cunningham writes, "is really a queen!" (76).

3. Ben Franklin would also influence Hemingway, who read *The Autobiography of Benjamin Franklin* in high school, kept copies of it at his Cuba and Key West homes, and, like Ben Franklin, taught himself to write by imitation (Reynolds, *Young Hemingway* 240).

4. These facts, well known to Hemingway scholars, are of particular interest when contrasted with Franklin's experience. Franklin from a young age *chose* the costumes and pageantry of the theatre, and shed them only at the *insistence* of his father.

5. Interestingly, Pa Frumpkin, the policeman, who never took a day off from work, never complained, and was emotionally guarded, abided almost exactly by Papa Hemingway's masculine code.

6. Though Franklin frequently boasted of his sexual prowess, claiming to have bedded scores of native women in a single night, the writer and journalist Martha Gellhorn, Hemingway's third wife, has provided the only written account of Franklin having (possibly) slept with a woman. During the Spanish Civil War, Gellhorn observed that "a Swedish girl, who spoke seven languages and wore men's clothes, sometimes came and joined [Franklin in his room]" (Moorehead 113).

7. Hemingway claims here that the experience of watching the bullfights had turned one "Mrs. S. T.," who had received a convent education, into an "alcoholic nymphomaniac" (*DIA* 498).

8. Franklin's paperwork and permissions troubles are mentioned in Hemingway's first two dispatches from Spain.

9. To note, Franklin began calling Hemingway "Papa" during the Spanish Civil War (Meyers 240).

10. Had Hemingway really believed Franklin was a child molester, he would not have allowed Franklin to accompany Pauline and nine-year-old Patrick to a Mexican bull ranch in August 1937 (Reynolds, *1930s* 196).

Works Cited

Brand, Anthony. "The Photographs in *Death in the Afternoon*." *A Companion to Hemingway's* Death in the Afternoon. New York: Camden House, 2004.

Brian, Denis. *The True Gen.* New York: Grove Press, 1987.

"Brooklyn Matador Kills Two Bulls in Spain; Seville Throng Carries Franklin in Triumph." *New York Times* 11 June 1929: 1.

Bruccoli, Matthew J., ed. *The Only Thing That Counts: The Ernest Hemingway/Maxwell Perkins Correspondence, 1925–1947.* New York: Scribner, 1996.

Capellan, Angel. *Hemingway and the Hispanic World.* Ann Arbor: UNI Research P, 1977.

Conrad, Barnaby. "With Cape And Sword." Rev. of *Bullfighter from Brooklyn,* by Sidney Franklin. *New York Times.* 9 Nov. 1952. 7.

Cunningham, Patrick. *A River of Lions.* Santa Barbara: Neville, 1991.

Delaplane, Stanton. "He Was a Right Guy and the Woman with Him Was Good Looking." *San Francisco Chronicle* 31 Jan. 1941: 13.

Eby, Carl P. *Hemingway's Fetishism: Psychoanalysis and the Mirror of Manhood.* Albany: State U of New York P, 1999.

"Franklin, In Court, Testifies on 'Bull.'" *New York Times* 21 Dec. 1934: 29.

Franklin, Sidney. *Bullfighter from Brooklyn.* New York: Prentice-Hall, 1952.

———. "My Life as a Yanqui Torero." *True* June 1960: 120.

———. "Sidney Franklin's Rebuttal." *Toros* Oct. 1962: 21.Gajdusek, Robert E. "Sacrifice and Redemption: The Meaning of the Boy/Son and Man/Father Dialectic in the Work of Ernest Hemingway." In *One Man Alone: Hemingway and* To Have and Have Not. Ed. Toni E. Knott. New York: UP of America, 1999. 95–111.

Hemingway, Ernest. *The Dangerous Summer.* New York: Scribner, 1960.

———. *Death in the Afternoon.* New York: Scribner, 1932.

———. *Ernest Hemingway: Selected Letters, 1917–1961.* Ed. Carlos Baker. New York: Charles Scribner's Sons, 1981.

———. *In Our Time.* New York: Scribner, 1925.

———. *The Sun Also Rises.* New York: Scribner, 1926.

———. *Under Kilimanjaro.* Kent, OH: Kent State UP, 2005.

Koch, Stephen. *The Breaking Point: Hemingway, Dos Passos, and the Murder of José Robles.* New York: Counterpoint Press, 2005.

Leff, Leonard J. *Hemingway and His Conspirators: Hollywood, Scribners, and the Making of American Celebrity Culture.* New York: Rowman and Littlefield, 1997.

McAlmon, Robert, and Kay Boyle. *Being Geniuses Together, 1920–1930.* 1938. Revised with Supplementary Chapters and an Afterward by Kay Boyle. San Francisco: North Point Press, 1984.

McCormick, John. *Bullfighting: Art, Technique, and Spanish Society.* New Brunswick, NJ: Transaction Publishers, 1998. Rev. ed. of *The Complete Aficionado.* 1967.

Mellow, James R. *Hemingway: A Life Without Consequences.* 1992. Cambridge, MA: Da Capo Press, 1993.

Meyers, Jeffrey. *Hemingway: A Biography.* New York: Harper and Row, 1985.

Moorehead, Caroline. *Gellhorn: A Twentieth-Century Life.* New York: Henry Holt, 2003.

Raeburn, John. *Fame Became of Him: Hemingway as Public Writer.* Bloomington: Indiana UP, 1984.

Reynolds, Michael. *Hemingway: The 1930s.* New York: Norton and Co., 1997.

———. *The Young Hemingway.* New York: Basil Blackwell, 1986.

Ribalow, Harold, and Meir Z. Ribalow. *The Jew in American Sports.* New York: Hippocrene, 1985.

Ross, Lillian. *Reporting.* New York: Dodd Mead, 1981.

Samuelson, Arnold. *With Hemingway: A Year in Key West and Cuba.* New York: Random House, 1984.

Sherwood, Lyn. Personal interview. 19 Dec. 2005.

Smith, Rex, ed. *Biography of the Bulls: An Anthology of Spanish Bullfighting.* New York: Rinehart and Co., 1957.

Spilka, Mark. *Hemingway's Quarrel with Androgyny.* Lincoln: U of Nebraska P, 1990.

Voss, Frederick. *Picturing Hemingway: A Writer in his Time.* New Haven: Yale UP, 1999.

5

A Creative Spiral

From Death in the Afternoon *(1932) to* The Dangerous Summer *(1960)*

Beatriz Penas Ibáñez

As we read in *The Dangerous Summer,* it took until 1953 for Hemingway to return to Spain after his last assignment in 1938, during the Spanish Civil War. In 1953, he returns not so much to watch the Spanish bullfights again as to end what he saw as his exclusion: "I had been away for fourteen years. A lot of that time though was like being in jail except that I was locked out; not locked in" (*DS* 3). Six years later, in writing *The Dangerous Summer,* Hemingway says that 1953 was a "historic" year (6).

For many reasons, Hemingway's 1953 return to Spain became a point of inflexion; it meant the end of an exile and, symbolically for him, the return to an altered (perverted) Eden. In coming back to Spain—and then to Africa—Hemingway was retracing his steps, going back on a reconnaissance trip around the scenarios he had experienced in the 1920s and 1930s and reconciling himself to the changes brought about by the wars.[1] He was revisiting cherished places and times and reinscribing—from a 1953 perspective—events that had been essential to him in the past. By doing so, he was both engaging in a process of self-refashioning and subjecting his Text[2] to a restyling process. Hemingway was actively pursuing the onset of experiential recurrence, starting on a trip back and forth in time that would bring his past to the present and his present to the past in a movement of reappropriation and cleansing conducive to personal renewal and a surge of creativity. And Hemingway's effort was rewarded. There is a clearly noticeable and characteristic postmodern quality to the texts he produced after World War II, when he had time to go back to Europe and see it as changed as he was changed. This last phase of his career, brought about by a spiral of literary and experiential recurrence, had as an outcome a body of original writing—symbiotically fictional and autobiographical in status—that can be considered the postmodern development of Hemingway's always evolving writing.[3]

For Hemingway, the 1953 trip to Europe and Spain was historic also because he met Antonio Ordóñez for the first time. This, and the fact that the author already knew Antonio's father from the 1920s, made the 1953 occasion memorable, a point where past and present experiences met in a series of recurrences—not mere repetitions[4]—that would trigger Hemingway's creativity. In 1953, Hemingway saw side by side two men, the exhausted old bullfighter Cayetano Ordóñez,[5] known as Niño de la Palma, and his young son Antonio, a rising sun (/son) in the taurine world and for Hemingway a source of creative energy. Antonio, who would grow to be a sensational bullfighter in 1959, inspired the writing of *The Dangerous Summer.*

Hemingway again saw Antonio in Madrid in 1954 and 1956. We know from sources such as Castillo-Puche that in 1956 Hemingway not only came to see Antonio fight in Logroño and Zaragoza, he also came to visit Pío Baroja (1872–1956)[6] before the old novelist died on 30 October. Hemingway stayed in Madrid afterward to attend the Spanish master's funeral and say a prayer for him[7] (Castillo-Puche 194–96). Three years later, when Hemingway came again to Spain—for the last time in his life—in the summer of 1959, he came both to see Antonio and the bullfights and for something else.

Hemingway's project for 1959 incorporated a novelty: he would be spending the summer in Andalusia. It was a convenient location not far from the homes of the two bullfighters, Antonio Ordóñez and Luis Miguel Dominguín, whose mano a mano bullfighting tour he wanted to watch. To that point, Hemingway's travel in Spain had taken place mainly in the north: the region between Pamplona and Madrid in the 1920s and in his 1953, 1954, and 1956 visits. During the civil war in the 1930s, and again during his visits in 1953, 1954 and 1956, he had traveled to Madrid, Zaragoza, Teruel, and Valencia. In 1959, however, Hemingway altered his customary pattern of action by centering his stay in Andalusia, in the Spanish province of Málaga. La Cónsula, Bill Davis's villa, was to be Hemingway's base of operations while he followed and once again, after a lapse of many years, wrote about the bullfights. The modern Spanish bullfight had been a theme in Hemingway's 1920s and 1930s writing that climaxed in *Death in the Afternoon;* in 1959, he revisited that theme, which climaxed again in the writing of *The Dangerous Summer.* Here Hemingway associates bullfighting with a set of parallel meanings and metaphors, principally war and the fight for predominance in the literary arena. The bullfight and its parallels in Hemingway's prewar writing, such as *Death in the Afternoon,* are directly alluded to and refashioned in *The Dangerous Summer* to suit Hemingway's new writing agenda, one in which Andalusia plays an important role. Andalusia is certainly a beautiful part of Spain, but *The Dangerous Summer* at first obviates this to focus on other, more significant truths, particularly the region's differences from the area around Madrid. For one thing, Hemingway resents that he does not understand the Andalusian dialect. Like Pío Baroja and the Spanish writers of the 1898 generation—the Spanish literary generation he identified with on the basis of shared ideas on life and literature—Hemingway loves the "clear, beautiful Spanish" and "harshness of La Mancha and Castille" (*DS* 23, 36). Hemingway says so in *The Dangerous Summer* in what becomes a particular homage to Castille, the land of castles and of Don Quixote. He also pays subtle homage to the Spanish writers of the generation of 1898 (his slightly older contemporaries), and especially to their maestro, the then recently buried Pío Baroja. These writers considered the dry, fertile soil of Castille an emblem for the best qualities of the Spanish earth and soul. The values Hemingway associates with the Spanish earth of Castille are fertility under a dry, apparently barren, surface; the capacity of its people to endure bravely under hardship; a taste for clarity through simplicity of expression; and a nobility of feeling under an outward appearance of harshness. They are also the qualities that Hemingway defends in *Death in the Afternoon* (192) and again in *The Dangerous Summer* (73), in relation to both Spanish bullfighting—classicism and contention—and American writing and the writer's texts, which Hemingway imbues with meanings hidden within his apparently straightforward style.[8]

Andalusia, vibrantly colorful and flowery, emblematized a different set of values. Fantasy, unrestrained imagination, a touch of craziness, and a taste for metaphor and the language of the baroque were objects of admiration to a second generation of Spanish writers, the generation of 1927, whom Hemingway knew well but with whom he did not closely identify, in spite of his nearness to them in age. This is probably because they were poets, not novelists. García Lorca and Rafael Alberti are the most famous members of this younger group of poets: Lorca had been killed by the fascists during the Spanish Civil War, but by 1959 Alberti was living in exile and could visit Hemingway in his Cuban home in 1960, as María Teresa León, Alberti's wife, tells the reader in her memoirs, *Memoria de la Melancolía.* They all knew each other from civil war times in Madrid (León 316–19; Fuentes 141). *The Dangerous Summer* mentions García Lorca once in passing and alludes indirectly to his best poem, the elegy "Llanto por la muerte de Ignacio Sánchez Mejías." The allusion takes place in the middle of a revealing passage, while Hemingway and Bill Davis are crossing the

Despeñaperros pass as they travel from Andalusia up through the mountains to Castille and Madrid. The passage from the lower to the higher land is, literally, the passage from Andalusia to Castille, while symbolically, it represents an ascent from Lorca's imaginary universe to Baroja's. And it is there, once they are in Castille–La Mancha, that Hemingway stops to visit Manzanares, the town in whose plaza Ignacio Sánchez Mejías was fatally wounded. The narrative lets Hemingway pass by the bullring without stopping. No respects explicitly paid, no overt gesture of homage.[9] He prefers to walk among the local people and sit for breakfast at a tavern, where he hears a warning from the man at the bar: "You never speak badly of anything you don't like. Not now" (*DS* 24).

The comment takes place on a trivial occasion and in a displaced context; Hemingway and the man at the bar are talking about what they like and dislike in the matter of wine. But the more general political meaning of the Spaniard's words is inescapable both for Hemingway in the narrative and for his readers. The man at the Manzanares bar is aware of self-censorship, and expresses, in an exercise of understatement, the need for him to repress criticism of his—also political—dislikes. Moreover, Hemingway, his American guest at the bar, understands him perfectly because he feels trapped in a similar situation. Internal or self-censorship is doubly repressive when it exists side by side with external or official censorship. Both kinds of censorship affected Hemingway on his 1950s visits to Franco's Spain. The latter, official censorship in Spain, impinged on Hemingway's Spanish readership in that they could not read English and had to make do with the very poor translations available at the time. LaPrade has studied the official censorship of Hemingway's translated work into Spanish during the dictatorship. Hemingway was aware of these issues. He could come to Spain in 1953 as an American tourist, he could meet Spanish writers who respected him as a literary model, but he would have to keep a low political profile. As the opening paragraph of *The Dangerous Summer* puts it, "I might honorably return to Spain if I did not recant anything that I had written and kept my mouth shut on politics" (1).

Hemingway was doubly aware of censorship. It affected him when he traveled as a foreign visitor in Spain during the fifties and also, probably more profoundly, as an American national having to come back from Cuba to the United States in the post-MacCarthyist years. In *The Dangerous Summer,* Hemingway addresses these two instances of censorship differently, foregrounding Spanish censorship while dealing with American censorship more subtly. He deals with censorship in Spain explicitly, since the book is about the past and present of the Spanish bullfights and about the effects of the Spanish Civil War on Spanish society. Hemingway tackles the latter instance of censorship, in America after the McCarthy era, indirectly, by using an American narrator and coprotagonist in *The Dangerous Summer*. The Americanness of narrators and protagonists in the Hemingway Text does not disappear while they travel to and in Spain; it is only less visible because it remains in the background while we see them come and go, watching and criticizing the bullfight. The American vantage point and the submerged meanings that accompany it always balance the non-American nature of the Spanish surface themes and characters. Both *Death in the Afternoon* and *The Dangerous Summer* are explicitly concerned with the modern Spanish bullfight and the bullfighters' changing styles, but they are also concerned with changing Spanish and American social ways and with Spanish and American writers and generational changes in how they write as they reflect on Hemingway's own stance among them.[10] Valerie Hemingway's memories of Hemingway in the summer of 1959 include recollections of the different generations of writers who occupied Hemingway's mind at the time and about which he liked to give her his informed critical opinions. Internal evidence for the parallel between bullfighting and writing can be deduced from the juxtaposition of the two themes in *Death in the Afternoon*. In *The Dangerous Summer* the parallel is explicitly stated in dialogue between Ernesto Hemingway and Antonio Ordóñez. There are times when Antonio and Ernesto stress the sameness of their two arts and professions and make them one—writing—in their discourse. Ernesto reports that "[Antonio] was very pleased, always, to call the faena writing" (*DS* 51–52).[11] At other times, the two men, again in conversation, stress the sameness of their arts in taurine terms, as when Antonio and Ernesto go to Ronda, the cradle of the bullfight, to be awarded the gold medal by the town mayor in honor of the centenary of Pedro Romero. On that occasion, Antonio combines the two arts into one—bullfighting—in saying to Ernesto: "We're toreros, aren't we?'" (*DS* 58–59).

While *Death in the Afternoon* explored the analogies between the bullfight and literary writing at length and in depth through a persistent but largely implicit juxtaposition, *The Dangerous Summer* presents these issues in the inverse manner. The text does not explore the analogy between bullfighting and narrative writing at length, because this was already done in the earlier text and Hemingway can rely on his readers' intertextual recall. He can rely on this now, after the wars, because his celebrity grants him his readers' familiarity with the design of the Hemingway Text. Nevertheless, he playfully leaves room in his text for explicit statement of the homology within the fiction: it is voiced in conversation by the central characters, the literary personas of Antonio Ordóñez and his friend, the celebrated writer Ernesto Hemingway. This is a textual strategy typical of *The Dangerous Summer*'s postmodern construction. The surface text, explicit about the *one* overt subject of bullfighting, includes a design of allusions to the submerged themes—the Spanish Civil War and literature—that is coherent within the fictional world represented by the overt narrative, but whose deeper significance is gained in reference to *Death in the Afternoon.*[12]

Both before and after the wars, the Spanish bullfight theme corresponds to the sociopolitical and literary themes. In *Death in the Afternoon,* these themes earned parallel treatment on the textual surface of the bullfight, but the metaphorical association remained unstated. This is one of the main sources of difficulty in what is usually regarded as an "unclassifiable" genre-mixing book (Reynolds, "Brief Biography" 32). *The Dangerous Summer,* on the other hand, explicitly states the sameness within difference between two arts, *la lidia* and literature, and two artists, Ordóñez and Hemingway. Hemingway's concern with art extended from the artist bullfighter to the artist writer, no matter where each artist is from, Spain or America. His interest in Spain and modern Spanish writing was an extension of his interest in America and modern American writing and in the successive generations, older and younger, with which he had lived—Gertrude Stein, Ezra Pound, and F. Scott Fitzgerald, as well as J. D. Salinger, Carson McCullers, and Truman Capote (V. Hemingway 58). This is what his readers need to know and this is what Hemingway teaches them while they read his bullfight books: that they must bring within their interpretative horizon not only what Hemingway says about the decadence of Spanish bulls and bullfighting styles, but also what Hemingway silences regarding the decadent Spanish and American lifestyles and their corresponding literary styles in modern times. Surely it cannot be coincidental that both Hemingway texts on the Spanish bullfight were written at periods of crisis affecting Hemingway as well as the countries he loved most.

Hemingway published *Death in the Afternoon* in 1932, only three years after the 1929 Wall Street crash, and the socioeconomic ideological crisis became evident in the changed American lifestyles and writing styles of the ensuing years. Spain also felt the effects of the financial crash; the late 1920s and early 1930s were a time of social and political upheaval, a revolutionary phase in Spain's history, initially leading to the Second Republic, and then to the civil war (1936–39) and Franco's long dictatorship, which ended only with his death in 1975. At the same time these years also fostered intense intellectual production by the best generations of American and Spanish writers in modern times: the Lost Generation in the United States and the so-called generations of 1898 and 1927 in Spain, which included such authors as Pío Baroja, Valle Inclán, Unamuno, Ortega y Gasset, Antonio Machado, García Lorca, and Rafael Alberti. These generations were writing the books that now represent twentieth-century American and Spanish culture. For Hemingway, the early 1930s was a difficult period for personal reasons also; his father had committed suicide in 1928. The financial failure, and eventually a loss of confidence in powerful fatherly models seem to be the underlying sources of Hemingway's generalized dissatisfaction in *Death in the Afternoon*. In the book, Hemingway criticizes earlier forms of writing as weak, proposes himself in the role of the "strong" creative artist and writer (see Bloom), and places himself and his name in the place and the name of his literary fathers, rather than his biological, father.[13]

In *Death in the Afternoon,* Hemingway "articulate[s] a modernist version of the idea of tradition and fame" (Penas Ibáñez, "Very Sad" 156). Some before him, Hemingway knows, sought mastery in the art of writing and failed, others achieved temporary acclaim, and only a few became great, influential masters, maestros whose work is still valid in our time. For Hemingway, this knowledge is associated with his need to dominate the twentieth-century literary scene, and, as happens with all strong artists, this need prompts a rejection of his immediate predecessors, except Pound and perhaps Joyce. Gertrude Stein, Sherwood Anderson, and Scott Fitzgerald were all first his friends and then his enemies. The list of authors derogated in *Death in the Afternoon* includes Waldo Frank, William Faulkner, T. S. Eliot, Jean Cocteau, Aldous Huxley, Oscar Wilde, and Walt Whitman. Others are only impersonally alluded to through mention of their schools, with Hemingway declaring, "All schools only serve to classify their members as failures" (*DIA* 100). That preceding generation made its own judgement about those who followed them, patent in old lady Stein's famous remark, "You are all a lost generation." (Her verdict on Hemingway's work specifically was that it was "*inaccrochable*"—literally, "unhangable," as of a picture, but in this case implying that his work was unpublishable.) *Death in the Afternoon* plays witness to Hemingway's acute awareness of his own need and that of his generation to overcome the readers' prejudice, the older generation's prejudice. In *Death in the Afternoon,* Hemingway defends not just the bullfight but also his own writing from his contemporaries' misunderstanding. In *The Dangerous Summer,* Hemingway likewise defends his writing, old and new, from misunderstanding, but in this case he is defending it from the misunderstanding of both an English-speaking readership—general and specialized—that he wants to fend off, and a Spanish readership, especially those Spanish would-be writers who look up to him as a model—particularly after Baroja's death—and cannot find his texts except in very poor translations that fail to do justice to his style.[14]

This defensive posture leaves *The Dangerous Summer* permeated by a tone of discontent similar to that of *Death in the Afternoon*. It is a general kind of dissatisfaction that reflects the downward trajectory that Hemingway sees developing from "the good old days" down to the insignificant present. When reading, for example, the following passage in *The Dangerous Summer,* we know that something is missing from the scene: "The road was very bad and the country was sad in the gray light. The Ebro that had meant as much to us at one time as the Marne or the Aisne looked equally unhistoric. . . . The day was starting sad for me" (*DS* 69). Hemingway is comparing what he sees to what he remembers, what he feels to what he believes he used to feel, and the result is sadness. His melancholy results from an awareness of the passage of time and the changes, external and internal, it brings about: the loss of past experience, the dulling of emotion, the not-caring, the unreliability of memory. "Memory, of course, is never true," Hemingway had written in *Death in the Afternoon* (100). Now, after so many years, he reconsiders the idea and updates it: memory may be unreliable regarding insignificant details—for instance the more potent cars and improved roads: "The distances were all smaller, as usual" (*DS* 64)—but it is totally reliable with respect to the central aspects of the subject that originally made an experience memorable. Such aspects retain their heartfelt quality as lived experience. In 1959, Hemingway returns to Spain to see both the bullfights and the Spanish Civil War sites: "There were certain places that I liked to show to Bill for their incredibility; to show them as museum pieces of the impossible in war. . . . When I saw them I could not believe them myself although the original memory of them was sharper than any photograph" (*DS* 65).

Hemingway perceives an analogous process in the decadence of both the postwar fascist society and the modern Spanish bullfight. We see this in his descriptions of the theatricality of the new style of bullfighting, the insignificance of the bulls, the less-than-brave bullfighters who want to fight young, undeveloped bulls to minimize the danger, and the manipulation of the horns of the better bulls to save the bullfighters and deceive the spectators. This is the general state of affairs that Hemingway resents in *The Dangerous Summer.* Against this decadent background, the figure of Antonio Ordóñez is portrayed with unmistakable admiration and joy: admiration and joy for him and for his style with the cape and muleta, which kept "the old heart-stopping rhythm" of the *passes* as it should be—moving, honest, classical and true (*DS* 61)—and admiration for his way of killing *recibiendo,* "the greatest way to kill" (*DS* 130), the dangerous moment of truth in a corrida when the bullfighter shows what he is worth. Hemingway praises Antonio's style as "classical," "warm," "Bach-like purity of style and timing," "pure as mathematics," and "as exciting and as stirring as love" (76). This praise recalls in its terms what *Death in the*

Afternoon described as the necessary qualities of a work of art. Hemingway's final compliment is to claim that Antonio "made poetry of movement" (105). Antonio and Ernesto each takes pride in his own métier and they acknowledge each other and their respective professions, for they know they are two of a kind: artists, and the best men in their respective professions despite the difficult times and the prevalent decadence. Against this, Luis Miguel's style—full of artificial tricks, set-ups, and faking—may appeal to the new majority taste of his followers but is worthless to the true connoisseur. To Hemingway and the true aficionado, "there was no magic in it" (*DS* 61).

Because they are primarily fighters, the two matadors, Antonio Ordóñez and Luis Miguel Dominguín, can be made to play several roles in *The Dangerous Summer.* One role is connected to Hemingway's literary aesthetics: here Antonio represents an aesthetics of truth, while Luis Miguel represents illusion and untruth. This is a long-standing seminal contrast in the Hemingway Text, dating all the way back to *In Our Time* (1925) and resurfacing in different guises throughout Hemingway's work, but more essentially so at its most creative moments. *Death in the Afternoon* and *The Dangerous Summer* mark the second and third climactic points in the spiral of creativity developed by Hemingway from beginning to end.

A second role played by the two matadors reflects Hemingway's ethical stance in the face of what he saw in Spain before and during the civil war and what he sees in the 1950s, when the effects of the civil war are painfully felt by the man and the writer. The 1959 duel between Antonio Ordóñez and Luis Miguel Dominguín is fratricidal, between brothers-in-law who are each made to stand for one of the belligerent bands in the Spanish Civil War: the young Antonio is portrayed as a reincarnation of the best old Spanish (Castillian) values, his character design being a synthesis of novelty and tradition, an example of goodness that can avoid the danger of destruction only through self-insulation against the sinister surrounding circumstances. In contrast, Luis Miguel is portrayed as a middle-aged son of Spain immersed in, and contaminated by, the prevailing fascist climate.

From the beginning, *The Dangerous Summer* distinguishes between Antonio and Luis Miguel both directly and indirectly. Luis Miguel Dominguín and Ernesto Hemingway do not take pride in each other. Because they are not equal, there is no mutual admiration. For a while, Luis Miguel seeks to emulate the writer, and the narrative reports the narrator's thoughts on Luis Miguel's opinion: "[Luis Miguel] thought about taking up writing. If Ernesto could write, I think he reasoned, it must be easy. I explained there was nothing to it if you did it right and told him how I did it. So for a couple days we each wrote in the mornings and he brought what he wrote down to the pool at noon" (*DS* 11). The possibility of one-directional admiration is ruled out by Luis Miguel's vanity. So he will eventually invade Ernesto's territory, derogating the maestro and his work by saying, "What a man Ernesto would be if he could only write" (*DS* 99).

The writing and publication of *The Dangerous Summer* closes a difficult decade not only for Hemingway and for anti-McCarthyist Americans but also for the Spaniards. Franco's regime had been recently accepted into the international community. Now a member of the United Nations and an ally of the United States—through an exchange of military bases for international support—Spain initiated a path to modernization that would take two long decades to realize. At that moment in the late fifties, the state of affairs in the country was sinister, and Hemingway clearly recognized that. He saw a hypocritical government and a society operating on the false assumption that the past was over and that everybody had agreed to be happy with things as they were. Another related assumption was that Franco was a leader loved by the entire Spanish people. Those challenging these assumptions, by their attitudes or even by their mere presence (since censorship reduced the probability of open verbal challenge) were considered sources of embarrassment and company to be avoided. *The Dangerous Summer* hints at this situation through its masterly deployment of irony and understatement.

For Luis Miguel Dominguín, being friends with Hemingway, the American celebrity and friend of the Republic, could be wonderfully thrilling but also uncomfortable on certain public occasions. For instance, Hemingway, in his role as a narrator, complains about the dangers that having rich and important friends and too much social life may bring Antonio Ordóñez. When Antonio and Luis Miguel are in Bilbao for their last corrida together, Hemingway contrasts Bilbao's society with that of Madrid: "It was not the sinister social life of Madrid" (*DS* 124). This is the only time that the word *sinister* appears in *The Dangerous Summer;* knowing Hemingway's preference for the mot juste, we realize how accurate the adjective is. A little later, we learn that at their last corrida in Bilbao, Antonio and Luis Miguel, together with Jaime Ostos, have a special spectator: "There were many high dignitaries of the government present. Doña Carmen Polo de Franco, the wife of the head of the state, was in the presidential box with a party from San Sebastián" (*DS* 125). "The three matadors," Hemingway continues, "went up to the presidential box to pay their respects to Doña Carmen Polo de Franco. Luis Miguel, who is a friend of the Generalissimo's son-in-law and shoots with the head of the state, had sent his compliments and his excuses. But his leg felt well enough for him to go up to the high box. Or if it did not he still went up anyway and then he had to come down again. The next bull was his" (*DS* 128). Here Hemingway is telling us a truth about Dominguín's motives that can be learned just by watching the matador's revealing (re)actions to political power. They form part of a scene crafted by Hemingway to show an unsavory truth about a friend without directly stating it.

Hemingway trusts the reader and aficionado to know that the interruption of the bullfight so the bullfighters can go on a diplomatic errand to the Generalísimo's wife is an irregularity. The fact that the Generalísimo's wife is in the president's box is also irregular; only experts in the bullfight should be there to govern the proceedings. The bullfighters' subjection to rules beyond those of the corrida is a political statement and a statement on changed priorities. The natural dominators at the plaza, the matadors, are made to play the role of the dominated bull. It was embarrassing for Luis Miguel to have Hemingway witness his compliance with unspoken rules external to the world of the bullfight but relevant now in a changed postwar Spain.

The Dangerous Summer is a difficult text, more politically oriented than it seems at first sight. The attentive reader may find apparently insignificant scenes pregnant with hidden criticism that can be read between the lines. Later in the text, for instance, Luis Miguel is badly wounded and taken to the plaza infirmary to be operated on. Hemingway cannot go to be with him there because, as he says, "there was no way to get to the infirmary from where we sat in the first row of seats and the police would not allow anyone in the passageway so I stayed and watched while Antonio took over Luis Miguel's bull" (*DS* 129). This passage might be read either literally, as a true narrative of the sequence of moves and motivations explaining Hemingway's behavior in the plaza or indirectly, as an excuse for Hemingway's staying away from Luis Miguel at the infirmary in order to watch Antonio's faena. Of the possible interpretations for Hemingway's absence from the infirmary, Luis Miguel will be shown to believe the one that casts the worst light on Hemingway's character. This and similar misunderstandings on Luis Miguel's part indirectly construct him for the reader as lacking true knowledge of the world. This scene demonstrates Hemingway's technical expertise at censoring his text for a positive reason, to save a friend's face. Later in the text, when the afternoon is over and Antonio has changed, he and Hemingway go to the Bilbao Clinic, where Luis Miguel is resting. They find Luis Miguel in a crowded room.

> There were half a dozen people present, and Luis Miguel was being gracious to them through his suffering. . . .
>
> "I'm sorry I couldn't get to the infirmary," I said. "How's the pain holding?"
>
> "It's so-so, Ernesto," he said very softly.

> "Manolo will ease it."
> He smiled gently. "He has," he said.
> "Can I take any of these people out?"
> "Poor people," he said. "You took so many before. I missed you."
> "I'll see you in Madrid," I said. "Maybe if we go some of them will go."
> "We all look so nice together in the rotogravures," he said.
> "I'll see you at Ruber's." Ruber's was the hospital.
> "I've kept the apartment," he said. (*DS* 134)

This is the closing scene of *The Dangerous Summer,* one which is difficult precisely because of its apparent insignificance. It seems to be a simple, agreeable conversation between friends, but it is actually a complex interaction between two sophisticated men who disagree on essential points. Analysis of the conversation reveals the vast distance between Luis Miguel's words and his meaning and says everything about a way of being and acting that Hemingway considers sinister. Luis Miguel does not want to, or cannot, ask the people around him to leave the room. Hemingway offers to do it for him, but Luis Miguel declines, saying, "'Poor people,' . . . [y]ou took so many before. I missed you.'" He seems to be referring to the fact that no one was with him in the infirmary. Unaware that the police prevented everybody in the passageway from going to the infirmary, Luis Miguel supposes that Hemingway was the one who asked people to go away, depriving Luis Miguel of company. This is another misunderstanding on Luis Miguel's part. His belief that Hemingway would assume that responsibility without asking shows that he does not know Hemingway. But this suspiciousness is masked by Luis Miguel's gentle smiles and soft tone. Hemingway does not correct him on the point and says good-bye, hoping someone will follow suit—that's what he actually says to Luis Miguel. Luis Miguel insists that he likes being accompanied because it looks good in the photos for the press. Hemingway says good-bye again, announcing that he will visit Luis Miguel again at the hospital to which the matador is being transferred. Luis Miguel does not agree; he mentions his flat, implying it is a better place for Hemingway to visit him. A surface reading may rest at the point where Luis Miguel would seem to be inviting Hemingway to visit him at his flat, a more private place than the hospital rooms. Yet such literal reading would leave unnoticed an important textual clue. For a reader aware of contrasts, the allusion to the flat in Madrid can have another, more sinister, more consistent reading. Luis Miguel fears Hemingway's presence at Ruber's, because his friends in Madrid are rich and belong to the Marquis of Villaverde's circle. Luis Miguel does not want to risk having these people, especially Franco's son-in-law, the marquis, his friend and a physician at home at Ruber's, meet Hemingway the author of *For Whom the Bell Tolls,* in his company; it would not be proper for them to appear together in the rotogravures.

In ironic contrast, Antonio likes having Hemingway around on all occasions, as after his wounding in Aranjuez. When he is at the Hospital Ruber in Madrid, where he is attended by Dr. Tamames, Antonio is accompanied only by his wife, his mother, and Hemingway. The rest of the people, his banderilleros and picadors and others, wait outside in the hall, in another room, or come and go. "Visitors came and went leaving messages and cards. Miguelillo [Antonio's attendant] kept everyone but the family out of the room" (*DS* 48). So Ernesto is considered family and he, in the narrative, draws a family resemblance between the values Antonio represents and his own. And unlike Luis Miguel, Antonio is given a minimum of sedation, for he is returning to the bullfights as soon as possible. "Antonio was sweating heavily with the pain and he held his gray lips together. He did not want to open his lips but his eyes kept asking for Tamames to come" (48). The contrast with Luis Miguel's scene at Bilbao's hospital is revealing. Antonio is truly suffering, but Miguel is sedated, "snowed," even if he does not openly admit it. Antonio is true as a man, husband, friend, and fighter, while Luis Miguel is all words and vanity, a faker.

As is clear from their contrasting images, the two protagonists in this grotesque[15] tragedy serve more than one purpose. In the first place, they help to expose—rather than articulate—one theme central to Hemingway's Text since the 1930s: the necessity for art and for the artist of authenticity. Hemingway's manifesto in defense of the strict mutuality of truth and art was articulated in *Death in the Afternoon.* Since the 1930s, Hemingway had been interested in the way in which truths and illusions affect the lives of artist writers, both as individuals and as members of communities: families, friends, coworkers, parties, and countries. "The Snows of Kilimanjaro" (1936)[16] and *The Dangerous Summer* both symbolically explore the complex relationship between vain illusion and solid truth and the destructive effects that blindness to truth has on the individual, his private life, and his work. Harry in "The Snows of Kilimanjaro" and Luis Miguel's fictional construct in *The Dangerous Summer* both expose the dangers of reducing one's life to a lie. By elevating an illusion to the category of the actual, they come to live by it. All these texts stress the idea that the creative artist—be he Hemingway, the artist writer, or Antonio, the artist bullfighter—must know experientially the real-life difference between truth and delusion so as to be able to transmute their knowledge into fictions that are still illusions but believable and true for the reader.

The uniformity of Spanish cultural life and its politicization during the dictatorship was obvious to Hemingway. Any unwanted surplus of meaning had to be kept at bay. Censorship was one of the most important means of control at the time. The younger generation of Spanish writers liked Hemingway's work and learned from him, but his books were difficult to find in either English or Spanish, and not many young people could read English, as they could not travel abroad easily and as the universities had not yet recovered from the diaspora of intellectuals following the Spanish Civil War. These stifling conditions were likely to affect the quality of the writing being produced in Spain at the time, and Hemingway was much aware of it. We can see that clearly in Castillo-Puche's report on Hemingway's responses at the time of Pío Baroja's death and funeral, ranging from respect toward Pío Baroja to detachment from the not-exiled Spanish writers attending Baroja's funeral. The work of the postwar Spanish generation of fiction writers was bound to be poorer than that of the generations of 1898 and 1927, if only for want of freedom to read the leading contemporary authors, both national authors in exile and foreign authors, and to select themes and speak the truth about them. Nevertheless, a few Spanish writers (notably Camilo José Cela, future Nobel Prize-winner and a censor between 1943 and 1944) seem to have managed to circumvent the difficulties by profiting from a secure position analogous to that of the fictional police inspector in *The Dangerous Summer.*[17] The opening scene of *The Dangerous Summer* shows how even in the worst of circumstances there is room for exceptions. In 1953, a police inspector at the border simply addresses Hemingway while he goes through the customary routine, checking that the tourist is the famous American writer. When this point is settled, the inspector tells the author that he has read all his books. The passage might indicate that Hemingway's books do not manage to cross the border and are retained at the customs post, where they can be read only by some of the men on duty there. But it might indicate that, despite the censorship and related regulations, Hemingway's texts not only have reached a man in a position to confiscate Hemingway's books, but have permeated part of the social and literary fabric. This latter meaning might be the most important one if we judge by the natural way in which the inspector acknowledges, without fear of sanction, that he has read Hemingway's work. This man may be an active agent of a repressive regime of censorship, but he keeps enough individual freedom to avoid being a "dumb ox."[18] Hemingway seems to suggest here, and throughout *The Dangerous Summer,* that Spain is still Spain, and there is yet hope for its future.[19]

Antonio and Luis Miguel serve to expose the consequences of the civil war on Spanish life and art that Hemingway would not address more directly. The iceberg principle that he formulated in *Death in the Afternoon* helped him to keep the word given in 1953 to his Spanish friends in Cuba, veterans from the Spanish Civil War, "[to keep his] mouth shut on politics" when he came to

Spain (*DS* 1). Although *The Dangerous Summer* displaces the theme of the civil war to the textual margins, it raises the issue by alluding to the conflict. Such passages are neither long nor specifically a part of the primary narrative, the bullfight story, a quite banal duel between members of a decadent generation, Antonio Ordóñez and Luis Miguel Dominguín. The truly tragic fratricide, the three-year strife between the sons and daughters of the Spanish land, is allotted little textual space in *The Dangerous Summer* beyond the diminished mock-heroic form of a mano a mano fight, a fight between brothers-in-law and matadors, a fight for preeminence in their profession and an *entente cordiale* for money. In Hemingway's words, "the rivalry [between Antonio and Luis Miguel] was beginning to shape up like a civil war and neutrality was becoming increasingly difficult" (*DS* 58). These words signal the presence of a wider context, war, displaced from the textual surface of *The Dangerous Summer*, but an integral, though subdued, part of its overall design. Each man stands for a civil war faction: Luis Miguel, a well-off middle-aged bullfighter who does not need to fight for a living, one on Franco's side, represents the powerful group with whom he associates in *The Dangerous Summer*, the rich and beautiful city men owning land in the country upon which they hunt and others toil. Antonio is the hard-working young family man with honest plans to buy some land and work it. He is suntanned from working at the farm, not, like Luis Miguel, from sitting by the swimming pool. This characterization is steadily enforced throughout *The Dangerous Summer*. The ideological scheme follows the lines traced by *The Spanish Earth*. The true man and the vain one are Hemingway's implicit emblems for the men that fought in the Spanish Civil War and their motivations. Hemingway makes the duel between Antonio and Luis Miguel end as the civil war should have ended had things been different. Hemingway's engaged literary reconstruction somehow manages to correct the past.[20] It may be a sad consolation, but a consolation at least.

The Dangerous Summer stands as a narrative of reminiscence, artistic precisely because its author remembers the past as it was and knows the present as it is, but chooses to let both, the most significant memories of the past and the most significant facts of the present, remain untold, omitted from a text that is highly selective, a text that adds and subtracts, displaces and misplaces, and thus lets shared memory and fact become the point where the reader's imagination and knowledge meet the writer's. *The Dangerous Summer*'s peculiarity as an autobiographical narrative of reminiscence, what makes it "anti-narrative," is that the reminisced is scarcely represented in the overt narrative; it appears instead in displaced thematic contexts. The bullfight tour, following Antonio Ordóñez from Zaragoza to Valencia, across Teruel, and up to Barcelona, gives Hemingway the excuse and the chance to visit—unchecked—the Spanish Civil

War sites along the Ebro Front. The war appears in the form of collateral allusions that are marginal to the overt narrative, the bullfight narrative about Antonio and Luis Miguel's rivalry. Yet even with the Spanish Civil War pushed to the margins, Hemingway manages to make his understated views retrievable by his readers. For this, Hemingway relies on shared reminiscence. The reader's recall is triggered by the poignancy of a sudden experience of recognition in a passing allusion to a particular geographical name, Teruel: "A big part of the road to Teruel had never been rebuilt properly since the Civil War. It was narrow, cut-up blacktop, dangerous to drive with any speed at night but it was the only way for us to cut through to the Mediterranean" (63). It is a recognition of repetition and recurrent pattern, also an intertextual coincidence: suddenly, something is/reads like it was before for the writer and others, except for a little something or somebody missing or added, a measure of difference which brings with it a feeling of loss and a longing to recover, even if in a displaced mode and form, what there was and is no more.

Hemingway revisits Spain and the bullfights in order to build a balance between the amount of recurring reminiscence and the amount of recent experience that will together form *The Dangerous Summer* and make it as true as Hemingway wanted it to be: "I wanted to come over and write the truth, the absolute truth, about [Antonio's] work and his place in bullfighting so there would be a permanent record; something that would last when we were both gone" (*DS* 34–35). It is a desire for literary truth that started at the beginning of Hemingway's career and sustained him—in transformed guises—until its very end.

In an inverse movement, Hemingway brings the reader of *The Dangerous Summer* to revisit a past text, *Death in the Afternoon*, in a present one, and see a younger version of the writer, his narratorial persona addressed by means of an impersonal second person "you," from the evolved perspective of an older and more ironic memoirist. The awareness of aging is also part of this imaginary trip from past to present and back from present to past. When Hemingway, Mary, and their group go to the Irati forest from Pamplona in July 1959, they are happy, the text says:

> Finding the country unspoiled and being able to have it again and share it with the people that were together that July I was as happy as I had ever been and all the overcrowding and the modernizations of Pamplona meant nothing . . . The wine was as good as when you were twenty-one, and the food as marvelous as always. There were the same songs and good new ones that

> cracked and suddenly pounded onto the drums and the pipes. The faces that were young once were old as mine but everyone remembered how we were. The eyes had not changed and nobody was fat. No mouths were bitter no matter what the eyes had seen. Bitter lines around the mouth are the first sign of defeat. Nobody was defeated. (*DS* 80)

The same preoccupation can be read in *Death in the Afternoon,* where Hemingway writes: "Pamplona is changed, of course, but not as much as we are older. I found that if you took a drink that it got very much the same as it was always. I know things change now and I do not care. It's all been changed for me. Let it all change. We'll all be gone before it's changed too much . . . We've seen it all go and we'll watch it go again (*DIA* 278). We see here the power of words to re-create a moment of (self)awareness taking place in the middle of an act of reminiscing. Already in 1932 a young man's narrating voice looks back at a past only ten years removed from the present and projects this retrospection into the future with an older man's prospective knowledge: nothing ever remains the same, and the feeling of loss that change brings will hit him several times in the future through the recurrence of similar experiential and creative cycles. Decades later, an older man's narrating voice will remind the reader of *The Dangerous Summer* that that young man was right, that it is memory and the awareness of memory's workings that allow the artist to forge a creative answer to cyclical loss, his work and his ability to re-create the past and bring it back to life for the little while that the writing and the reading last. Sad but fine is the modernist writer's ambivalent emotional answer to the paradoxical nature of art, which is creative and destructive. From very early and until the very end, Hemingway recognized his need to go along with the stream of time and accept the changes that time brings, an acceptance without bitterness but that embraced novelty and introduced novelties even in what seemed an already perfect style, [21] novelties that could be called the postmodern developments of a modernist writer who was never lost or trapped within one and just one generation.

Notes

1. After the two world wars of 1914–18 and 1939–45 and the Spanish Civil War of 1936–39, Europe's tremendous losses became apparent. Early modern European colonial powers had already suffered the gradual loss of their empires, a process that for Spain culminated in the 1898 Spanish-American war over Cuba. A whole generation of Spanish writers is called "the generation of 1898" on account of this date's significance. For the modern colonial powers, especially Britain and France, World War II would play a similar role fifty years later.

2. I am using the capitalized expression *Text* in the specific sense used by Comley and Scholes in the opening pages of *Hemingway's Genders: Rereading the Hemingway Text.*

3. We can cite here the whole body of writing produced between the mid-1940s and 1960, including *A Moveable Feast, Under Kilimanjaro,* and *The Dangerous Summer,* which would count as literary—rather than historical—autobiographical writings, and the rest of his postwar writing, which would be autobiographical literary fictions. The status of Hemingway's postwar writings can be said to be guided by a kind of narrativity configuring Hemingway's diverse successive forms of being in successive narrative redescriptions of his own self and others (see Ricoeur).

4. The difference between recurrence and repetition is one of essential importance for understanding Hemingway's relation with the past as perceivable in his nonfiction. His literary memoiristic writing, from *Death in the Afternoon* (chapter 20 is "all that the book is about") to *The Dangerous Summer,* relies on intertextual recurrence—rereading the past from a different position in a renewed writing present—for one more redefinition of the writer's identity and of his role within the literary tradition.

5. Cayetano Ordóñez, Niño de la Palma, who was in the list of matadors mentioned in chapter 18 of *Death in the Afternoon,* earlier served as the model for Pedro Romero, the bullfighter with whom Lady Brett falls in love, in *The Sun Also Rises.*

6. Pío Baroja, a leading member of the literary generation of 1898, is considered the greatest novelist in twentieth-century Spanish literature. Hemingway admired the man's honesty and his brand of literary realism. The older writer was an individualist, opposed to the effects of industrialization on the modern urban and human landscape. A master of dialogue and a literary impressionist, Baroja, his ideas, and his sober precision of expression serve as the perfect Spanish match for Hemingway's achievements in English.

7. On this occasion Hemingway complained to Castillo-Puche about the cowardice of some of the Spanish people—authors mainly—at the civil cemetery: "They are ashamed of praying and then they will kill others for not praying" (Castillo-Puche 195; my translation). This revealing passage makes clear that Hemingway saw behind appearances and understood perfectly the "sinister" fascist atmosphere in Madrid and its effect on the cowardly souls of Baroja's public mourners.

8. It is Hemingway's idea that good texts are deceptive: they mean more than they say, and their "surface-to-bottom" narrativity resembles an iceberg (Penas Ibáñez, "A Pragma-Stylistic Contribution" 230–31): "If a writer of prose knows enough about what he is writing about he may omit things that he knows and the reader, if the writer is writing truly enough, will have a feeling of those things as strongly as though the writer had stated them. The dignity of

movement of an iceberg is due to only one-eighth of it being above water. A writer who omits things because he does not know them only makes hollow places in his writing" (*DIA* 192).

9. Valerie Hemingway writes that Hemingway knew Lorca's poem "Llanto por Ignacio Sánchez Mejías" (1935) and "could recite the lines by heart" (V. Hemingway 44).

10. A full interpretation of the bullfight and the homology that *Death in the Afternoon* draws between bullfighting, literary writing, and the literary scene can be found in Penas Ibáñez ("Very Sad"). The same interpretation and homology apply to *The Dangerous Summer.* In both books, the readers find implicitness to be the central structural narrative device, one which, at certain levels, could operate as self-imposed censorship.

11. The full passage is as follows:

> [Antonio asks] "Did you write well?"
> [Ernesto replies] "Some days very well. Some days not so good."
> "I'm the same way. There are days when you can't write at all. But they have paid to see you so you write as well as you can."
> "You've been writing all right lately."
> "Yes. But you know what I mean. You have days too when it isn't there."
> "Yes. But I always force it and I use my head."
> "So do I. But it's wonderful when you really write. There's nothing better."
> He was very pleased, always, to call the faena writing.
> We talked about all sorts of things: the different problems of the artist in the world he lives in; technical things and professional secrets; finance; sometimes economics and politics. (*DS* 51–52)

12. In the postwar texts, the Hemingway reader notices an increase in textual self-reflexivity, accompanied by a more pervasive but also more hidden use of intertextuality, all of which results in a special kind of displaced iceberg textuality—still omissive, but more allusive.

13. Early in *Death in the Afternoon,* the reader is made indirectly aware of the deepest source of anxiety—the lack of a good father—underlying the narrative design; the narrator confesses to studying the bullfight "as a man might, for instance, study the death of his father" (*DIA* 3).

14. The research conducted under my supervision at the University of Zaragoza on the Spanish translation of Hemingway's work supports the point that the translations available at the time were poor and must have undermined Hemingway's critical reception in Spain. See, for instance, Rodríguez Pazos.

15. I use the word in its technical sense, as it is used in association with the theatre of the grotesque, created by the Galician author Don Ramón María del Valle Inclán, a renowned member of the generation of 1898. Hemingway's literary autobiography embeds a grotesque trio—Ernesto, Antonio, and Luis Miguel—and a grotesque tragedy à la Valle Inclán, which reflects its absurdity on the absurdity of an earlier tragedy, the Spanish Civil War and the strange role played by the neutral democracies.

16. See Penas Ibáñez ("Hemingway's Ethics") for a detailed analysis of these aesthetic tenets in "The Snows of Kilimanjaro."

17. See Twomey's chapter in the present book for more details about the political situation in Franco's Spain at the time of Hemingway's visits in the 1950s.

18. My allusion is to Wyndham Lewis's April 1934 *Life and Letters* article, "The Dumb Ox: A Study of Ernest Hemingway" (rpt. in Meyers). Lewis makes an excellent critical evaluation of the meaning of the ox in *DIA* and, more generally within Hemingway's ideological frame, the ox as the passive modern American to whom things are done. Nevertheless Lewis is partial when he forgets that the pattern is incomplete without the active bull, and becomes insulting when he compares Hemingway to the ox for his lack of political commitment. Malcolm Cowley's criticism is more careful and does not deprive *Death in the Afternoon* of its sociopolitical implications.

The caption to the photograph "the Ox" that accompanies the text reads: "While here we have the ox built for beef and for service who might have been president with that face if he had started in some other line of work. He differs from the fighting bull in this, as well as in his general shape . . . He may work hard all his life or he may be made into beef early in his career, but he will never kill a horse. Nor will he ever want to. Hail to the useful ox; a friend and contemporary of man." (*DIA* np).

19. In María Teresa León's memoirs, we find a telling passage recollecting a visit she made with the poet Rafael Alberti to the Hemingways' home, the Finca Vigía, in Cuba in 1960. She gives us a glimpse of Hemingway's general impressions about Madrid and Spain after spending his 1959 dangerous summer there. He told the Albertis: "I went back to see all that again and it is no good, nothing like our times" (León 317, translation mine).

20. This concept is not far from Jameson's idea that narrative often comes as an imaginary solution to real problems.

21. Eby provides an invaluable analysis of the dynamics and the meaning of transformation in *The Garden of Eden* (1986). Eby applies his analysis to the masculine-feminine psychological transformations of the characters. Eby's analysis can also be applied to the dynamics of change of the Hemingway text in its modernist (masculine) and postmodernist (feminine) forms. The postmodern narrative forms (like *The Garden of Eden*) function, like Catherine, as mirrors creating an infinite regression of reflections, and infinite transformations (Penas Ibáñez "Looking Through Garden's Mirrors").

Works Cited

Bloom, Harold. *The Anxiety of Influence: A Theory of Poetry.* Oxford: Oxford UP, 1973.

Castillo-Puche, José Luis. *Hemingway: Entre la vida y la muerte.* Barcelona: Destino, 1968.

Comley, Nancy R., and Robert E. Scholes. *Hemingway's Genders: Rereading the Hemingway Text.* New Haven: Yale UP, 1996.

Cowley, Malcolm. "A Farewell to Spain." *New Republic* 30 Nov. 1932: 76–77; rpt. in Meyers 1982: 164–70.

Eby, Carl. "'He Felt the Change So That It Hurt Him All Through': Sodomy and Transvestic Hallucination in Late Hemingway." *Hemingway Review* 25.1 (2005): 77–95.

Fuentes, Norberto. *Hemingway in Cuba.* Secaucus, N. J.: Lyle Stuart, 1984.

Hemingway, Ernest. *The Dangerous Summer.* London: Hamish Hamilton, 1985.

———. *Death in the Afternoon.* New York: Scribner, 1932.

———. *Green Hills of Africa.* New York: Scribner, 1935.

———. *In Our Time.* New York: Boni and Liveright, 1925.

———. "The Snows of Kilimanjaro." *Esquire* Aug. 1936: 27, 194–201. Rpt. in *The Complete Short Stories* by Hemingway. New York: Scribner, 1991. 39–56.

———. *True At First Light.* London: William Heinemann, 1999.

Hemingway, Valerie. *Running with the Bulls: My Years with the Hemingways.* New York: Ballantine Books, 2005.

Jameson, Fredric. *The Political Unconscious: Narrative as a Socially Symbolic Act.* Ithaca: Cornell UP, 1981.

LaPrade, Douglas. *La Censura de Hemingway en España.* Salamanca: Ediciones de la Universidad de Salamanca, 1991.

León, María Teresa. *Memoria de la melancolía.* Barcelona: Laia-Picazo, 1977.

Lewis, Wyndham. "The Dumb Ox: A Study of Ernest Hemingway." *Life and Letters* 10 (April 1934): 33–45. Rpt. in Meyers: 186–209.

Mandel, Miriam B., ed. *A Companion to Hemingway's* Death in the Afternoon. New York: Camden House, 2004.

Meyers, Jeffrey, ed. *Hemingway: The Critical Heritage.* London: Routledge and Kegan Paul, 1982.

Penas Ibáñez, Beatriz. "Hemingway's Ethics of Writing: The Ironic Semantics of 'Whiteness' in 'The Snows of Kilimanjaro.'" *North Dakota Quarterly* 70.4 (2003): 94–118.

———. "Looking Through the Garden's Mirrors: The Early Postmodernist Hemingway Text." *North Dakota Quarterly* 65.3 (1998): 91–104.

———. "A Pragma-Stylistic Contribution to the Study of Narrativity: Standard and Non-standard Narrativities." In *Theorizing Narrativity.* Ed. John Pier and José Angel García Landa. New York: Walter De Gruyter, 2008. 211–51.

———. "Very Sad but Very Fine": *Death in the Afternoon*'s Imagist Interpretation of the Bullfight-Text." In *A Companion to Hemingway's* Death in the Afternoon. Ed. Miriam B. Mandel. New York: Camden House, 2004. 143–64.

Reynolds, Michael. "Ernest Hemingway 1899–1961: A Brief Biography." In *A Historical Guide to Ernest Hemingway.* Ed. Linda Wagner-Martin. Oxford: Oxford UP, 2000. 15–50.

———. *Hemingway: The American Homecoming.* Oxford/Cambridge: Blackwell, 1992.

———. *Hemingway's Reading 1910–1940: An Inventory.* Princeton: Princeton UP, 1981.

Ricoeur, Paul. *Du Texte à l'action. Essays d'herméneutique II.* Paris: Éditions du Seuil, 1986.

———. "L'imagination dans le recit et dans l'action." *Savoir, Faire, Espérer: Les Limites de la raison.* Bruxelles: Publications des Facultés Universitaires Saint-Louis, 1976. 207–28.

Rodríguez Pazos, Gabriel. "Not So True, Not So Simple: The Spanish Translations of *The Sun Also Rises.*" *Hemingway Review* 23.2 (2004): 47–65.

Twomey, Lisa. "Ernest Hemingway—¿Amigo de España?" In *Hemingway's Spain: Imagining the Spanish World.* Ed. Carl P. Eby and Mark Cirino. Kent: Kent State UP, 2015. 28–43.

6

Bulls, Art, Mithras, and Montherlant

Ben Stoltzfus

While Hemingway was living and working in Paris, he visited Spain frequently and came to love that country as much as France, if not more. At the end of 1923, he wrote to his friend James Gamble, saying that Spain was "the very best country of all" (*SL* 107). He also wrote to William D. Horne, an American Red Cross ambulance driver who, like Hemingway, had been in Italy in 1918 and who later, in 1920–21, had been his Chicago roommate, saying that the best times he had had since the war were at the Pamplona feria. He described the corrida as "the most beautiful thing" he had ever seen (*SL* 88).

In 1925, Hemingway wrote to Max Perkins, his editor, saying that he wanted to write a book on bullfighting and illustrate it with good photographs (*SL* 156). That proposed book eventually became *Death in the Afternoon.* Meanwhile, he went to Pamplona a third time and transformed his experiences there with his friends into *The Sun Also Rises*—a novel that incorporates the fiesta of San Fermín and the climactic moment of Pedro Romero's faena with the second bull.[1]

In his three major books on bullfighting—*The Sun Also Rises, Death in the Afternoon,* and *The Dangerous Summer*—Hemingway describes the corrida as tragedy and the *toreo* as art.[2] First and foremost, however, overriding his love for Spain and his enthusiasm for the corrida, was his dedication to writing. That he was able to meld all three into his art—Spain, the corrida, and writing—is an example of his creative genius. Hemingway assimilated the discipline and spectacle of bullfighting, even as he forged a language that would mirror the rich cultural heritage of Spain and its deep roots in a mythical Mithraic past.[3]

Death in the Afternoon, as many commentators have noted, is not only about bullfighting. Nancy Bredendick points out that its subject matter is death—the death of bulls, horses, and human beings—and that Hemingway "explores the philosophical, emotional, and artistic implications of death" (209). Edward F. Stanton notes that *Death in the Afternoon* evolved into a book on Spain, Spaniards, Spanish life, and the whole culture (93). Miriam B. Mandel and Amy Vondrak both emphasize the book's postmodern diversity. In addition to being a travelogue and a manual on bullfighting, it incorporates a range of genres, including journalism, the short story, drama, parody, humor, biography, autobiography, lexicography, history, criticism, scientific description, folklore, translation, and prose poetry (Mandel 258).

Even if *Death in the Afternoon* is a kaleidoscope of genres, or perhaps because it is, it is essentially and unavoidably about writing. Many critics agree on this, although they differ on how Hemingway links writing to the book's other themes. Peter Messent says that "writing and bullfighting . . . are linked in symbiotic connection throughout the book" (123). Hilary K. Justice observes that "Hemingway's metacritical project . . . resides in the complex analogy between the art and business of bullfighting and the art and business of writing" (239). Beatriz Penas Ibáñez asserts that Hemingway's interest in bullfighting is subordinated to his interest in literature ("Very Sad" 143), while according to Brendendick, *Death in the Afternoon* is a "book about writing a book" (234), the ultimate in self-reflexive art. "Its taurine dicta," she says, "are congruent with dicta on the art of writing" (206). *Death in the Afternoon* is, after all, the book in which Hemingway develops his iceberg theory of writing. Stanton notes that the work itself is like an iceberg, one whose tip looks like a manual on bullfighting but "whose submerged body contains the deeper levels of life, death, sacrifice, and renewal" (117).

Despite Hemingway's emphasis on writing, his corollary purpose in writing *Death in the Afternoon* was to give the corrida its just due as an art form. A poem and a painting survive in time, and music can be revived whenever we replay a Beethoven quartet, but a great faena, says Hemingway, is as fleeting as a dream. *Death in the Afternoon* seeks to honor the art of the faena, and goes further. It serves, among other things, as an apologia for the cult of death and the pleasure of killing, beliefs that are, generally speaking, alien to Anglo-Saxon audiences. Hemingway shifts the observer's attention from the blood and gore of the event to the matador's performance and the spectacle. Not that Hemingway eschews the violence: bulls bleed; horses are gutted, spilling their entrails; and matadors are sometimes killed. Nor does Hemingway hide the obvious: the ultimate death of the bull. In building toward this climax, however, he emphasizes the beauty and artistry of the performance.

Although Hemingway believes that bullfighting is an art, he sees it as an impermanent art. It is impermanent, he says, because, unlike most other arts, the artistry is in the performance. When it ends, nothing remains except a few dead bulls, a horse or two, and perhaps an injured matador. Unlike a great sculpture or a great novel, artifacts that we can point to repeatedly and say, "Yes, this is art," the bullfight is ephemeral. Its art, like that of the dance, is in the visual moment, and when the moment ends, the art is over, remaining only as a mnemonic trace. Hemingway's goal was to lend permanence to the traces of memory, to restore their intensity and, insofar as writing can lend permanence to such things, to give the corrida its just due as an art form.

Hemingway envies the permanence of sculpture, and he strives to give his writing about the bullfight a sculptural hardness. But not all sculpture is equal. In *Death in the Afternoon,* he says that he knows of "no modern sculpture, except Brancusi's, that is in any way the equal of the sculpture of modern bullfighting" (99). In *The Dangerous Summer,* Hemingway also compares bullfighting to music, poetry, painting, mathematics, and writing, as in the following passages taken from an account of Ordóñez's performance: "With the muleta, he *sculptured* his passes gently and slowly making the whole long faena a *poem*" (*DS* 170). "It was the closeness and the slowness that *carved* the figure and made each pass seem *permanent*" (171). "Antonio was doing it all to music and keeping it as pure as *mathematics* and as warm, as exciting and as stirring as *love*" (*DS* 130; my emphasis throughout). But if Antonio's performance is a poem, as stirring as love, as precise as mathematics, and as moving as music, it is because of his superior artistry, his courage while facing death, and his ability to communicate these sensations to the observer.

Hemingway compares the *toreo* to the works of Velásquez, Goya, Cervantes, and Lope de Vega (*DIA* 73). He describes the three acts of the corrida as though we were at the theater (*DIA* 96, 98), and when he refers to the event as tragedy we think of drama and Shakespeare. Finally, when Hemingway says that the goring of the horses is comedy—"the death of the horse tends to be comic while that of the bull is tragic" (*DIA* 6)—we become aware of all the actors on the program, and the sun, the sand, the blood, and the shadows, in addition to the bull, the horses, the matador, the picador, the banderillero, the *puntillero,* the peon, and the president also play their roles. Furthermore, and tellingly, "Charri, a rotund, hard-drinking Basque who was devoted to Antonio and followed all of his fights, had the old Shakespearian role of the Fool" (*DS* 119).

Hemingway believes that bullfighting is an art and, conversely, he incorporates the aesthetics of bullfighting into his writing. Not only does he think of bullfighting as an art, he also equates the skill of a great matador with the skill of a great writer. In doing so, he stresses the ability, discipline, courage, honor, honesty, rhythm, pacing, movement, action, drama, comedy, tragedy, emotion, and ecstasy of both artists. In due course, he illustrates each one of these categories, and we come to understand how they function in bullfighting and in art. Skill, rhythm, and courage in dominating the bull combine to generate the emotion in the matador and in the observer, and it is this emotion that Hemingway equates with the effect produced by a great work of art. Maera "gave emotion always and, finally, as he steadily improved his style, he was an artist" (*DIA* 79). This artistry is the "real thing," says Hemingway, and it is "the sequence of motion and fact" that make the emotion (2).

Stanton points out that if Hemingway learned from Cézanne how to write about country, he learned from the *toreo* how to make writing a performative art (*Hemingway and Spain* 29–30). Hemingway's "prose of ecstasy," he says—a prose that has "emotional and spiritual intensity"—has the "pure classic beauty" of a brilliant faena (*DIA* 206–7). Death unites man and bull in the "aesthetic and artistic climax of the fight" (247), and this moment of tragedy, in the arena and on the page, produces the ecstasy that is both emotional and spiritual. Not only that, but the emotional appeal of a great faena "is the feeling of immortality that the bullfighter feels," which is also the emotion "that he gives to the spectators" (213). In *The Sun Also Rises,* Hemingway describes Romero's performance as giving "real emotion, because he kept the absolute purity of line in his movements . . . through the maximum of exposure" (168). Inferior matadors, unlike Romero, use tricks in order to exaggerate the danger: they twist themselves like corkscrews, they raise their elbows, and they lean against the flanks of the bull after the horns have passed (*SAR* 167–68). Tricks or not, every bullfighter exposes himself to death. The difference between the good ones and the bad ones is in the degree of exposure, the manifest skill, and the eventual reprieve from death. These are the qualities that provide the emotion for the matador and the observer. No wonder that Hemingway describes Antonio's purity of style and timing as Bach-like.

Although *The Dangerous Summer* stresses the rivalry between Miguel Dominguín and Antonio Ordóñez, Hemingway, in this sequel to *Death in the Afternoon,* again equates bullfighting with writing while emphasizing both as art. The writer, he says, is free to break the rules of syntax and grammar for artistic effect, but if he fakes in order to cover up his incompetence or lack of knowledge, he mystifies where there is no mystery. He has failed to master his craft and he substitutes overwritten journalism or a false epic quality for good writing (*DIA* 54). Having talked about the fakery of bullfighters—about matadors who do not keep the absolute purity of line but simulate the appearance of danger in order to fake the emotional appeal (*SAR* 168)—Hemingway praises the artist who "writes clearly" because "any one can see if he fakes" in order to cover a "lack of knowledge" or ability (*DIA* 54). Ordóñez, in his purity of line and absence of fakery, was clearly an artist, as the following passage from *The Dangerous Summer* makes clear: "He took the bull with the muleta so suavely, so simply, and so smoothly that every pass seemed to be *sculptured.* He made all the classic passes and then seemed to try to *refine* them and make them *purer* in line and more dangerous as he *purposely* shortened his naturales by bringing his elbow in to bring the bull by him closer than it seemed any bull could be passed. It was a big bull, entire, brave and strong and with good horns and Antonio made the most complete and *classic* faena with him that I had ever seen" (94; my emphasis).

It was on 30 May 1959, during this fight in Aranjuez, that Ordóñez was gored.[4] Hemingway was on hand for his recovery and convalescence. During one of their many conversations on various topics they discussed the crafts of writing and fighting: the fact that some days were better than others and that during the good days you could do certain things without forcing it. "It's wonderful when you really write," says Ordóñez. "There's nothing better." Hemingway's aside to the reader—an aside full of meaning—tells us that Antonio "was very pleased, always, to call the faena writing" (*DS* 102–3).

Not only are artists happy when the juices are flowing, they also alter reality in order to make it conform to their inner vision of things. Hemingway did it, he says, in order to paint a truer portrait of the world and it is a process that necessarily incorporates the observer. The artist's role, says Hemingway, is to communicate the emotion of lived experience, and he must do it simply and without fakery and to the best of his ability. To fulfill his vision, the artist does not simply mirror reality, he invents it, and when he invents correctly he produces a work of art. Hemingway applies all this to one of Ordóñez's fights, during which he invents the bull, much as an artist invents his work.

On this occasion, Ordóñez has drawn a worthless animal that is hesitant with the horses and does not charge frankly. At one point in the different sequences, he picks up the bull with the cape, delicately and suavely, fixes him, teaches him, and encourages him by letting him pass closer and closer. Antonio *fabricates* him into a fighting bull, and you see it happen. In his enjoyment and knowledge of the bull, he seems to be working in the bull's head until the bull understands what is wanted of him. All of this is done in "slow motion [as] in a picture or a dream" (*DS* 72), and, after he places the sword, Antonio guides the bull's death as he had guided his one performance in his short life. When it is over, Antonio asks: "'Contento Ernesto?'"

"'You know,' I said. 'Everybody knew. You had to make him. You had to invent him'" (*DS* 73). In his writing and in conversation Hemingway frequently calls attention to the artist as a person who invents, as someone who transforms the ordinary into the sublime and, in the process, invents the reader by getting inside his or her mind and fabricates the emotion to which the reader will respond.

In bullfighting, a superior performance is both art and tragedy because it ends in the death of the bull and because it reenacts in ritual form the mystery of life and death. The matador performs a work of art, and he plays with death, bringing it closer and closer with each veronica (pass with the cape) which, if he is an artist, shows his domination of the bull. These are moments of immortality that the matador proves to himself and to the observer, and at the moment of truth "he proves it with the sword" (*DIA* 213). "Killing cleanly and in a way which gives you aesthetic pleasure and pride has always been one of the greatest enjoyments of a part of the human race" (*DIA* 232).

So the matador, like the writer, is an artist; the faena is comparable to writing, and the *toreo* is tragedy. But in Spain, the death of the bull goes beyond art and tragedy, incorporating myth, religion, ritual, and the cult of the bull throughout history. What we read in Hemingway on this subject is the tip of the iceberg. To experience the seven-eighths below the iceberg's surface, we need to go to the works of Henry de Montherlant, particularly *Les bestiaires* (1926) and *Le chaos et la nuit* (1963). Hemingway owned the original French edition of *Les bestiaires* (Paris: Grasset), and he borrowed the 1927 English translation (*The Bullfighters*) from Sylvia Beach's Paris bookstore, Shakespeare and Company (Mandel 113).

Les bestiaires recounts the initiation into bullfighting of a young matador, Alban de Bricoule. While learning the *toreo,* he falls in love with Soledad, the daughter of a rancher who raises bulls. They meet, and she promises her favors to him if he will fight a very dangerous animal. Despite his youth and inexperience, Alban's pride goads him to overcome his fear and he confronts the bull, but, having killed it, he rejects Soledad because he objects to her capricious frivolity that would have him risk his life in order to submit to her sexuality. In addition to the love story, however, the real subject matter of the novel is the corrida, which is presented in all its vitality as ritual and sacrifice—a ritual inherited from the cult of Mithras.[5]

In order to write about Mithraism, Montherlant borrowed heavily from the two volumes by the Belgian scholar Franz Cumont, entitled *Textes et monuments figurés relatifs aux mystères de Mithra.* Mithras, or Mithra, as he was called by the Persians, is the Roman name for the Indo-Iranian god Mitra. He is the god of light between heaven and earth, and he is also associated with the sun. According to Noel Swerdlow, a leading Mithraic scholar at the University of Chicago, Mithraism is the ancient Roman mystery cult that began during the early Roman empire and flourished from the second through the fourth centuries of the Common Era. Although the exact origins of cult practices remain controversial, the earliest datable evidence comes from the hills surrounding the valleys of the Rhine and Danube rivers, where, in little grottos, soldiers of the Roman frontier legions were initiated into the rites of Mithras. Relics of Mithraic rituals, including inscriptions, mosaics, frescoes, statues, and bas-reliefs, litter central and southeastern Europe, central Italy, and Rome itself. The most celebrated are the reliefs of Mithras slaying the bull, and the best-known examples of the tauroctony are the reliefs from Heddernheim and Osterburken, in Germany. They depict Mithras astride the bull, with his left knee on its back and his right leg along the animal's hind leg, pulling its head up by the snout with his left hand while he plunges a sword into the bull's shoulder with his right hand. The youthful Mithras wears a tunic, a Phrygian cap, and a billowing cape. He is sometimes depicted looking over his shoulder at a bird, possibly a raven. The reliefs also include busts of a male sun in the upper left and a female moon in the upper right. A scorpion grasps the bull's genitals and a dog leaps toward the wound. A snake slithers on the ground and shafts of wheat spring from the bull's tail (Swerdlow 48).

In tracing the history of Mithraism, scholars such as Roger Beck and David Ulansey argue strongly for its astrological origins. Still others, notably Ernst Renan, see a close link between Mithraism and Christianity. In a review article, however, "On the Cosmical Mysteries of Mithras," Swerdlow dismisses Mithraism's astrological origins and its links with Christianity (58–63).

Even though Mithraism had a wide following from the middle of the second century to the late fourth century CE, the belief that Mithraism was the prime competitor of Christianity is, according to Alison Griffith, blatantly false. She argues that Mithraism was only one of several cults imported from the eastern empire and that the major competitor to Christianity was the combined group of imported cults and Roman cults subsumed under the term *paganism.* In the final analysis, Mithraism failed as a religion because it was polytheistic, because it excluded women, and because, like other mystery cults, its central figure was mythical and not historical. Swerdlow maintains that Mithraism had more in common with Freemasonry, Dungeons and Dragons, and the Loyal Order of Moose than with Christianity which, at the time, was attracting converts in the major cities of the empire (48).

Although Christianity prevailed in the West, a vestigial Mithraism survives in Spain and the south of France, where the cult of the bull, the sun, and blood sacrifice remains alive to this day. As Hemingway's books on the corrida demonstrate, he was drawn to the ritual because of its emphasis on death and killing, but it is Montherlant, not Hemingway, who incorporates Mithraism into his writing. Hemingway may well be alluding to the cult when he says that "the sun is very important. The theory, practice and spectacle of bullfighting have all been built on the assumption of the presence of the sun" (*DIA* 15). But the sun will always be present, and it will also rise over the Iberian peninsula with or without Mithraism. Mithraism is never mentioned in Hemingway's descriptions of the *toreo,* whereas Montherlant alludes to it frequently and directly. Furthermore, as a former matador and a scholar of the cult, he gives the reader an insider's appreciation of both.

Montherlant wrote *Les bestiaires* in Paris in the summer of 1925, the same year that Hemingway was writing *The Sun Also Rises,* and both novels were published in 1926. It is interesting to note that *The Dangerous Summer,* although not a novel, resembles *Les bestiaires* more closely than *The Sun Also Rises* or *Death in the Afternoon.* In *Les bestiaires* and *The Dangerous Summer,* both writers describe numerous bullfights over a period of time, and the lyricism of the former book spills over into the latter, written thirty-three years later.

Montherlant's narrative and Alban's narrative overlap as the author re-creates the past in the present. An evocative description of the novice bullfighter depicts him on his horse, looking at the blue sky, the expanse of buttercups in the fields, and the dazzling black of the bulls. At this moment, Alban compares himself to the Acheans, who tamed their horses, and he thinks of himself as a link in a chain of events dating back to Homer (*Bullfighters* 74, *Les bestiaires* 52). Alban feels that the cult of Mithras is still alive in him and, in his mind's eye, he sees a youth dressed in diaphanous robes with Ganymede's cap on his head. He sees Mithras doing battle with the Sun and, from the depths of the struggle, he senses an emergent love. Like Mithras before him, Alban forms an alliance of friendship with the Sun and feels fortified. Then, with the help of his dog, Alban imagines hunting the Sacred Bull, vanquishing it, and dragging it back to his lair, where he receives an order from the Sun, through the voice of the crow, to kill the animal. Alban now understands the love that has to kill in order to fulfill itself (71).

According to the legend, Mithras kills the Sacred Bull, and from the blood comes wine; from the marrow, wheat and all vegetables; and from his sperm, every beast useful to man. This one bloody act engenders all good things on Earth, and the Bull's horn is a symbol of plenty. Alban believes that in due course, at the end of time, Mithras will come again to sacrifice the Sacred Bull, and this time the sacrifice will not engender life on Earth as it did before but the resurrection of the body and the soul, accompanied by eternal punishment or reward (*Bullfighters* 71). Alban thinks of redemption, and he evokes the cults of Mithras and Cybele and the sacrifices of the Bull throughout the ages, sacrifices that produced two ideas of mystical generation: the generation of love through strife and the generation of abundant life by the act of killing. The Apocalypse refers to sinners "washed in the blood of the Lamb," and in St. John we learn that "the blood of Christ doth purify us." As *Les bestiaires* melds Mithraism and Catholicism, Alban is overcome with religious feelings which, he says, made the men of Thessaly, Crete, Egypt, Persia, and Asia Minor, thousands of years before his era, bow down before the deified Bull (*Bullfighters* 72–73).[6] While contemplating the taurine landscape, Alban feels stirring within him the same zeal that swept the Roman legions off their feet. Recalling that Mithras was born from a rock, he thinks of the stones in the Rhône Valley, the Roman roads, and the amphitheaters of southern France.

In keeping with Mithraic doctrine, Alban loves the bulls too much not to kill them, and he feels that he must possess them in order to be free. Such possession is but a variation of primitive sacrifices, when people adored the animals they hunted and killed. Was not the bull Apis the most perfect example of the godhead in animal form? And was he not in due course drowned by the priests in a fountain dedicated to the Sun (*Bullfighters* 70–71)? Alban is reminded of Mithras's contract with the Sun, and Montherlant notes that Frenchmen of the Midi, like Spaniards, still adore the bull and associate the animal with the sun (*Bullfighters* 12). Alban believes that he is a solar child and that he, like Mithras, was born in sacred blood; that Mithraism and Christianity are connected and that the bullfight is the visible manifestation of this union.[7]

This mythology is arguably still alive today in the minds of bullfighters and aficionados. It is perhaps difficult to generate much enthusiasm for the corrida as a bloody spectacle without an appreciation of the cult of Mithras and the mythology that accompanies it. I'm surprised that, in arguing so eloquently for the beauty, tragedy, and art of the corrida, Hemingway did not incorporate the Mithraic cult into his writings, but perhaps he couldn't without violating his own iceberg theory of writing.

In Montherlant's novel, Mithras is everywhere, present in great detail. One evening, Alban borrows a book on the art of bullfighting from his mentor—a book in which one chapter, entitled "Bullfights and the Church," catches his eye. Montherlant's purpose here is to educate Alban and the reader, and we do indeed learn many things. We learn that in the teachings of Mazdaism the bull was the first living thing created; that the Indra of the Veda was the Divine Bull, like Marduk, Neneb, and Anu in Babylon, or Horus in Egypt; that Heliopolis was a center of worship for the Bull of Râ; and that the bull was celebrated by bullfights six thousand years ago, in Crete, the cradle of pre-Hellenic civilization; that in Boetia there was probably a cult of Poseidon in the form of a bull, the Bellower; that in Thessaly, bull-catching resembled the Spanish corrida or the bull games of the Camargue; that at Eleusis, young men fought with bulls; and that in the Tauria of Ephesus, they identified with the god, calling themselves "bulls." We also learn that in Greece, Jupiter assumed the form of a bull in order to seduce Europa; that Pasiphaë fell in love with a white bull and thus became the mother of the Minotaur; that Dionysos of the mysteries was portrayed in the form of a bull; and that during the spring festivals, the women of Elea sang a famous hymn of the divine bull: "Come hither, divine Labor, borne upon your ox-hoofs! Come hither, divine bull, O bull, showering blessings upon us!" Alban learns that countless representations of bulls exist throughout Spain that are associated, according to Diodorus Siculus, with the voyage of Hercules, who built Seville, and presented cows to a native princeling; these representations bear witness to the living and sacred nature of bulls in Spain ever since (*Bullfighters* 164–65).

Alban also learns that Seville was loyal to Julius Caesar and that Caesar introduced bullfighting to Rome, where it remained popular until the end of the Renaissance; that the sacrifices of bulls and the cult of Mithras, the Bull-Slayer, soon followed; that the emperor Julian, as a devotee of Mithras, celebrated his mysteries in Constantinople; and that Christianity and Mithraism, because of their similarities, had struggled bitterly for supremacy. Alban remembers a passage in a book by the French historian Ernst Renan, in which he argues that had Christianity failed as a religion, the world would belong to Mithras, and states that the Mithraic clergy accused the Christians of plagiarism because they substituted the blood of the Lamb for the blood of the Bull (*Bullfighters* 166–67).

Alban learns that in the sixteenth century Pope Pius V issued many decrees concerning the *agitatio taurorum* that forbade the staging and attending of fights, and he had even excommunicated toreros. This ban was withdrawn by Gregory XIII and reimposed by Sixtus V, but the Academical Council of the University of Salamanca refused to obey it, saying that Spaniards had bullfighting in their blood, and that to interdict the practice would do them great harm. So Clement VIII, in a supplementary decree, recognized bullfighting as a school for courage and an important part of Spanish tradition. He lifted the decree of excommunication for bullfighting, except for clergymen who had performed in the ring. Henceforth, the survival of Mithraism and its union with the Catholic Church in Spain were assured, and bullfighting, the symbol of this treaty, has lasted until this day. Until recently, no canonization, no transference of relics to a new church, could take place without a bullfight honoring the occasion.[8]

Bishops often organized bullfights at their own expense, dignitaries of the Church attended, and the dean of the chapter of Burgos even wrote and published a book on the *toreo.* Two hundred bulls were killed when Saint Theresa was canonized, in order to commemorate the two hundred convents she had founded. For the canonization of Saint Ignatius of Loyola, the Jesuits asked the Seville Chapter to put on a "dazzling" *toreo* right after the religious ceremony. The canonizations of two Jesuit saints, Aloysius of Gonzaga and Stanislas Kostka, were also honored with bullfights. The pope himself celebrated the Jubilee of 1500 in Rome, on Saint Peter's Square, with a huge bullfight. In Calderon's time, the first performance of Mass by a young priest was celebrated with a bullfight. Under Ferdinand VII, it was not unusual for a young girl on the eve of taking the veil to go to a *toreo* and make a few passes with a young bull. At the festival preceding the election of a convent abbess, the nuns organized small fights and played bullocks with the cape. Representations of *suertes* were carved on the choirs and the transepts of cathedrals, notably the cathedrals of Plasencia and Cordova (*Bullfighters* 167–68).

On one occasion, so that bad weather would not spoil the afternoon fights in Salamanca, three hundred masses were said to honor the souls in purgatory. A brotherhood in Cacerès, formed to honor the Virgin, admitted no one who could not work the bulls on horseback. And Roa, having escaped the plague, pledged to pay for four bulls to be sacrificed every year, "for the love of God." There are many additional examples of the coexistence of Mithraism and Catholicism in Spain, and the festivals reveal the persistence of ancient beliefs in the sacredness of the bull—beliefs that are still alive today (*Bullfighters* 169–70).

Montherlant multiplies these examples in order to demonstrate the pervasive historical influence of Mithraism on Spanish culture. Hemingway, like the Spanish, identified with the killing of bulls as a source of ritual pleasure and understood the profound spiritual connotations of tragedy. It is odd, therefore, that he does not write about Mithraism and the corrida, as Montherlant does; nor does he mention the Frenchman, despite the fact that he had read his book and owned a copy of it. Why did Hemingway fail to acknowledge Montherlant's influence? Montherlant's writing explores themes that Hemingway later developed in *Death in the Afternoon* and *The Dangerous Summer,* namely, the bullfight as tragedy, as art, as poetry, as music, as emotion, as love, as dream, as slow-motion film, and as the economy of mastery. Writers are frequently reluctant to acknowledge debt, and this may explain Hemingway's silence.

Here, for the sake of comparison, are some examples from *Les bestiaires.* Alban is in the arena, and because he "knew what [the bull] was going to do he could dominate this beast." And, "a man can really conquer only what he loves, and conquerors are tremendous lovers. Even as a poet in the throes of inspiration, or a composer improvising, Alban *shaped* the bull" (*Les bestiaires* 221–22; emphasis in original, my translation). The key concepts are domination, love, poetry, music, and the shaping of the bull, concepts that Hemingway also used in *Death in the Afternoon* and *The Dangerous Summer.* Here is another example from *Les bestiaires:*

> As in all art, mastery in the end produced simplicity. The ritual passes were made soberly and with great dignity, appearing as easy as *actions in a dream,* endowed with the superhuman grandeur and freedom of *slow-motion films.* It became manifest to all that in the center of the arena a sovereign power was at work, with a detachment verging on disdain: the sovereignty of the man was obvious to all. It was no longer a combat; it was a religious incantation, wrought in chaste gestures, lovelier than those of *love* itself, *subduing crude spectators* as well as the bull, and *bringing tears to the eyes.* (*Les bestiaries* 222; my translation and emphasis)

Once again, the familiar Hemingway themes are present. Not only does the matador dominate the bull, not only are his actions as easy as in a dream, or as grand as those in a slow-motion film, but the fight also becomes a religious act that brings tears to the eyes of the spectators. Every emotional element is present, including the essential link between the matador and his audience, as well as the writer and the reader. This is already the so-called prose of ecstasy, and it was written in 1925, seven years before the publication of *Death in the Afternoon.*

Because Montherlant is writing from the point of view of an experienced fighter, his style develops a voluptuous and sensuous rhythm that transforms the struggle between man and beast into an act of love—an act in which the death of the bull is also an orgasmic climax:

> Henceforward there was not a series of passes, but one continuous pass, one tragic comingling of two beings confounded in one, one single brutal and continuous embrace. . . . That body was made for his body, and each movement of the man was attuned to every movement of the beast; man and beast

> locked together within the evolving spaces of their displacements; and the withheld laughter, the eyelids lowered at the culminating point of the exquisite sensation, the passion animating the gestures—it is the god and his priest constructing their impending communion, enclosing it in a nuptial dance. (*Les bestiaries* 216–17; my translation)

This description not only communicates Montherlant's personal experience, it also reveals his admiration for Juan Belmonte, who sometimes, when training, fought bulls naked. In the Pléiade edition of the *Album Montherlant,* there is a pen-and-ink drawing by Montherlant of a naked Belmonte fighting a bull (Sipriot 117). Belmonte had developed a fighting style to accommodate a chronic illness that prevented him from moving his legs, and for which he substituted arm movements. These changes brought him much closer to the bull than usual—so close, in fact, that each pass left froth and slaver on the man. Belmonte himself acknowledged this closeness as highly erotic (Sipriot 116–17).

Montherlant's description is both erotic and religious, and he combines the two into a moving and voluptuous Mithraic ritual that extols the bull's regenerative blood as an act of worship and love. In the following passage, in which Alban has already dedicated the bull to "the unvanquished Sun" (*Les bestiaires* 219; my translation), "he saw the path of sunlight between his hand and the withers shining in their golden blood; and he saw the sword as a longer beam from the sun which smote the very body of Mithras.... The purifying life blood flowed like water from the double wound" (*Les bestiaries* 223; my translation). Montherlant has incorporated poetry, drama, eroticism, and Mithraism into *Les bestiaires,* and he communicates the layered dimensions of this background to the reader. The fight and voluptuousness, says Montherlant, are like brother and sister. Mithras wields the sword of the Ram, the sign of Mars, and he rides the Bull, the sign of Venus (*Bullfighters* 83).

In both *Death in the Afternoon* and *The Dangerous Summer,* Hemingway equates bullfighting with art. But the missing dimension in both books is Mithraism, and we are indebted to Montherlant for descriptions that communicate the *toreo* not only as art, but also as religious spectacle, regenerative act, and sensual experience. The invisible seven-eighths of the iceberg in Hemingway's three works about bullfighting is foregrounded and highly visible in Montherlant's *Les bestiaires.*

Notes

1. Pedro Romero is the fictional name of the real bullfighter Cayetano, and a faena is the work done by the matador with the muleta. The muleta is the heart-shaped scarlet cloth that is used to defend the man and tire the bull as the matador performs a series of passes.

2. *Toreo* means the art of fighting bulls, and the corrida almost always ends with the death of the animal and sometimes of the matador. The event is a quintessentially Spanish performance, and Hemingway describes it as tragedy, and not sport (*DIA* 16), because death unites man and bull "in the emotional, aesthetic and artistic climax of the fight" (247). See Allen Josephs for an insightful account of the role and meaning of bullfighting in Spanish culture and in Hemingway's thinking and art. Josephs notes that *toreo* in Spain is frequently described "as the tragedy of the death of the bull" (229).

3. Mithras is a god mentioned in Sanskrit and old Persian documents. The cult of the bull was the foundation of Mithraism, and that legacy has been passed down through the ages and transmuted into the tragedy and spectacle of bullfighting in Spain. Mithraism and Christianity developed simultaneously, and they share common symbols: blood, wine, and the sun. In Catholicism, the eucharistic wine represents the blood of Christ. The host recalls the solar circle. In Spain, all three symbols converge around the bull, which bled, was sacrificed, and worshipped as a god for millennia.

4. In 1959—the year of the "dangerous summer"—Hemingway followed the rivalry between two great matadors, Luis Miguel Dominguín and Antonio Ordóñez, from one corner of Spain to the other. What made the rivalry so personal was that Carmen, Antonio's wife, was also Luis Miguel's sister. Month after month, from May to September, Hemingway describes the competition between the two men and the eventual triumph, at least in Hemingway's mind, of Ordóñez. Their dueling is intense, and while it lasts both matadors are gored several times.

5. For historical information and references on Mithraism, I am indebted to Francesca Rochberg, Professor of History at the University of California, Berkeley.

6. All the translations from *Les bestiaires* that appear in the text are mine.

7. In linking Mithraism to Christianity, Montherlant draws heavily on the theories of Renan and Cumont, and all three were unaware of archeological evidence and Mithraic scholarship done since 1960. Cumont's works were published in the 1890s and *Les bestiaires* in 1926.

8. Again, Montherlant is drawing heavily on the theories of Cumont and Renan, and is unaware of recent scholarship that downplays the struggle for supremacy between Mithraism and Christianity. Ironically, the *toreo* illustrates the melding of the two, not their opposition.

Works Cited

Beck, Roger. *Planetary Gods and Planetary Orders of the Mysteries of Mithras*. Leiden: E. J. Brill, 1988. Etudes préliminaires aux religions orientales dans l'empire romain. 9.

Bredendick, Nancy. "'¿Qué tal, hombre, qué tal?' How Paratexts Narrow the Gap Between Reader and Text in *Death in the Afternoon*." In Mandel 205–34.

Cumont, Franz. *Textes et monuments figurés relatifs aux mystères de Mithra*. 2 vols. 1896. Brussels: H. Lamertin, 1899.

Griffith, Alison. "Mithraism." *Exploring Ancient World Cultures*. 1996. Web. 10 December 2005.

Hemingway, Ernest. *The Dangerous Summer*. New York: Scribner, 1960.

———. *Death in the Afternoon*. New York: Scribner, 1960.

———. *Ernest Hemingway: Selected Letters, 1917–1961*. Ed. Carlos Baker. New York: Charles Scribner's Sons, 1981.

———. *The Sun Also Rises*. New York: Scribner, 1926.

Ibáñez, Beatriz Penas. "'Very Sad but Very Fine': *Death in the Afternoon*'s Imagist Interpretation of the Bullfight-Text." In Mandel 143–64.

Josephs, Allen. "Hemingway's Spanish Sensibility." In *The Cambridge Companion to Hemingway*. Ed. Scott Donaldson. New York: Cambridge UP, 1996. 221–42.

Justice, Hilary K. "'Prejudiced Through Experience'; *Death in the Afternoon* and the Problem of Authorship." In Mandel 237–56.

Mandel, Miriam B., ed. *A Companion to Hemingway's* Death in the Afternoon. Rochester: Camden House, 2004.

Messent, Peter. "'The Real Thing'? Representing the Bullfight and Spain in *Death in the Afternoon*." In Mandel 123–41.

Montherlant, Henry de. *Les bestiaires*. Paris: Gallimard, 1954.

———. *The Bullfighters*. Trans. Edwin Giles Rich. New York: Dial, 1927.

Renan, Ernst. *Marc-Aurèle et la fin du monde antique*. Paris: Calmann Lévy, 1882.

Sipriot, Pierre, ed. *Album Montherlant*. Paris: Gallimard, 1979.

Stanton, Edward F. *Hemingway and Spain: A Pursuit*. Seattle: U of Washington P, 1989.

Swerdlow, Noel. "Review Article: On the Cosmical Mysteries of Mithras." *Classical Philology* 86 (1991): 48–63.

Ulansey, David. *The Origins of the Mithraic Mysteries*. New York: Oxford UP, 1989.

Vondrak, Amy. "'The Sequence of Motion and Fact': Cubist Collage and Filmic Montage in *Death in the Afternoon*." In Mandel 257–79.

7

"At Five in the Afternoon"

Toward a Poetics of Duende *in Bataille and Hemingway*

David F. Richter

> *"Being-toward-death is the anticipation of a potentiality-of-being of that being whose kind of being is anticipation itself, . . . the possibility of understanding one's ownmost and extreme potentiality-of-being, that is, as the possibility of authentic existence."*
>
> —Martin Heidegger, *Being and Time*

> *"If it—learning to live—remains to be done, it can happen only between life and death. Neither in life nor in death alone."*
>
> —Jacques Derrida, *Specters of Marx*

In a short essay about the Spanish poet Federico García Lorca and the importance of death in Spanish art and culture, fellow poet Pedro Salinas states that the "destination of nearly all the characters that Lorca creates, whether in his ballads or in his dramas, is death" (5–6). Salinas shows not only that death is the cornerstone of Lorca's poetics, but also that it is central to Spanish culture and the construction of Spanish identity. Salinas calls this the "culture of death," which is manifested in a heightened interest in mortality, although that inclination is not purely nihilistic or negative in nature. It is, rather, as Salinas continues, "a conception of man and his earthly existence, in which the awareness of death functions with a positive sign; it is a stimulus, and not a hindrance, to living and acting, and it makes possible an understanding of the full and total meaning of life" (9–10). Death becomes, for Lorca, an enabling force, an impetus for creation, and a motivation for contemplation.

Other intellectuals, including the American writer Ernest Hemingway and the French thinker Georges Bataille, also experienced Spanish culture firsthand and were likewise captivated by the invigorating force of death and its implications for artistic expression. Hemingway, for example, maintains that through an understanding of death one can further appreciate and experience an enhanced life. Indeed, his works related to Spanish culture and bullfighting exhibit a profound consideration of death and the graceful artistry that gives rise to an aesthetic rooted in deathly tones. Several writings by Bataille likewise focus on Spanish cultural elements of pure emotion and artistic sovereignty. In works that treat Iberian culture and in an essay on Hemingway's *For Whom Bell Tolls,* Bataille elucidates the anguish that persists in iconic Spanish art forms. In short, it is through the lens of art and death that Lorca, Hemingway, and Bataille understand the pleasures of existence. As Salinas concludes, the culture of death in Spain always involves the consideration of dying for the sake of living.

Duende and the Culture of Death

Lorca approached the "culture of death"—along with its importance in the inspiration of artistic creation—through the figure of the *duende,* a goblin-like spirit that is manifest in distinct art forms. In a lecture entitled "Play and Theory of the Duende," first delivered in Buenos Aires in 1933, he declared that "the *duende,* then, is a power, not a work. It is a struggle, not a thought" (García Lorca, *Search* 49). He highlighted the relationship between Spanish culture and *duende* by suggesting that "Spain is moved by the duende, for it is a country of ancient music and dance where the duende squeezes the lemons of death—a country of death, open to death. Everywhere else, death is an end. Death comes, and they draw the curtains. Not in Spain. In Spain they open them. . . . A dead man in Spain is more alive as a dead man than anyplace else in the world" (*Search* 55). For Lorca, the *duende* appears only when death is possible, and it is for this reason that poetry, the Andalusian gypsies' *cante jondo* (deep song), and bullfighting play a central role in the Lorquian aesthetic. The tight link between artistic forms and the reality of death is likewise one of the essential components of Hemingway's attraction to Spain in the early 1920s, and that interest led him to the writing of various texts on bullfighting, including *Death in the Afternoon* (1932) and *The Dangerous Summer* (1959–60). In the opening pages of *Death in the Afternoon,* for example, Hemingway asserts that Spain was the only place where one can see violent death now that the war is over and states that he went to Iberia precisely to learn how to better understand death and to write about it more effectively (*DIA* 2–3). An appreciation of *duende,* then, is essential to understanding Hemingway's fascination with the bullfight and Spanish culture.

Death remained a constant preoccupation throughout Lorca's life and became the central point of consideration in nearly all of his poetic and dramatic texts. Seeking to preserve the feelings and emotion of primitive art forms, Lorca assisted the Spanish musician Manuel de Falla in organizing a festival in the summer of 1922 to commemorate Andalusian *cante jondo. Duende* functions as the vital mediator between artist and receptor in deep song; it is the strength that gives emotion and passion to the work of art. The dilutions of modernized versions of *cante jondo* apparent in flamenco, however, show that it has lost the anguished and emotive aspects that come from the painful life experience of the marginalized gypsy culture. The loss of this artistic aura is analogous to the decadence of modern bullfighting, a problem Hemingway noticed and described, in which bullfighters display a diminished interest in killing passionately and artistically. Hemingway argues that the modern variants of the bullfight are a profane rendering of the art form without ritual and emotion, inartistic expressions by bullfighters "who require a special, almost made-to-order bull" (*DIA* 86). What is certain concerning *duende* (regardless of whether or not Lorca was accurate in his historical analysis of *cante jondo*),[1] is its affinity toward death. It is this aspect of artistic creation as an expression at the limits that Lorca signals in his lectures on *cante jondo* and *duende,* reflections that involve a poetics of *duende* as the work of art evokes the pain, suffering, grace, and emotion of a discarded culture.

Of the relatively few artistic manifestations in which *duende* is most potent, Lorca declares that the *duende* is "at its most impressive in the bullfight, for [the artist] must fight both death, which can destroy him, and geometry—measurement, the very basis of the festival. The bull has his orbit, and the bullfighter has his, and between these two orbits is a point of danger, the vertex of the terrible play" (*Search* 59). In the elegiac poem "Lament for Ignacio Sánchez Mejías," Lorca traces his own attraction toward and repulsion from the contemplation of death, a death that strikes at five in the afternoon, "a las cinco de la tarde." Lorca's four-part poem focuses on the poet's bullfighter friend, who was fatally wounded in Manzanares on 11 August 1934, and it examines the gravity of the instant of death. Through the inspiration of an ominous source that appears with the presence of a lurking destruction, Lorca notes how there is death on all clocks—in the shadow and in the sun—at five in the afternoon. With a vertiginous mix of times and spaces (including the temporal frames of the goring, death, and corporeal decomposition; and the physical spaces of the bullring, bleachers, hospital, and grave), "five in the afternoon" becomes in Lorca's poem what Hemingway and others refer to as "the moment of truth" (*DIA* 68), the moment of encounter between man and bull, the moment of death. In this text of somber denial, Lorca recognizes the ritualistic and sacrificial importance of the event:

> *The cow of this ancient world*
> *was running her dreary tongue*
> *over snoutfuls of blood*
> *spilled across the sand* (Collected Poems 67–70)[2]

In sacrificial fashion, "Ignacio mounts the steps, / shouldering his full death" (77–78), and in the moment of communal frenzy and ritual sacrifice, the blood of the fallen spills over the stands, covering the "bloodthirsty masses" (91).

With image after image alternating with the incantatory refrain "a las cinco de la tarde," Lorca shows that five in the afternoon is the hour of tragic death and corporeal decomposition, and subsequently, the moment of reflection and remembering. Lorca re-members the artistic nature of Ignacio's perceptive bullfighting since, as the poetic voice recognizes at the end of the poem's second part,

> *No prince ever was in Seville*
> *that could even approach him,*
> *no sword like his sword,*
> *no heart so truly a heart.*
> *Like a river of lions*
> *the marvel of his strength,*
> *and like a marble torso*
> *the contour of his prudence.*
> . . . .
> *What a great fighter in the ring!*
> . . . .
> *How harsh applying the spurs!*
> *How tender toward the dew!* (102–9, 114, 117, 118)

Lorca's text pinpoints the emotion and grace with which the fallen bullfighter approached his art, metaphorically attributing to Ignacio not only the strength of lions and the valor of a warrior but also the beauty of classical sculpture and a sensitivity toward nature. Hemingway recognizes similar qualities when he writes of great bullfighters such as Juan Belmonte and José Gómez Ortega (Joselito), who were "intuitive genius[es]" and "great artist[s]" (*DIA* 69). Clearly for Lorca and Hemingway, when bullfighters such as Sánchez Mejías, Belmonte, and Joselito fought, they did so with the highly charged grace and artistry enabled by *duende.*

La emoción, *Sovereign Art, and the Impossible*

When the French thinker Georges Bataille visited Spain in 1922, as an exchange student at the School of Advanced Spanish Studies (later called the Casa de Velázquez), he was fascinated by the emotion and treatment of death transmitted by dancing, singing, bullfighting, and Spanish painting (most notably the works of Francisco de Goya and Juan de Valdés Leal). During his eight-month sojourn in Spain, Bataille experienced Spanish culture through attendance at both the bullfight in Madrid in which Manuel Granero was gored to death and the *cante jondo* festival in Granada. While only minimal information concerning his stay in Spain survives, three letters to his sister Marie-Louise Bataille (dated between February and September 1922), as well as a 1946 publication entitled *Actualité* (*Current Events*), inform our understanding of his experiences there. In the last of these sources, *Actualité,* Bataille maintains that pure emotion coupled with anguish (evident in the bullfighting spectacle and the *cante jondo* festival) best describe Spanish culture. Bataille describes his encounter with Spanish culture and recalls that he "then began to understand that uneasiness is often the secret to the most intense pleasures. The Spanish language designates the sort of exaltation that underlies this anguish with a precise word, *emoción:* this is exactly the feeling that is given when the bull's horns miss, *by an inch,* the body of the *bullfighter*" ("Concerning *For Whom the Bell Tolls*" 120).[3] Bataille also comments on the emotion evoked by a dancer that he saw perform in Spain and the ecstatic—but agonizing—delight that she displayed: "The dancing, essentially the miming of an anguished pleasure, exasperates a defiance that suspends breathing. It communicates an ecstasy, a sort of suffocated revelation of death and the feeling of touching the impossible" (122). His experiences in Spain, and the impact that Spanish culture provided during this visit, later led to the conception of some of Bataille's most influential writings, including the 1928 short novella *Story of the Eye,* other essays on bullfighting and Spanish art, and an insightful analysis of Hemingway's *For Whom the Bell Tolls.* What is constant in his reflections on Spain, whether in his personal letters, creative writings, or theoretical analyses, is the predominance in Spain of a heightened sense of emotion and anguish. In Hemingway's estimation, this aesthetic anguish is most prevalent in the "complete, imaginative, artistic, and emotional performance with the muleta" (*DIA* 206), the scarlet-colored cloth used to defend the torero through a series of passes and also to aid the bullfighter in preparing the bull for the moment of truth.

Bataille's writings, like those of Lorca and Hemingway, are profoundly motivated by the presence of death in bullfighting. In *Story of the Eye,* drawing on his own witnessing of the event, Bataille describes the death of Manuel Granero, during which one of the bullfighter's eyes was viciously gouged out. The protagonist relates how "Granero was thrown back by the bull and wedged against the balustrade; the horns struck the balustrade three times at full speed; at the third blow, one horn plunged into the right eye and through the head . . . under a blinding sun; men instantly rushed over to haul away Granero's body, the right eye dangling from the head" (*Story* 64). According to Michel Surya, "this mutilation gripped and fascinated" Bataille and provided "the most disturbed pleasure" (43). The enchantment with which Bataille describes the enucleation of Granero approaches what he deems sovereign or transgressive art, that is, art that freely captures emotion and inner experience. For Bataille, the emotive properties of arts like bullfighting resist limitations and seek to communicate an excess of unrestricted expression. The pleasurable anguish felt during the tragic bullfighting scene in Madrid, an anguish also evident with the appearance of *duende,* was augmented months later at the *cante jondo* festival in Granada.

Through his reflections on *cante jondo,* Bataille further explores the communication of an expression at the limits of the possible, which gives voice to an excess of emotion. On 13 and 14 June 1922, Bataille traveled south to Lorca's hometown of Granada in order to attend the *cante jondo* music festival and tournament. Surya comments that one of the most important events that contributed to Bataille's early thinking was "the *cante hondo* tournament he attended in Granada and the appearance of a flamenco singer, [Diego] Bermúdez" (43). Twenty-four years later, Bataille recorded his impressions concerning this event in his article, "Concerning *For Whom the Bell Tolls* by Ernest Hemingway," appearing in the journal *Actualité,* which Bataille edited. The journal did not survive long, producing only this single 1946 number, subtitled "Free Spain," an issue dedicated exclusively to Spanish politics, economy, art, and culture. The volume includes several significant pieces, including a preface by Albert Camus; articles by Jean Camp, Maurice Blanchot, and Bataille; a translated version of chapter 19 of Hemingway's *For Whom the Bell Tolls* (to which they gave the title "The Smell of Death"); and the short *Puppet Play of Don Cristóbal,* written by Lorca.

Bataille's article on Hemingway in *Actualité,* however, deals more with Spanish culture and his own experiences in Spain in 1922 than it does with Hemingway. The references to Hemingway seem to serve, rather, as a pretext for Bataille to expound on the persistence of death in Spanish art and literature. For example, the French thinker focuses on Andalusian deep song and the impact of the *cantaor* Bermúdez at the *cante jondo* fesitval. "After some guitar chords, while seated on the stand, . . ." Bataille recalls, Bermúdez "sang—rather, he threw out his voice in a sort of excessive, rending, prolonged cry which, when you thought it was drained, reached, in the prolongation of a death moan, the unimaginable" ("Concerning *For Whom the Bell Tolls*" 124). Lorca's biographer, Ian Gibson, details the same events by suggesting that "the great surprise of the festival was the performance of Diego Bermúdez Cañete, 'el Tenazas' ('Pincers'), an old *cantaor*, almost forgotten, who, so it was said, had walked to Granada all the way from Puente Genil, in the province of Cordova, a cross-country hike of some eighty miles. Bermúdez sang the first night with powerful *duende* and carried all before him" (115). Bataille's and Lorca's common interest in events such as bullfighting and *cante jondo* music demonstrates a shared contemplation of the relationship between the arts, pure emotion, and death. Denis Hollier affirms that for Bataille, "Spain is the locus of . . . death, the country of death agony. A sort of internal transgression of the laws of European geography" (53). For both Lorca and Bataille, the focus on death in art stems from Nietzsche, as they both appeal to the primitive Dionysian drives of marginalized cultures and the irrational irruptions of desire and emotion pertaining to the presence of *duende*.

The affirmative aspects of Spanish emotion and the meditations on death are analyzed at length by Bataille in his article on Hemingway. What distinguishes the Spanish people, and what interested Bataille in their culture, is their openness to death and the manner in which this openness affords them an authenticity toward life and its numerous possibilities. Much like Salinas's "culture of death," Bataille's vision of a Spanish "culture of anguish" appreciates artistic expression at the extreme limits of experience, constantly in the face of death. The French intellectual proposes that "the *culture of anguish* of which I have spoken gives an outcome to the will of the impossible that the people give themselves . . . *the nostalgia for the impossible*" ("Concerning *For Whom the Bell Tolls*" 123). For Salinas and Bataille, whether through a culture of death or of anguish, the reflection on experience at the limits is supremely positive in its affirmation of sovereign existence. Bataille concludes that "anguish is not a negative and suppressible suffering, but rather, a fashioning of being essential to man, without which we do not have the happening of anything but an inauthentic experience" (125). For these thinkers, part of living more authentically involves living at one's limits and having a nostalgia for the nearness of death; indeed, it requires seeking what Hemingway refers to as "the feeling of immortality," just as the bullfighter "is playing with death, bringing it closer, closer, closer, to himself" (*DIA* 213).

An examination of the other texts that Bataille, as editor, includes in the 1946 single-issue journal *Actualité* offers insight into the interest in Spanish culture displayed by other early twentieth-century foreigners, and the inclusion of Hemingway's text in the volume on a "Free Spain" highlights that fascination. It is clear that

Bataille and other Parisian intellectuals of the 1940s felt a kinship with Spain and a longing for the Republic that preceded Franco's fascist rule there. Spain's loss of democracy was a loss experienced by all of the European community, since it failed to respond adequately (Surya 365). Bataille's inclusion of Lorca's *Puppet Play of Don Cristóbal* in *Actualité* draws attention to the *Puppet Play*'s subversive thematic and structural nature. Through the use of crude language and dark humor, which the metaliterary "author" informs us in the prologue might unsettle, the play questions the parameters of propriety in artistic representation. The persistent erotic references to body parts and fluids in the *Puppet Play,* along with the "performance" of the subversions the text exposes, make this text of great interest to Bataille, who strove for sovereign literature. In Lorca's short text, the theatrical representation breaks with mimetic art and presents a methectic, or real-life, presentation in which the borders of fiction and reality are annihilated.[4] Lorca presents this "real life" dramatic scenario through recourse to the artificiality of puppetry and through "adult themes" of death and eroticism. Traditionally, these puppet plays would be designed for audiences of children, but Lorca subverts cultural values by transgressing those theatrical norms and expectations.

While Bataille states, in the introductory note to Lorca's text included in *Actualité,* that the Spaniard was not a political poet *per se,* he does find the poet's work relevant since it searches for liberation in both political and aesthetic contexts. He appreciates, furthermore, the manner in which Lorca puts into art the essence of Spanish identity: "In the entire world's opinion, the greatest of all living painters is Pablo Picasso. And, without the torturing of the rebels, a free Spain would count among its own perhaps the greatest poet . . . The poetry of García Lorca is marked with the most intimate traits of Spanish character. It is not by chance that it evokes death, and the death of a *bullfighter*—nor is it by chance that it evokes the harshness of *cante jondo*" (*Actualité* 88). In *Actualité,* the French thinkers yearn for freedom in Spanish sociopolitical constructs and artistic expression. They highlight the efforts of Spanish anarchists who display what Bataille called "the most onerous expression of *an obstinate desire for the impossible*" ("Concerning *For Whom the Bell Tolls*" 124).

Giving Emotion and the Smell of Death

Much as Lorca's theory of *duende* elucidates Bataille's writings in and about Spain, the allure of death is also key to Hemingway's work. In his memoir *Being Geniuses Together,* American writer and publisher Robert McAlmon reflects on one of Hemingway's first encounters with death in Spain in the early 1920s and the fascination that this experience provoked. McAlmon recounts that while traveling with Hemingway by train from Paris to Madrid, the train stopped briefly at a station. There, on top of a flatcar on an adjacent train track, the two travelers noticed, in McAlmon's words, "the maggot-eaten corpse of a dog. I, feeling none too hale and hearty, looked away, but Hemingway gave a dissertation on facing reality. It seemed that he had seen in the war the stacked corpses of men, maggot-eaten in a similar way. . . . He tenderly explained that we of our generation must inure ourselves to the sight of grim reality" (178). Hemingway indeed went to Spain to understand the reality of death more intimately, and this initial experience in the Iberian country underscores the overarching theme of decomposition and death that permeates much of his Spain-inspired works.

In *Death in the Afternoon* and *The Dangerous Summer,* the aficionado of Spanish culture and bullfighting demonstrates a sustained interest in the permanence of death and also the aesthetic aspects of the encounter between man and bull. For Hemingway, "any man can face death but to be committed to bring it as close as possible while performing certain classical movements . . . is more complicated than just facing death" (*DS* 141). The Hispanist Allen Josephs draws the following conclusion when considering the interest in death shared by Lorca and Hemingway: "Death—the awareness of death, the possibility of death, the certainty of death—is the essential element in the *fiesta* sense of life . . . As Lorca had written in his essay on *duende,* 'Spain is the only country in the world where death is the national spectacle' . . . It was precisely for that reason that the young Ernest Hemingway would spend so much time in Spain seeking a purity of emotion in the atavistic spectacle of death in the afternoon, a purity he could find nowhere else" (153). Hemingway, like Lorca and Bataille, approaches the bullfight with a sense of nostalgia for a more primitively artistic mode of bullfighting that had been partially lost in the modern age. He notices how bullfighters of a past epoch gave much emotion when they fought, performing graceful acts of great difficulty and killing with passion and desire. In contrast, the bullfight in the modern era is seemingly dominated by smaller bulls and a lack of artistic ability, coupled with a near-impotence at the moment of the kill.

In a short essay on the sacrificial nature of bullfighting, Lorca concludes, "They say that the torero goes to the ring to earn money, prestige, glory, applause . . . but this is not true. He goes to the ring to be alone with the bull, an animal he both fears and adores, and to whom he has much to say" (*Search* 84). Hemingway similarly reveres the solemn encounter between man and bull in the bullfighting spectacle. In *Death in the Afternoon,* he describes the communal moment of union as a fusion of two discontinuous beings. In the days of pure bullfighting, when the killing of the bull was performed with artistic passion—or with *duende*—the man and bull became one flesh. Hemingway relates that the matador "provoked the charge by bending one leg forward and swinging the muleta toward the bull, letting the bull come until the man and bull become one figure as the sword goes in; . . . there coming a moment when they are joined by the sword" (*DIA* 238). When killing in this fashion, the aesthetic and ritualistic properties of the fight reach their pinnacle simultaneously, in ecstatic fusion. Hemingway further recognizes the importance of the culminating instant of contact, since "the beauty of the moment of killing is that flash when man and bull form one figure as the sword goes all the way in, the man leaning after it, death uniting the two figures in the emotional, aesthetic and artistic climax of the fight" (*DIA* 247).

Hemingway's treatment of the limits of emotion and aesthetics in the authentic bullfight echoes the themes of sovereign and transgressive literature developed in Bataille's writings on Spanish culture. Hemingway refers to the bullfight as an event that evokes a mystical rapture, "as profound as any religious ecstasy; moving all the people in the ring together and increasing in emotional intensity as it proceeds, carrying the bullfighter with it, he playing on the crowd through the bull and being moved as it responds in a growing ecstasy of ordered, formal, passionate, increasing disregard for death" (*DIA* 206–7).[5] The symmetry between death, ecstasy, and eroticism is further traced in *Death in the Afternoon* in the story of two young gypsy children who seek to avenge the death of their fourteen-year-old brother, who died at the horns of a particular bull. The two gypsies follow the bull around Spain for two years, until they finally encounter it at a slaughterhouse, ready to be butchered:

> The two gypsies were at the slaughter-house and the young man asked permission, since the bull had killed his brother, to kill the bull. This was granted and he started in by digging out both the bull's eyes while the bull was in his cage, and spitting carefully into the sockets, then after killing him by severing the spinal marrow between the neck vertebrae with a dagger, he experienced some difficulty in this, he asked permission to cut off the bull's testicles, which being granted, he and his sister built a small fire at the edge of the dusty street outside the slaughter-house and roasted the two glands on sticks and when they were done, ate them. They then turned their backs on the slaughter-house and went away along the road and out of town. (*DIA* 25)

The perverse pleasures found in gouging out the bull's eyeballs, spitting in the eye sockets, castrating the bull, and finally eating the testicles, find similar treatment in Bataille's *Story of the Eye*.

The fascination with corporeal decomposition and putrefaction is emphasized most directly in the passage by Hemingway that Bataille includes in *Actualité*. The text of interest for the French philosopher contemplating a "Free Spain" in

1946 was chapter 19 of *For Whom the Bell Tolls.* This chapter was translated by Bataille's lover, Diane Kotchoubey, and included nearly in its entirety.[6] As their title for the excerpt, "The Smell of Death," indicates, this chapter deals with the events surrounding Pilar's description, to Robert Jordan and the rest of the rebel group, of the odor of death present moments before the goring of certain bull-fighters. "I saw death there as plainly as though it were sitting on his shoulder," Pilar affirms. "And what is more he smelt of death. . . . The odor of death was so strong on Manolo [Granero] that it almost made Blanquet [his assistant] sick" (*FWTBT* 251). When others in Pilar's company doubt her ability to, in fact, smell death, she tells of the experiences that led to her olfactory assumption: "And it was on that afternoon that the bull *Pocapena* of the ranch of Veragua destroyed Manolo Granero against the planks of the barrier in front of *tendido* two in the Plaza de Toros of Madrid. I was there with Finito and I saw it. The horn entirely destroyed the cranium, the head of Manolo being wedged under the *estribo* at the base of the *barrera* where the bull had tossed him" (*FWTBT* 252). The details of the events as related by Pilar are startlingly similar to the description in Bataille's *Story of the Eye,* published twelve years earlier.

Rédouane Abouddahab suggests thematic and ideological points of contact between Bataille's *Story of the Eye* and another of Hemingway's novels, *The Sun Also Rises,* published in 1926. Abouddahab shows how Bataille's novel is informed by Hemingway's treatment of anguish and death and how biographical information concerning both writers strengthens conclusions regarding issues of influence. In fact, Bataille and Hemingway frequented similar circles of avant-garde thinkers in Paris in the 1920s and both entered into collaborations with associates that included Raymond Queneau and André Masson. Abouddahab also asserts that both *The Sun Also Rises* and *Story of the Eye* explore the "profound communion between eroticism and the sacred, the great play between life and death, and the capacity of this 'culture of anguish' (according to Bataille) to channel the excess through its joyous ritualization" (62–63).[7] Moreover, a like theme is evident in chapter 19 of *For Whom the Bell Tolls.*

A final reference to chapter 19 of *For Whom the Bell Tolls,* which Bataille included in *Actualité,* further elucidates these writers' common obsession with death and putrefaction. While Robert and Pilar discuss the possibility of being able to "smell death" and approximate what it might smell like, Pilar notes that it is similar to the smell of rotting flowers:

> When thou seest a refuse pail with dead flowers in it plunge thy nose deep into it and inhale so that scent mixes with those thou hast already in thy nasal passages. . . . [Then] thou shouldst go on to the Jardín Botánico where at night those girls who can no longer work in the houses do their work against

> the iron gates of the park. . . . [A]nd there, on a dead flower bed that has not yet been plucked out and replanted, and so serves to soften the earth that is so much softer than the sidewalk, thou wilt find an abandoned gunny sack with the odor of the wet earth, the dead flowers, and the doings of that night. In this sack will be contained the essence of it all, both the dead earth and the dead stalks of the flowers and their rotted blooms and the smell that is both the death and birth of man. . . . [W]hen thou inhalest deeply, thou wilt smell the odor of death-to-come as we know it. (*FWTBT* 255–56)

In a June 1929 article entitled "The Language of Flowers," originally published in the avant-garde review *Documents* (also edited by Bataille), Bataille explores similar desublimated properties of flowers, including their putrefaction and recourse to decay. In this article, Bataille states that "in fact, after a very short period of glory the marvelous corolla rots indecently in the sun, thus becoming, for the plant, a garish withering. Risen from the stench of the manure pile . . . the most ideal is rapidly reduced to a wisp of aerial manure" (*Visions* 12). This shows the inevitable destruction of forms once "*elevated,* noble, sacred" (*Visions* 14), the loss of beauty to decay, and the stench that is ever-present in putrefaction. In *Actualité,* nearly twenty years after the publication of *Story of the Eye,* Bataille returns his interest, or obsession (through Hemingway), to the death and stench of the matador Granero.

On Living

The characteristics of sovereign literature afforded artistic expression through the presence of *duende* are also evident in the literary structure of the texts discussed here. For Miriam B. Mandel, "*Death in the Afternoon* is a confusingly transgressive book, for it blurs the distinctions between genres, . . . [M]ore aggressively and insistently than any of his earlier work, it mixes, blurs, and finally breaks through the limits implicit in concepts like subject, style, genre, research, and invention" (6, 8). In other words, Hemingway's text artistically performs the liberated and Dionysian, yet precise, ritual of bullfighting to which it makes constant reference. For Edward Stanton, whose book *Hemingway and Spain* provides detailed cultural and biographical insight into Hemingway's time in Spain, the structure of *Death in the Afternoon* succinctly supports the thematic treatment of bullfighting. According to Stanton, the "real structure of the book is to be found deep below its surface, in a profound, irrational undercurrent of primordial images and symbols embedded in the rhythmic, ecstatic prose" (98).

Here form and content meld as Hemingway effects his narrative in a nearly inebriated fashion. Stanton underscores the importance of *duende* in the inspiration for such writing and recognizes the powerful emotions that are evoked through the representation of death inherent to bullfighting (100–101).

What is instructive about Lorca's, Bataille's, and Hemingway's reflections on the deaths (and smells) of bullfighters is the communal aspect that death acquires. The Lorquian critic Andrew Anderson affirms this jointure between the representation and reality of death: "The theme of death looms large in almost all of Lorca's literary output, and many 'deaths,' physical and emotional, literal and figurative, poetically portrayed and imaginatively apprehended, are rendered therein" (233). In the poem Lorca dedicated to the memory of Ignacio Sánchez Mejías, the death and personal loss alluded to are real. Anderson proposes further that the death Lorca faces in his poem may "also be read as a hyperbolic meditation on everyman's life and death" (233). Thus, the contemplation of death is not merely a contemplation of a figurative death or merely of the death of the *other* (bull or bullfighter), but also of *my own death.* For Beatriz Penas Ibáñez, "what interests [Hemingway] in the bullfight is not the bull's fate, but the human fate that the bull symbolizes. . . . [I]t symbolizes their own death" ("'Very Sad'" 145).

This authentic consideration of death is literal, and it outlines an instructive ethical correspondence among these writers when considering John Donne's words that Hemingway uses as an epigraph to *For Whom the Bell Tolls:* "Any mans death diminishes me . . . by this consideration of anothers danger, I take mine owne into contemplation." In essence, with death as the catalyst for their artistic creation, Lorca, Bataille, and Hemingway engage in a questioning of what it means to live authentically and in a community. Penas Ibáñez suggests that for Hemingway, "the goal to be achieved by literature is effective communication of an experience which, due to the existence of a common ground of human feeling and emotion, is bound to produce an equivalent experiential impact on the reader" ("Between" 641). As do Bataille's writings concerning the once-free Spain and Lorca's writings on bullfighting, Hemingway's novels demonstrate how one's encounter with death is experienced and contemplated by all.

When examining Bataille's and Hemingway's writings in and about Spain under the Lorquian lens of the theory of *duende,* the roots of bullfighting culture move beyond superficial considerations of sport or entertainment. Lorca's inclinations toward *duende* show a central preoccupation and fascination with the primordial drives of the human psyche (most importantly, that of the death drive) and reveal insightful nuances about the inspiration of artistic creation. By studying Lorca's theory of *duende* and the interest in death that it signals, we notice how the references to bullfighting and death in the writings of Bataille and Hemingway illuminate the cultural importance of death in Spain. More than just evoking a feeling of sadness or loss, a profound consideration of death lays the foundation for a powerful way of experiencing emotion, art, and living. In the work of Lorca, Bataille, and Hemingway, *duende* and death are considered artistically and theoretically as enabling forces. As Andrew Anderson concludes, "the bullfighter, in confronting death at close quarters in the ring, experiences life, at least for the while he is living it, all the more intensely: risk gives one a real sense or heightens the experience of being alive" (236). Regardless of their different nationalities, languages, and literary interests (whether poetry, narrative, or philosophical inquiry), in their passionate treatment of death and bullfighting, Lorca, Bataille, and Hemingway *give* much emotion and *have* much *duende.*

Notes

1. In fact, Félix Grande shows in *García Lorca y el flamenco* that the Spanish poet does err in several of his assumptions regarding the history of *cante jondo.*

2. References to Lorca's "Lament for Ignacio Sánchez Mejías" come from the revised bilingual edition of *Collected Poems,* edited by Christopher Maurer. Here and elsewhere in this essay, parenthetical documentation refers to line numbers when citing Lorca's verses.

3. Translations of Bataille's *Actualité* essay are my own, although for each citation I indicate the corresponding page number from the French volume. Citations of other texts by Bataille come from published translations of his works.

4. In *Homo Ludens,* an anthropological study of play elements in culture, the Dutch historian Johan Huizinga examines how certain types of play have effects outside the parameters of the game. Echoing Greek understandings of ritual and theater, Huizinga refers to this break from mimetic representation as methexis (14–15).

5. In *Inner Experience* (1943) and *Eroticism* (1957), Bataille writes extensively about the correspondence between mysticism and erotic swoons.

6. Curiously, the first nineteen lines and the last five lines of the chapter are omitted.

7. Translations of Abouddahab's essay are my own.

Works Cited

Abouddahab, Rédouane. "L'œil et le soleil: Bataille avec Hemingway." *Revue Française d'Études Américaines* 84 (2000): 61–76.

Anderson, Andrew. *Lorca's Late Poetry: A Critical Study.* Leeds: Francis Cairns, 1990.

Bataille, Georges. "Concerning *For Whom the Bell Tolls* by Ernest Hemingway." *Actualité: L'Espagne libre* (1946): 120–26. Ed. Georges Bataille.

———. *Story of the Eye.* Trans. Joachim Neugroschel. San Francisco: City Lights, 1987.

———. *Visions of Excess: Selected Writings, 1927–1939.* Ed. and intro. Allan Stoekl. Trans. Allan Stoekl, Carl R. Lovitt, and Donald M. Leslie Jr. Minneapolis: U of Minnesota P, 1985.

García Lorca, Federico. *Collected Poems.* Ed. Christopher Maurer. Trans. Catherine Brown, et al. New York: Farrar, Straus, and Giroux, 2002.

———. *In Search of Duende.* Ed. Christopher Maurer. Trans. Norman Di Giovanni, et al. New York: New Directions, 1998.

Gibson, Ian. *Federico García Lorca: A Life.* New York: Pantheon, 1989.

Grande, Félix. *García Lorca y el flamenco.* Madrid: Mondadori, 1992.

Hemingway, Ernest. *The Dangerous Summer.* Intro. James A. Michener. New York: Scribner, 1985.

———. *Death in the Afternoon.* 1932. New York: Simon and Schuster, 1996.

———. *For Whom the Bell Tolls.* New York: Scribner, 1940.

Hollier, Denis. *Against Architecture: The Writings of Georges Bataille.* Cambridge: MIT, 1992.

Huizinga, Johan. *Homo Ludens: A Study of the Play-Element in Culture.* Boston: Beacon, 1970.

Josephs, Allen. *White Wall of Spain: The Mysteries of Andalusian Culture.* Ames: Iowa State UP, 1983.

Mandel, Miriam B. Introduction. *A Companion to Hemingway's* Death in the Afternoon. Ed. Mandel. Rochester, NY: Camden House, 2004. 1–17.

McAlmon, Robert. *Being Geniuses Together, 1920–1930.* 1938. Revised with Supplementary Chapters and an Afterward by Kay Boyle. New York: Doubleday, 1968.

Penas Ibáñez, Beatriz. "Between Melancholia and Jubilant Novatio: Ernest Hemingway's Modernist Ambivalences." In *De Baudelaire a Lorca: Acercamiento a la modernidad literaria.* Ed. Kurt Reichenberger, et al. Vol. 3. Kassel, Germany: Reichenberger, 1996. 637–57.

———. "'Very Sad but Very Fine': *Death in the Afternoon*'s Imagist Interpretation of the Bullfight-Text." In *A Companion to Hemingway's* Death in the Afternoon. Ed. Miriam B. Mandel. Rochester, NY: Camden House, 2004. 143–64.

Salinas, Pedro. "Lorca and the Poetry of Death." *Hopkins Review* 5.1 (1951): 5–12.

Stanton, Edward. *Hemingway and Spain: A Pursuit.* Seattle: U of Washington P, 1989.

Surya, Michel. *Georges Bataille: An Intellectual Biography.* Trans. Krzysztof Fijalkowski and Michael Richardson. London: Verso, 2002.

8

"It was all there . . . but he could not see it"

What's Dangerous about The Dangerous Summer

Suzanne del Gizzo

The "danger" in the title of *The Dangerous Summer* ostensibly refers to the perils faced by matadors Antonio Ordóñez and Luis Miguel Dominguín in their mano a mano during the *temporada* of 1959. It was indeed a dangerous season for them; each matador was gored three times. But even a cursory reading of the book reveals that the narrative is preoccupied with the notion of danger outside as well as inside the bullring; from the familiar dangers (for Hemingway at least) of fame, money, and success to a range of physical dangers, such as the death-defying late-night drives between bulls, the prop planes flown by matadors with no pilots' licenses (*DS* 177), or even Hemingway's odd decision to climb into a cage with a recently trapped wolf (53). None of these dangers, however, is the most interesting in *The Dangerous Summer:* the most significant danger in the book lies in Hemingway's attempt to return to a site of previous artistic and personal satisfaction without recalibrating his perspective to account for his present realities.

Many of Hemingway's writings from the last decade of his life—*A Moveable Feast* and *Under Kilimanjaro* are notable examples—focus on such returns and are thus often considered exercises in nostalgia. William Kennedy notices a similar nostalgic quality in *The Dangerous Summer;* in his *New York Times* review, he observes that the book seems to be a concerted effort by an aging Hemingway "to re-create [a] past when he was living . . . well and writing . . . well" (33). Along the same lines, John Raeburn describes the book as "a sentimental journey, the return of an aging man to the scene of youthful triumphs" (164).

The Dangerous Summer, however, stands apart from *Feast* and *Under Kilimanjaro* in that it is ostensibly a journalistic book about the present—the 1959 bullfight season. Unlike *A Moveable Feast*, which Hemingway composed in part simultaneously with *The Dangerous Summer*, this second bullfighting book is not characterized simply by nostalgia for a time remembered or a place from the past; rather, Hemingway's past seems to intrude on his attempts to observe the present. Typically, nostalgia is an exercise of memory and desire that entails an idealization of the irrecoverable past; nostalgic endeavors involve a complex act of projection, in which the idealized past mingles with dissatisfactions in the present to create a distorted but stable, coherent, and harmonious version of that past.

But *The Dangerous Summer* is anything but a stable, coherent, and harmonious text. Hemingway constantly diminishes or evades his present realities, specifically his age, his celebrity, and the changes to Spain that have taken place since he first fell in love with it in the 1920s. In fact, *The Dangerous Summer* functions like nostalgia in reverse, as Hemingway attempts to use the past to restructure his present.

The 1959 trip to Spain came at a difficult time for Hemingway. It coincided with the beginning of what was arguably his last bout of depression, the one from which he did not recover. After World War II, Hemingway faced a variety of challenges, among them his own advancing age, an expanding list of health problems, and the increased commercialization and commodification of both his own image and the world around him. His fame as a writer and cultural figure had intensified after he was awarded the Nobel Prize in 1954. He appeared on nearly fourteen mass-market magazine covers between 1950 and his death in 1961, as well as in numerous advertisements for products ranging from Ballantine Ale and Parker Pens to Pan-American Airlines. Although he welcomed the approbation and attention, there is evidence in his unpublished writing from this period that he also felt increasingly limited and trapped by the hyper-masculine public persona they created. Even by post–World War II standards, however, Hemingway was particularly petulant in the months leading up to that dangerous summer of 1959. Biographer Michael Reynolds notes that January 1959 was the beginning of a "dark trip down" to "new found depths" (321). Hemingway's experiences that summer made it clear that "the aging, traumatized celebrity who followed the bulls in 1959 was very different from the ambitious, eager young man who had followed them in the 1920s and 1930s" (Mandel 3). Reynolds argues that Hemingway simply did not realize "how hard the summer [of 1959] would be on him" as he endeavored to keep the same schedule as the matadors, who were approximately thirty years his junior (525). The trip, designed to invigorate Hemingway and remind him of his youth and vitality, in fact highlighted how much he had aged and how much his beloved Spain had changed, not only the obvious changes resulting from Franco's rule but also the changes to the culture of the bullfight, the raison d'être for his return. In the intervening years, the festival of San Fermín had become a tourist attraction and the bullfight itself had become heavily commercialized and, as far as Hemingway was concerned, artistically compromised.

Even after Hemingway returned home from the trip and began work on the manuscript, his problems continued. The trip may have made him aware of his own physical limitations, but it was his attempt to capture the summer in writing that confirmed problems with his ability to focus mentally. He found he could not control the flow of the words or sculpt his experiences into a meaningful, dynamic narrative. Recognizing this conundrum, Hemingway tried to frame it in familiar terms in a letter to his wife, Mary, remarking that he was writing through and against another one of his "black ass" periods (Reynolds 333). But this time was different. His struggle left traces on the final product. As Kennedy remarks, "Hemingway's mind was out of control and would get progressively worse. His vaunted ability to leave out what was irrelevant, his great talent for synthesis, were malfunctioning" (33). For these reasons, Kennedy speculates that Hemingway "turned . . . the mano a mano . . . into a quest for, and a statement about, his own youth, his own heroism, his own art, his own immortality; for he was dying, psychically and artistically, and he seems to have intuited that" (1). But for my purposes, the issue is not simply Hemingway's compulsion to make a statement about himself and his art in the last years of his life, but the curious way this statement is presented in *The Dangerous Summer.*

Unlike a typical nostalgic narrative, which aims for comfort and harmony by compensating for the present by reimagining the past, Hemingway's repeated and strained attempts in *The Dangerous Summer* to re-create the past and deny the present in front of him ultimately served to reveal, rather than obscure, his current anxieties. For example, he *almost* completely erases indications of aging or physical infirmity, choosing instead to highlight his fitness by emphasizing the physical demands of the *temporada* and by identifying with the younger bullfighter, Antonio Ordóñez. In addition, although Hemingway's celebrity was such that he could not attend the 1959 fights in anonymity (as he had in the 1920s), and although the Spain surrounding him in 1959 was very different than the Spain of his youth (in part because of his use of it in his novels), he minimizes the realities of his celebrity and its impact on tourism (and the impact of tourism more broadly) in Spain throughout *The Dangerous Summer.* The result is a book that waffles between fleeting recognition of change in the present and complete denial of it. To account for this curious and unsettling aspect of the book, it may be helpful to read *The Dangerous Summer* as a narrative governed by the logic of disavowal.[1]

Disavowal is a psychological defense mechanism that allows one to cope with an "external reality" that is perceived to be unsavory or threatening (Laplanche and Pontalis 119). Generally associated with the behavior of fetishists (and Carl Eby's work has persuasively argued that Hemingway was indeed a fetishist), disavowal permits one to acknowledge something considered dangerous or threatening only on condition that he or she negate it immediately. The process is an attempt to master or control fear and anxiety. From this perspective, Hemingway's use of disavowal in *The Dangerous Summer* suggests that he was anxious about the changes he saw in himself and in Spain that summer; they represented a reality he was not prepared to confront. Moreover, the visibility of this process of disavowal is the reason the book does not function as a work of nostalgia. The present is too present, and Hemingway's efforts to diminish it are too disruptive and obviously evasive. As a result, disavowal leaves its mark not only on the content of the book (e.g., his denial of aging and his celebrity), but also on the narrative, in the repetitive structure of the story and the way Hemingway presents his identity as divided between his past and present, as well as between Ordóñez and Dominguín. In short, the practice of disavowal—both thematically and structurally—is what makes *The Dangerous Summer* dangerous for Hemingway.

Old age and the decline of his physical and mental health presented a particular challenge to Hemingway and his art because, as Stanley Cooperman aptly noted in 1965, "the virtues of the Hemingway hero had always been the virtues of the young" (217). As a result, Cooperman observes, Hemingway in his later works seems to be "searching for a posture which would enable him to *cope* with the fact of his own age" (217; my italics). *The Dangerous Summer* is one of these later works, but Hemingway's coping mechanism is problematically rooted in the defensive process of disavowal. Perhaps the most candid example of this occurs during a dinner at Marceliano's in Pamplona, when Hemingway observes: "The faces that were young once were old as mine but everyone remembered how we were. The eyes had not changed and nobody was fat. . . . Nobody was defeated" (*DS* 139). In three sentences, Hemingway acknowledges that he is older, but he simultaneously denies that age makes any difference in his or his companions' ability to experience the joys of the *temporada.* Hemingway finds evidence of their youth in two images that he will repeatedly associate with a denial of aging in his later work—unchanged eyes (and by extension, good eyesight, which was something Hemingway had always admired) and a svelte physique. The emphasis on unchanged eyes suggests that Hemingway and his companions' way of seeing has not been narrowed or compromised by age, both literally (no cataracts or glaucoma) and metaphorically. If the eyes are the windows to the soul, these souls are undefeated, betrayed only by their aging shells. In a similar vein, Hemingway's emphasis on his own and his companions' lean bodies counteracts the significance of their physical impairments; they are not flabby, a condition that Hemingway frequently regards as a sign of corruption by wealth and laziness (think of Harry's claim, in "The Snows of Kilimanjaro," that he is going on safari to save himself from a decadent and wealthy lifestyle and to "get back into training" ["Snows" 44]).

Another example of Hemingway's attempt to disavow his age occurs after he has spent a day at the beach with the young bullfighter Antonio Ordóñez and his cuadrilla. Hemingway claims that they were "dead tired and . . . went to bed early like worn-out healthy savages" (*DS* 154). The next day, Hemingway, concerned that they may have over-done the fun and worn out Ordóñez, who is facing a fight later that day, has a pointed exchange with the younger man:

> "Are you stiff?" I asked him.
> "Not at all."
> "Are your feet all right?"
> My own right foot was swollen from dribbling and kicking barefoot.
> "They're all right. I never felt better. . . ." (154)

Hemingway looks for signs of his own fatigue in Ordóñez, with whom, as I will demonstrate later, he strongly identifies throughout the book. Once the younger man denies these symptoms, the topic of discussion quickly changes to the weather conditions for the fight. These examples illustrate how Hemingway repeatedly and fleetingly mentions his age and signs of his aging only to deny their significance immediately.

At other times, however, Hemingway hints that he is not as fit as he would like to be. For example, he points out that Bill Davis, proprietor of La Consula and his host that summer, served as their self-appointed chauffeur. Hemingway frequently comments on Bill's ability to stay up all night in order to make the long drives between bulls, during which the fatigued Hemingway must catch up on sleep. He also makes an odd association between these long, dangerous drives and returning to one's youth when he writes: "The distances all seem longer than they are, the difficult parts of the road much worse than it is, the dangerous curves more dangerous and the steep ascents have a greater percentage of grade. It is like going back into your childhood or early youth" (*DS* 66). In other words, the older Hemingway experiences these drives as exaggerated, dramatic, and, of course, dangerous, but he is also aware that these are distorted perceptions resulting from his age. The demands put on him by the drives and, more broadly, by his experiences that summer seem to outpace his ability to keep up with them physically and mentally, making him feel like a child again in a world of unknown dimensions. In this way, Hemingway again indicates the significance of his age, which makes him feel out of control, disoriented, and childishly overwhelmed, but only in a circuitous way. More important, he seems to understand that the roads may not be as "dangerous" as they "seem"; it is his aging that is dangerous and causes the distortion.

Hemingway's anxiety and self-consciousness about his age reach their height when his wife Mary throws a huge party for his sixtieth birthday in the middle of the bullfighting season. Reynolds describes the party as "a fête richer than any of his previous birthdays. It began at 10:00 P.M. and continued on through the night, into the following morning, and through part of the day" (329). However, Reynolds also notes that "what should have been a triumph for Mary became another intolerable performance by Ernest, who either ignored her completely . . . or spoke to her in an abusive, sarcastic manner" (329). In *The Dangerous Summer,* this all-night extravaganza is summed up briefly in a couple of pointedly understated paragraphs. "It was quite a party," Hemingway comments, "and *I might not have noticed I was sixty* if Mary had not made it *so important and so pleasant.* But that party drove it in" (140; my emphasis). The "so important and so pleasant" drips with sarcasm, and the descriptive phrase that the party "drove it in" suggests an act of violence, since it resonates with the language Hemingway uses for killing a bull by "driving in" the sword. The next paragraph initially appears to be a non sequitur, in which Hemingway meditates on the need of bullfighters to confront death regularly, but the proximity of his consideration of death in bullfighting to his discussion of his sixtieth birthday suggests that he is fearful of aging because he associates it with the approach of death. Given the way age is presented in the book and his treatment of Mary that evening, it seems Hemingway might have preferred not to have been reminded of this momentous birthday.

In fact Mary, who was fifty-one that summer, often serves as a scapegoat for Hemingway's anxieties about his health and his age in *The Dangerous Summer.* Not only did he ignore Mary for significant stretches of that summer but he also presents her in the narrative as a drag on his good time, often insulting and annoying her by taking on younger female companions, notably Valerie Danby-Smith, whom he met in Pamplona that year (Reynolds 328). For Hemingway, Mary seems to represent his reality as an older, married man with physical limitations. As such, her presence taints and disrupts his efforts to re-create his past.

While Hemingway's tendency to ignore Mary fits the overall logic of disavowal in the text—she represents his present realities, so she is both acknowledged and negated—his presentation of her as an obstacle to his summer-long fiesta fits another related but distinct psychological defense mechanism, known as displacement. Displacement is a process by which concern about or anxiety over one matter is "transferred" or "cathected" onto something or someone else, with the goal of containing that concern or anxiety by distancing oneself from it (Laplanche and Pontalis 121, 123). From the beginning of *The Dangerous Summer,* Hemingway chronicles Mary's illnesses from her "bad cold" after San Isidro (*DS* 49) to her persistent fever in Córdoba (80), to her broken toe, incurred while swimming in the Irati (137). He points out that she increasingly opts out of the intense schedule, skipping fights to rest at La Consula (the home of Bill and Annie Davis) in order to recover from her various health problems. In the meantime, Hemingway seldom mentions his own health issues, or at most does so obliquely. When he recalls that George Saviers, "a doctor friend of ours from Sun Valley" (*DS* 137), cared for a wound Antonio Ordóñez received when running with the bulls in Pamplona, for example, he does not bring up the fact that Dr. Saviers was also treating him for a kidney disorder around that time (Baker 547). Hemingway also fails to mention the cocktail of drugs he was taking for his various ailments, a staggering list that included Serapasil, Doriden, Ritalin, Eucanil, Seconal, and Oreton-M (Reynolds 321–22).

But perhaps the most consistent and striking way Hemingway attempts to disavow his aging and fatigue in 1959 is through his identification with Antonio Ordóñez in the rivalry at the heart of the book. What is interesting about Hemingway's identification with Ordóñez is the extent to which it is achieved through his denigration of Luis Miguel Dominguín, Ordóñez's brother-in-law and rival in the bullring that summer. As James A. Michener points out in his introduction to *The Dangerous Summer,* Hemingway's bias against the older bullfighter is so noticeable and extraordinary that, in his opinion, the book "stands as an unwarranted attack on Dominguín" (16). Hemingway's unfairness to Dominguín, however, provides insight into the way he works to obscure his all-too-obvious similarities to the older bullfighter, who, in his words, will be "destroyed" by the end of the book (*DS* 189, 193).

Hemingway chooses his side from the first time he meets Dominguín and Ordóñez in 1953. During a visit to Dominguín's farm, Hemingway takes in the accoutrements of success displayed by the newly retired bullfighter, including a "new-built swimming pool" and a "bronze life-size statue of Luis Miguel" (*DS* 53). Hemingway latches onto this statue, remarking that it is "a rare thing for a man to have around his own finca in his own lifetime, and I thought Miguel looked better than his statue although his statue looked just a little bit nobler" (53). For a reader sensitive to Hemingway's value system, his singling out of these objects serves as a thinly veiled verdict that the man had become decadent and soft; he has succumbed to a comfortable life measured not in bulls killed but in objects owned and displayed. This image of Dominguín is juxtaposed with Hemingway's first meeting with Antonio Ordóñez in the previous scene, which takes place in the bullfighter's room after Hemingway has watched him fight. Hemingway's descriptions of Ordóñez are vital and sensual as he approvingly describes his dark eyes, mischievous grin, and his "scar welts on the right thigh" (52). He also notes that the younger matador extends a left hand in greeting because the right hand had been badly cut by a sword (52). Unlike Dominguín, whose greatness must now be symbolized and memorialized by things he owns while his physical presence becomes less "noble," Ordóñez's greatness is still being written on and through his young body. Almost immediately, then, Hemingway distances himself from the retired, wealthy, older matador softened by success and wealth and aligns himself with the younger one, who is still in the dangerous fight.

The mechanics of Hemingway's allegiances in the mano a mano are complex and rooted in the overall logic of disavowal that governs the book. Freud, who pioneered the theory, explicitly observes that disavowals are predicated on a split in the ego, in which a part of the ego disavows the reality and a part acknowledges it (Laplanche and Pontalis 119). As a result, Freud observes in *An Outline of Psycho-Analysis* that disavowals are always "half measures, incomplete attempts at detachment from reality" in which the two parts of the ego hold two incompatible positions (204). In *The Dangerous Summer*, this split ego manifests itself, at least on one level, in Hemingway's attitudes toward the two bullfighters. Joseph Fruscione has argued that Hemingway's intense identification with Ordóñez is a form of "projective identification," a concept Fruscione borrows from Melanie Klein. According to Klein, "projective identification" entails "the splitting of the ego and the projection of parts of the self, into other people" (qtd. in Fruscione 74). In this reading, Hemingway "'takes possession by projection of' Ordóñez creating an 'extension of self' that makes him feel more empowered and less anxious" (Fruscione 82). In other words, Hemingway identifies with Ordóñez because he represents those values Hemingway most wants to be reminded of in himself—youth, bravery, and artistic purity. However, another, related symptom of this split ego is visible in Hemingway's attempts to distance himself from Dominguín and the problematic values the older matador represents—aging, fear in the ring, and trickery in his art.

Ordóñez emerges as the hero of *The Dangerous Summer* precisely because he is young and not yet fully established as a great matador; he is not yet corrupted by wealth, and in this regard he probably reminded Hemingway of his younger self. In fact, Ordóñez is described as hungry for recognition of his ability, a quality Hemingway fondly recalled about his younger self in a somewhat more literal as well as a metaphorical fashion as he drafted *A Moveable Feast.* Ordóñez, like the young Hemingway, is willing and able to take risks. Hemingway celebrates Ordóñez's drive to prove himself the greater fighter, explaining, "Antonio would do that or he would die" (*DS* 112). As the older, established matador, Dominguín lacks this hunger because he has fed off the fruits of success. He does, however, feel the fatigue and pressure of the mano a mano in ways that Hemingway probably understood more fully than he would admit. Hemingway writes of Dominguín: "It was one thing to live to be the number one in the world in his profession and have that be the one true belief in his life. It was another thing to be almost killed each time he went out to prove it and to know that only his wealthiest and most powerful friends, a number of beautiful women, and Pablo Picasso who had not seen a bullfight in Spain in twenty-five years still believed it" (195). Hemingway, with his established reputation, his commissioned article on the *temporada* for *Life* magazine, and his large entourage of wealthy and supportive friends, might easily have been talking about himself.

After all, by the time that Hemingway was suspiciously eyeing Dominguín's "new-built" swimming pool, he had already lived in Key West with a monstrous sixty-five-foot swimming pool that had cost a scandalous $20,000 (McIver 21). And although Hemingway did not have a statue of himself on his finca in Cuba, he was living in the shadow of his image on nearly fourteen mass-market magazine covers between 1950 and 1961. Besides, he had already toyed with that level of vanity; he had a bust of himself on display in his Key West house (Meyers 242). In addition, during the dangerous summer of 1959, Hemingway and Dominguín are pursuing similar goals and confronting similar setbacks. Both are attempting to return to sites of previous glory; much as Dominguín returned to the ring for the 1959 *temporada,* Hemingway returned to Spain, the place where, Kennedy reminds us, "he had become a mythic figure" (33). And much as Dominguín was nearly "destroyed" by this return to the bullring, Hemingway came to recognize, as the installments of *The Dangerous Summer* appeared and flopped in *Life* magazine, that he too had made a serious mistake in "doubling back" (Michener 16). For these reasons, Hemingway's insistent identification with Ordóñez and his denial of Dominguín are suspicious and strained.

Following the logic of disavowal, Hemingway does come close to acknowledging his similarities to Dominguín. At one point, he compares Dominguín's trick of hypnotizing a bull with his own "parlor trick" of hypnotizing chickens (*DS* 110). Through the word *trick*—something Hemingway despises in modern bullfighting as a sign of its corruption—the indirect comparison is made and reveals Hemingway's fear that he had begun to compromise his art to please his public and maintain his reputation. As he wrote in an undated fragment, probably from the 1950s[2]: "So now we have reached the point where we are ruled by photographers and agents of publishers and writing is no longer of any importance and all that matters is bull-shit and consent to unwanted publicity. . . . What does it profit a man to gain a prize which might be given to an old man who wants it or to someone who covets it if he loses respect for himself and if his work is destroyed each day through small politenesses?" (qtd. in Scafella 79). The "small politenesses," like Dominguín's "tricks," are Hemingway's concessions to a demanding audience he feels obliged to satisfy. Less than a page after discussing his chicken "trick," Hemingway sympathetically observes: "Luis Miguel had his place to maintain. He claimed to be the number one bullfighter and he was rich. That was weight to carry in the ring but he really loved to fight bulls and he forgot about being rich when he was in the ring" (*DS* 111). Yet, given the comparison Hemingway makes in *The Dangerous Summer* and elsewhere between bullfighting and writing, Luis Miguel's name can be replaced with Hemingway's and bullfighting with writing. Writing, for Hemingway, was now a "defensive" attempt to maintain his status, and that fact arguably tainted and compromised his intense love of his art.

Nonetheless, Hemingway cannot quite bring himself to own up to his similarities to Luis Miguel, because such a gesture would require him to admit to his decline and corruption as an artist. Moreover, Hemingway's critics, when writing later in his life or when discussing his later career after his death, have much the same feeling about him as he claims the crowd at Valencia had about Dominguín: "They were watching something happen to a man that they could not understand" (*DS* 151). After all, this is the period in which Hemingway worked on but did not finish approximately four different manuscripts, a record not unlike Dominguín's during the corrida in Valencia, when he tries but fails to kill a bull five times because he cannot "bring himself to drive [the sword] in" (151). Even Hemingway's brief mention of Pepé Luis Vásquez, another matador who came out of retirement for the 1959 season, suggests what he feared might be true of himself: "[Vásquez] had put on weight in retirement and the delicacies and embroideries of his style now, with his plumpness and the lack of any lighthearted quality in his work, seemed sad and pitiful and he was unable to conceal his fear" (77).

Given Hemingway's emphasis on youth, then, the central problem of the book is clear: there is no model for returning honorably and impressively to sites of previous success. This was something Hemingway had suspected from a young age, as can be seen in his 1922 article "A Veteran Visits the Old Front." But the problem is only partly one of time and age, or, as Cooperman puts it, the need to decide "what sort of heroism is possible as a man gets older" (217); it is also a problem of the way the world—and Spain in particular—had changed as a consequence of the rise in commercialization and commodification in the middle of the twentieth century. The book's two most persistent disavowals in this regard concern Hemingway's presentation of his own celebrity and his diminishment of the changes tourism had introduced to Spain, especially Pamplona.

Hemingway does briefly acknowledge his fame on occasion, as when he is nearly recognized by a guard at the Spanish border in 1953 (*DS* 44) or when he is invited to stay at the Marquis del Merito's place outside Córdoba (80), but for the majority of the book, he presents himself more or less as one of Ordóñez's cuadrilla. He follows the young matador from town to town, is given access to the dressing room, and helps tend to Ordóñez's wounds between and after fights. Even here, however, he alludes to his privileged status, such as when he leaves Ordóñez's dressing room after only a brief visit, aware that his behavior will set an example for others (82).

Media accounts and the research of biographers suggest that Hemingway's self-effacement in *The Dangerous Summer* does not exactly capture the truth of the season. Other accounts of the 1959 *temporada* relate that Hemingway was followed by the Spanish press nearly everywhere he went, that he and Mary were treated like "visiting royalty," and that Hemingway "was not averse to [the] publicity" (Baker 545). Mary's recollections of "Papa Sportif" (as she called him) during that summer are that they "were never alone" and rarely experienced any break from what she called the "circus" (Lynn 577). In addition, Hemingway traveled with a considerable cuadrilla of sorts of his own and spent time with a cross section of old and new friends, ranging from members of the bullfighting circuit to Hollywood acquaintances (Lynn 577).

He was also a noticeable presence at the bullrings. Carlos Baker recounts an occasion,when Hemingway offered a conspicuous demonstration of his clout:

on 24 May on the Plaza del Toros, despite a "sea of waving handkerchiefs," the president gave "no official recognition" of a young bullfighter's performance until Hemingway rose, "faced the President, and solemnly waved one of his own" (546). That gesture secured both ears of the bull for Segura that day. Similarly, biographer Kenneth Lynn claims that at Valencia, "promoters of the duel made much of the fact that Hemingway had been in attendance" in order to drum up publicity for the mano a mano (570). It turns out that, as in *The Dangerous Summer,* the rivalry between the matadors was only half of the attraction for the audience—watching Hemingway was the other. John Raeburn points out that the mano a mano received a great deal of attention in America as a result of Hemingway's involvement and that "journalists and photographers followed him as eagerly as they did the bullfights" (163). Thus when Hemingway observes, during one of the corridas, "Another thing that worried me was the many photographers and motion picture men present who had no previous bull ring experience" (*DS* 169–70), he is acknowledging that his presence generated a lot of publicity and interest without directly taking responsibility for it or admitting that his fame is a dangerous thing that may compromise the integrity of the fight. In fact, Spanish critic Jose Luis Castillo-Puche has suggested that Hemingway was "suckered" by fight promoters to help generate attention for the fights; he even contends that Ordóñez was "using" Hemingway to advance his own career (Kennedy 35). Whether or not Hemingway was exploited is hard to say, but the point remains that he was a far more noticeable presence during the *temporada* than he generally acknowledges in his book.

Hemingway probably downplayed his celebrity in Spain and his visibility as a public figure during the season for two complementary reasons. First, throughout the book, Hemingway associates celebrity status with corruption and decadence in one's art. Just as he wants to distance himself from Dominguín, he is likewise reluctant to suggests he too plays to the crowd or enjoys the attention he receives. Second, Hemingway arguably knew that his writing had played some role in the changes in Spain, particularly the changes in Pamplona and the festival of San Fermín, and he wanted to minimize not only those changes but also his sense of culpability for them.

A *New York Times* article by Robert Daley on the Pamplona fiesta of 1959 registers the impact of tourism on the city, using publication of *The Sun Also Rises* as the watershed date; it reads: "Pamplona before 1925 was a small country town surrounded by medieval walls, the streets narrow, dark and cool. Today it is a city of 85,000, the medieval walls are gone and the focus has moved to a new part of the city when [sic] its great wide boulevards and ugly new buildings"

(6). Daley continues, "In the old days, the fiesta was for the locals. . . . Today there are more than 40,000 tourists in town, many of them young Americans" (6). Daley also notes the decline in the quality of the fights, suggesting that the fights themselves are no longer the principal draw. Rather, the article implies that Hemingway's portrayal of the fiesta in *The Sun Also Rises* is attracting many of the visitors. Curiously, although Hemingway attended this same fiesta, he recounts it in startlingly different terms. He does not remark on the quality of the fights, but, again following the logic of disavowal, he notes, "I've written Pamplona once and for keeps. It is all there as it always was" (*DS* 136). He does concede that "forty thousand tourists have been added" (136), but he assures readers, "I was as happy as I had ever been and all the overcrowding and the modernizations at Pamplona meant nothing" (139).

Although Hemingway disavowed his celebrity by not taking any responsibility for Pamplona's popularity with tourists, Pamplona officials and other commentators have for quite some time recognized the writer's role in popularizing the festival of San Fermín. In a 1985 article, "Hemingway's Spain," James Markham quotes Pamplona's mayor, Julian Balduz, on this issue: "There is a debate over whether or not Hemingway was positive for the identity of sanfermines. . . . What happened is that Hemingway put the sanfermines at the disposition of the whole world, and the whole world doesn't fit into Pamplona" (15). It seems clear to everyone that Hemingway's portrayal of Pamplona in *The Sun Also Rises* was in large part responsible for those forty thousand tourists in 1959 (and the many others since that time). In *The Dangerous Summer,* however, Hemingway minimizes their presence and diminishes the effect of his work on the city, giving only a backhanded acknowledgment to the power of his celebrity when he declines to give the details of a location on the Irati "because we want to go back there again and not find fifty cars or jeeps have found it" (139).

The carnivalesque atmosphere of Pamplona does lead to the most pronounced rupture in Hemingway's attempts at disavowal. The festivities culminate in an exchange with a young man (Matt Carney, although he is not identified in the book), who expresses the wish that he had been at Pamplona with Hemingway thirty years earlier, "when you used to go into the country and know the people, when you used to know the Spaniards and care about them and their country and about writing and not waste your time sitting in a bar seeking adulation, making wise cracks with your sycophants and signing autographs" (*DS* 139–40). Although Hemingway attributes these scathing comments to Carney's anger over another matter and attempts to dismiss him and his observations, the episode stands out from the rest of the text because it offers an outsider's perspective on the summer that jibes with biographical accounts of the visit by suggesting that Hemingway enjoyed the publicity and was the cause of much of the attention that season. As Valerie Hemingway recalls, "Ernest, never given a moment's peace when in public, was besieged with requests to sign autographs and pose for photos" (V. Hemingway 34).

In addition, Carney's comments uncover the realities behind Hemingway's textual performance of the older, but still vital author revisiting with undiminished zeal one of the proving grounds of his youth and finding it all, like a good bull before the faena, "intact." The problem, as I have been arguing, is that this approach requires that Hemingway disavow the realities of his present. Although in recent years Hemingway has often been presented in terms of performances of masculinity, in *The Dangerous Summer* these performances become self-referential, and therefore more self-conscious, because the narrative's focus on the present highlights its problematic relationship to his past. Readers are left with the somewhat uncanny image of Hemingway retracing his own steps, as if he were taking a prepackaged Hemingway tour, complete with dinner at Marceliano's and a day trip to the Irati. The visible disavowal of his present realities—his age, his celebrity, the changes to Spain—makes the book feel vestigial and synthetic, because he registers those changes just enough that his insistence that nothing has changed seems forced and insincere.

Despite his insistence on his good eyes, Hemingway's inability to "see" or fully acknowledge his present realities compromised his ability to write the story of the 1959 *temporada. The Dangerous Summer* spiraled out of control during the drafting process, ballooning from a 10,000-word article for *Life* magazine (Michener 13) to a manuscript that ran more than 120,000 words (Reynolds 344). In addition, Hemingway missed multiple deadlines for the article and actively resisted suggested cuts by Mary and his friend A. E. Hotchner. The book betrays his struggles with word count and control. The narrative stagnates because of a nearly obsessive insistence on a chronological presentation of the *temporada.* Each venue seems to bleed into the next as the narrative becomes an endless cycle of preparing for a fight, the fight itself, a possible injury, a meal, and an all-night drive.[3] There is little that distinguishes one fight from another (at least for those readers who are not bullfight aficionados), and Hemingway seems almost existentially bothered about how to end the story as in *Death in Afternoon,* especially since no climactic death occurred or clear winner emerged during the mano a mano, which was to continue into the 1960 season.

This nearly flat narrative is further complicated by Hemingway's struggle with his persona and voice in the book. In creating a piece of "ego-journalism," in which his status as a long-standing aficionado, celebrated author, and cultural icon inspired readers' interest in the piece, Hemingway had to determine how best to represent himself and his relationship to the matadors, the *temporada,* and Spain. Rather than confront the changes to himself and to Spain by the late 1950s in *The Dangerous Summer,* Hemingway equivocates about them. The logic of disavowal that dominates the text is visible, then, not only in his thematic avoidance of his age and celebrity or in the splitting of his identity between Ordóñez and Dominguín (not to mention the also noticeable split between his present and past self) but also in structure of the narrative itself.

It is this strategy of disavowal that makes *The Dangerous Summer* dangerous for Hemingway as a writer. Such an approach compromises the aura of authenticity that generally characterizes Hemingway's texts, since disavowal requires an avoidance of reality and thus infringes upon his usual writing strategy. Disavowal requires exposure—the saying—in order to negate what is said. Such a gesture violates Hemingway's theory of omission and creates problems for his craft. His voice takes on an obliquely confessional tone, which creates a sense of disjunction or discontinuity in the book that in turn may lead readers to question his reliability and sincerity. In addition, the word count mounts as Hemingway is caught in a cycle of acknowledging and negating, a cycle that may also account for the book's repetitiveness and lack of narrative structure. Hemingway is attempting to resolve a struggle that cannot be resolved; he is trying to write against time and re-create the past by avoiding his present. Nonetheless, he knows that his present is not just like his past—just as he knows that he is like Dominguín or that simply saying "I'm not old" does not erase the years or make the feet swell less after a long day. Since disavowal is also predicated on a split in the ego, the process never fully works; one half of the split identity (the one aware of the reality) knows it did not work. The only option is to try the process again and again.

In the case of *The Dangerous Summer,* this repetitive aspect of disavowal contributes to the episodic structure of the narrative. Arguably, part of the reason Hemingway could not staunch the flow of words or give shape to the narrative is that he was motivated not simply by a desire to represent the mano a mano as he saw it, but also by a need to undertake a psychological exercise that entailed finding the right voice that would allow him to disavow fully the changes in himself and in Spain, which he perceived as threatening and dangerous. Michener explains in his introduction to the book that Hemingway seems torn between representing faithfully each corrida and fulfilling his assignment for *Life,* which was to be an "article about what it was like to go back [to Spain]" (13). In short, despite the ostensible focus on the showdown between Ordóñez and Dominguín, there is another agenda in *The Dangerous Summer,* and it is one personal to Hemingway. He attempts to conjure an image of his present self as very much like his past self through his portrayal of the mano a mano, and he can't quite get it to work. As Kennedy argues, Hemingway seems to have intuited his decline and is struggling with it through the representation of the 1959 *temporada.*

The Dangerous Summer, then, is a book about decay and decline—be it in the swollen feet of an aging writer or in the art of bullfighting—but it is also a book that attempts to deny this decay and decline, principally through its focus on the bright, exceptional figure of a young Antonio Ordóñez at the height of his powers and through the process of disavowal that informs the logic of the narrative. Michener's introduction reminds readers that such a denial is ultimately futile when he recalls that "in subsequent years I saw [Ordóñez] fight perhaps two dozen times and invariably he was disgraceful. Although others saw him fight well after 1959, the times I saw him he was pudgy and evasive, apparently terrified of any real bull he faced" (39–40). In 1959, however, it was Hemingway who was wrestling with the decline of his powers. *The Dangerous Summer* offered him an opportunity to explore a series of difficult and compelling (and yes, dangerous) questions about heroism and authorship in old age and in a celebrity-obsessed society, but unfortunately he does not work to answer them. Rather, he produces a flabby and evasive book that counteracts his strenuous efforts to present himself as youthful, vital, and at the height of his powers. Because he cannot face the real dangers, Hemingway manufactures other "dangers" he can handle (much like the shaved horns or misleading passes resorted to by decadent bullfighters) to distract the reader. Thus, the superficial emphasis on and proliferation of dangers in the book is a trick in the ring—something done to give the impression of danger—but the danger lies not in the perils Hemingway showcases but in those he disavows. As a result, I cannot help feeling about Hemingway a little as he does about Matt Carney, that young man who confronted him in Pamplona: "It was all there and he had been invited to it; but he could not see it" (140).

Notes

Acknowledgment: I would like to thank Carl Eby for his guidance on the psychological concept of disavowal and its relationship to ego-splitting and repetition. His comments inspired the use of disavowal as a frame for this essay.

1. It is worth noting that the word *disavowal* is a translation of the German *Verleugnung,* which is also sometimes translated as "denial." Laplanche and Pontalis prefer *disavow* to avoid confusion with *verneinen,* which they translate as "negate" (120). All of these ideas are closely related, and I will use all three words—*disavow, deny,* and *negate*—in this essay.

2. I suggest that this fragment was written in the 1950s because of the line: "What does it profit a man to gain a prize which might be given to an old man who wants it. . . ." I believe this line may refer to the award to an aging Winston Churchill of the Nobel Prize for Literature in 1953, a year when Hemingway believed he would win the prize; Hemingway did win the following year, 1954.

3. Miriam B. Mandel has suggested that Hemingway's plotting uses "markers of taurine acceptance and authority" to create a cultural and political geography of Spain (xxiii), but I would suggest that this subtext is not available as a structuring device for most readers of the book.

Works Cited

Baker, Carlos. *Ernest Hemingway : A Life Story.* New York: Collier, 1969.

Cooperman, Stanley. "Hemingway and Old Age." *College English* 20.3 (1965): 215–20.

Daley, Robert "Spanish Fiesta Gay Despite Bad Bullfights." *New York Times,* 12 July 1959.

Eby, Carl P. *Hemingway's Fetishism: Psychoanalysis and the Mirror of Manhood.* New York: State U of NY P, 1999.

———. "Re: Disavowal." Message to Suzanne del Gizzo. 23 July 2009. E-mail.

Freud, Sigmund. *An Outline of Psycho-*Analysis. In vol 23 of *The Standard Edition of the Complete Psychological Works of Sigmund Freud.* 24 vols. Ed. and trans. James Strachey. London: Hogarth Press, 1964. 141–207.

Fruscione, Joseph. "*Mano a Mano:* Rivalries in Spain and America: Hemingway vs. Faulkner in *The Dangerous Summer.*" *Hemingway Review* 28.1 (2008): 68–88.

Hemingway, Ernest. *The Dangerous Summer.* New York: Scribner, 1985.

———. *The Garden of Eden.* 1986. New York: Scribner, 1987.

———. "The Snows of Kilimanjaro." In *The Complete Short Stories of Ernest Hemingway: Finca Vigía Edition.* New York: Scribner, 1987. 39–56.

Hemingway, Valerie. *Running with the Bulls: My Years with the Hemingways.* New York: Ballentine Books, 2004.

Kennedy, William. "The Last Olé." *New York Times Book Review* 9 June 1985. 1, 32–33, 35.

Laplanche, J., and J.-B. Pontalis. *The Language of Psycho-Analysis.* Trans. By Donald Nicholson-Smith. New York: Norton and Co., 1973.

Lynn, Kenneth S. *Hemingway.* New York: Fawcett Columbine, 1987.

Mandel, Miriam B. *Hemingway's* The Dangerous Summer: *The Complete Annotations.* Lanham, MD: Scarecrow Press, 2008.

Markham, James M. "Hemingway's Spain." *New York Times* 24 Nov. 1985. A15.

McIver, Stuart B. *Hemingway's Key West.* 1993. Sarasota, FL: Pineapple Press, 2001.

Meyers, Jeffrey. *Hemingway: A Biography.* New York: Da Capo Press, 1999.

Michener, James A. Introduction. *The Dangerous Summer.* By Ernest Hemingway. New York: Scribner, 1985.

Raeburn, John. *Fame Became of Him: Hemingway as Public Writer.* Bloomington: Indiana UP, 1984.

Reynolds, Michael. *Hemingway: The Final Years.* New York: W. W. Norton and Co., 1999.

Scafella, Frank, ed. *Hemingway: Essays of Reassessment.* New York: Oxford UP, 1991.

9

Hemingway's Spain in Flames, 1937

James H. Meredith

Nunc lento sonitu dicunt, morieris
Now this bell tolling, softly for another,
Says to me, Thou must die
—"Meditation XVII," John Donne

For Stone

The year 1937 was crucial in the life of Ernest Hemingway. Excepting 1961, the year of his death, 1937 is arguably one of only five pivotal years in his adult life: 1919, marked by his jilting by his nurse, Agnes Von Kurowsky; 1926, the year his first marriage to Hadley broke up and he changed his emotional allegiance to his second wife, Pauline Pfeiffer; 1944, which marked not only the tumultuous breakup of his marriage to his third wife, Martha, and the beginnings of his relationship with his fourth and final wife, Mary, but even more significant, his surviving the Hürtgen Forest campaign with the US 22nd Regiment during World War II; 1953–54, the year of his last African safari and the two plane crashes that followed, which left him physically and emotionally devastated; and finally 1937.

That year, 1937, marked the beginning of dramatic changes in his immediate family and was also a time of emerging personal growth and, most certainly, literary regeneration and reconfiguration. It is almost too simple to say that 1937 was a year of dramatic change for Hemingway because nothing was ever completely simple for him, still, in terms of his various personal, public, and moral and literary lives, he did begin the year moving in one direction and ended it moving almost 180 degrees in the other.

Much as it was within Hemingway's life, 1937 was crucial in the life of the Second Spanish Republic and in Spain's overall national character. Although the notion that Spain had ever previously experienced a day of unity and coherence is clearly a myth, and although the conflict historically known as the Spanish Civil War had officially been raging in the Iberian Peninsula since June 1936, it was in 1937 that the Republic lost any chance of victory. One only has to look at the burgeoning rate of inflation that year to understand that the international marketplace gave the Republic little chance of winning. It was certainly the last year that a liberal democracy had any chance of emerging as the immediate outcome of the war, regardless of which side won, since Stalin and his Soviet apparatchiks and henchmen, sent to help the Spanish Republican forces, were gaining more influence over the levers of government and military power than the amount of actual manpower they supplied should have allowed.[1] Like Hemingway, Spain, too, began the year with a sense that overall victory was still as a possibility but ended it knowing that any such victory was impossible. It is no wonder, therefore, that Hemingway felt in complete sympathy with the times and people of Spain in 1937; the man and the republican nation were on parallel tracks of change.

The purpose of this article is to reiterate some of the key events of 1937, both in the life of Hemingway and in terms of the historical milestones of Spain, a country that was quite literally in flames during that year. Hemingway not only made two trips to war-torn Spain in 1937; he also made two more trips in 1938, but the circumstances of his first 1937 trip, in the spring, were dramatically different from those of his other visits to Spain during the Spanish Civil War. During that first trip, Hemingway was pulled away from Pauline and what she represented for him: a stable family life, children, and Key West, a closer connection to traditional Catholicism, and, above all, his more conservative modernist aesthetic and the breathtaking literary accomplishments that came out of that artistic vision. At the same time, he was pulled toward Martha Gellhorn, who was far more socially conscious and secular than Pauline, and this shift had already altered the direction of his life and the thrust of his subsequent work while attached to her, just as the tide had turned against the Republican cause during 1937.

In his 1940 introduction to Gustav Regler's *The Great Crusade,* Hemingway recalled that "the period of fighting," during the spring of 1937, "when we thought that the Republic could win . . . was the happiest period of our lives" (viii). Here one should take Hemingway quite literally, especially about his being at his happiest, for several reasons. First, he was involved in a scorching affair with Gellhorn while in the middle of a red-hot war zone, which seemed to be highly erotic, at least for Hemingway, if maybe not so much for Gellhorn.[2] (Gellhorn later had another wartime affair, with General James Gavin; she always enjoyed sex and life when they were most daring.) Second, Hemingway, for the first and possibly the only time in his life, was committed to a cause larger than himself that was not so much a fight for democratic liberalism in

Spain as it was a fight against the vicious tyranny of global fascism. Finally, and perhaps even more erotically for him, both experiences were intricately linked. One has to ask, then, who exactly does Hemingway mean by the "our" in "our lives"? Just how many people and personalities should be included in the "our"?

When 1937 began, Hemingway was living the good life on Key West, Florida. He had only just met Martha the month before in his favorite Key West bar, Sloppy Joe's, but already, by the beginning of 1937, he was emotionally attached to this extraordinarily alluring younger woman. At just twenty-eight, she was a writer of significant promise, who already had begun to receive nationwide attention for her 1936 book on the Great Depression, *The Trouble I've Seen.* On 13 January, they met for dinner in Miami and then took the train north together before going their separate ways in Jacksonville, Florida. Hemingway and Gellhorn quickly agreed to meet in Spain; both writers had been troubled by the recent turn of events in that country's republic. At the time, Hemingway was on his way to New York to help organize an ambulance service for the Medical Bureau of American Friends of Spanish Democracy and to sign on with the North American Newspaper Alliance (NANA). On that visit and a subsequent trip to New York, he also sought to assist in the production of *Spain in Flames,* a propaganda film about Spain's civil war supporting the Loyalist Republican government of Spain in its fight against global fascism. As a member of Contemporary Historians (together with other writers and intellectuals, including Archibald MacLeish, John Dos Passos, and Lillian Hellman), Hemingway, with Dos Passos, cowrote the script for *Spain in Flames,* which was directed by Joris Ivens, a member of the Communist International.

Besides the journalistic (one could even say propagandistic) writing he would do for NANA, which gave Hemingway the credentials and money he needed to finance his other work in Spain, it was the making of the *The Spanish Earth* that preoccupied him during the first visit to Spain, beginning on 14 March 1937. The events that occurred during that trip, including the battle scenes that Hemingway witnessed while helping Ivens film *The Spanish Earth* on the front line during March and April 1937, would shape and dominate his later literary achievements. These high points emerge primarily in the form of four NANA nonfiction dispatches ("The First Glimpses of War," "Shelling of Madrid," "A New Kind of War," and "The Chauffeurs of Madrid"); five short stories ("The Denunciation," The Butterfly and the Tank," "Night Before Battle," "Under the Ridge," and "Nobody Ever Dies"); a play, *The Fifth Column;* and the novel *For Whom the Bell Tolls.*

The events that occurred during Hemingway's trip include the battle for Madrid, which was in the middle of a five-month siege when Hemingway arrived in March; the battles at Guadalajara (Reynolds, *Chronology* 86), which turned out to be unsuccessful for the Loyalist cause; fighting at Morata, outside of Madrid (Reynolds, *1930s* 265), and fighting in the Guadarrama Mountains. This last took place at the same time that Germany's Condor Legion destroyed Guernica on 26 April 1937, with a devastating bombing attack. All of these events occurred before 9 May 1937, when Hemingway was on his way out of Spain, through Paris, to return to the United States. By that time, the filming of *The Spanish Earth* had concluded, and, for all practical purposes, Hemingway's literary vision of the war was complete. Hemingway would return to Spain in September 1937, picking up his life there where it had left off, living at the Hotel Florida in Madrid with Martha and observing the various battle lines along the Mediterranean coast of Spain. His mind, however, must already have been working on a novel about the events that had occurred in the spring.

Allen Josephs argues convincingly that *For Whom the Bell Tolls* was set during the actual Segovia offensive at La Granja de San Ildefonso in late May 1937, and, of course, textual evidence in the novel supports his contention. In *The Spanish Civil War,* Hugh Thomas notes that "the attack occasioned a quarrel between General Walter and Colonel Dumont, his subordinate of the 14th International Brigade, the attacking force, as to who was to blame for the ultimate [Republican] reverse. Since Dumont was supported by the French communists, Walter could do no more than protest against Dumont's vanity and inefficiency. The Russian air force in support of the Republic was not only ineffective, but bombed Republican positions. The failure of these two offensives sealed the fate of Bilbao" (668–69). It is interesting to note here that since Hemingway was not in Spain during this offensive, the war experiences of his protagonist in *For Whom the Bell Tolls,* Robert Jordan, could not have been anything Hemingway actually experienced. However, given his earlier experiences at the Spanish front, it was not hard for Hemingway to imagine the problems faced by Jordan and his Spanish comrades; he had seen similar ones in the spring of 1937. From the very beginning of the Spanish Civil War, the Republican effort had been rife with political intrigue and betrayal, not to mention military ineptitude. The offensive at La Granja was largely representative of how the war would eventually and ineffectually be lost by the Republicans. Antony Beevor, in *The Battle for Spain,* writes that "the operation failed partly because the nationalists appeared to have got wind of what was being prepared, but mainly because the republican command had greatly underestimated the speed of the nationalists' reactions and the effectiveness of their air power" (276). All aspects of the Republicans' failed offensive are conveyed in Hemingway's novel.

In the volume of his biography devoted to Hemingway's 1930s, Michael Reynolds notes that immediately after Hemingway first visited war-torn Spain in 1937, he became convinced of the need for group action and solidarity to overcome the well-organized, highly motivated, and powerful forces of evil in the world and inserted eight new pages into his final draft of *To Have and To Have Not* (*1930s* 269–70). These pages include the final words of the wounded and dying Harry Morgan:

> "One man alone ain't got. No man alone now." He stopped. "No matter how a man alone ain't got no bloody fucking chance."
>
> He shut his eyes. It had taken him a long time to get it out and it had taken him all of his life to learn it. (*THHN* 225)

While these are the final words of Harry Morgan, an American man who dies far from the battle lines of the Spanish Civil War, they are quite similar—a Huckleberry Finn version, if you will—to the words written by that Anglican minister, John Donne, in "Meditation XVII": "No man is an island, entire of itself; every man is piece of the continent, a part of the main." That meditation, of course, is Hemingway's source for the title of his novel about the last days and hours of Robert Jordan, the American who dies on the European continent. This revision is an illuminating example of how that one experience, his spring 1937 visit to the front of the Spanish Civil War, influenced two of his novels. It led to this major revision of *To Have and Have Not,* which brought together the various moral strands of the novel, and it would become the visionary core of *For Whom the Bell Tolls.*

In her biography, *The Hemingway Women,* Bernice Kert writes:

> All her life Martha remained grateful to Ernest for teaching her about the different sounds of gunfire and when to fall flat. He began to say that she was the bravest woman he had ever met, braver than most men, including himself. . . .
>
> Since courage had come to be the yardstick by which Ernest judged people, Martha's possession of this quality dramatically enhanced his admiration of her. She in turn saw him at his best. "I think it was the only time in his life," she remarked, "when he was not the most important thing there was. He really cared about the Republic and he cared about that war. I believe I never would've gotten hooked otherwise." (299)

The year 1937 was a year for both Hemingway and Spain that gave way to the new, but in a way that strangely resembled the old.

Notes

1. According to Thomas, the number of men provided by Russia in support of the Republican cause was between 2,000 and 3,000, which would have been about five percent of total combatant and noncombatant support from outside Spain. The Soviet Union did, however, provide one hundred percent of outside support to the Republicans for aircraft (1,320), tanks (900), and artillery (1,550) (Thomas 944).

2. Gellhorn's biographer, Caroline Moorhead, asserts that Martha wasn't as physically and sexually attracted to Hemingway as he seemed to be to her. See *Gellhorn: A Twentieth-Century Life* (New York: Henry Holt, 2003), 135-36.

Works Cited

Beevor, Antony. *The Battle for Spain: The Spanish Civil War, 1936–1939*. New York: Penguin, 2006.

Donne, John. "Meditation XVII. 1624. In vol. 3 of *The Works of John Donne,* vol. III. Ed. Henry Alford. London: John W. Parker, 1839. 574–75. Luminarium: Anthology of English Literature. Web. 6 Jan. 2015.

Hemingway, Ernest. *For Whom the Bell Tolls.* New York: Scribner, 1940.

———. Introduction. *The Great Crusade.* By Gustav Regler. New York: Longmans, Green, and Co., 1940.

———. *To Have and Have Not.* 1937. Garden City, NY: Permabooks, 1953.

Josephs, Allen. For Whom the Bell Tolls: *Ernest Hemingway's Undiscovered Country.* New York: Twayne, 1994. Twayne's Masterwork Studies.

Kert, Bernice. *The Hemingway Women: Those Who Loved Him—The Wives and Others.* New York: W. W. Norton, 1983.

Reynolds, Michael. *Hemingway: An Annotated Chronology.* Detroit: Omnigraphics, 1991.

———. *Hemingway: The 1930s.* New York: W. W. Norton, 1997.

Thomas, Hugh. *The Spanish Civil War.* Rev. ed. New York: Modern Library, 2001.

10

Tanks, Butterflies, Realists, Idealists: Hemingway, Dos Passos, and the Imperfect Ending in Spain of 1937–1938

Mark P. Ott

In a life that was often filled with turmoil and transition, Ernest Hemingway endured more than even he could have reasonably expected from 1937 to 1938. Those years would mark the end of his marriage of Pauline Pfeiffer and the beginning of his life with Martha Gellhorn; they would mark his exhaustion and abandonment of the short story form, as he found it an inadequate repository for the experience of the Spanish Civil War; and they would mark the end of his twenty-year friendship with John Dos Passos, ostensibly because of the naïveté, idealism, and sentimentalism Dos Passos displayed during the Spanish Civil War over the execution of his translator, José Robles, as a fascist spy.

Hemingway's experience in the Spanish Civil War brought on a personal and artistic transformation, the struggles of which can be seen in the imperfections and awkwardness of "The Butterfly and the Tank." Composed between July and September 1938 and drawing on occurrences in Madrid in the winter of 1937, the story first appeared in the December 1938 issue of *Esquire* magazine.[1]

For the reader, the story could be described as perhaps more interesting than satisfying, especially when compared with short fiction Hemingway wrote in the 1920s. Indeed, no scholar has come forward to agree with John Steinbeck's assessment, stated in a letter to Hemingway, that "the story is one of a very few finest stories in all time" (qtd. in Johnston 183). According to Robert Paul Lamb, "Clearly, Hemingway was emotionally too close to the material to digest it and transmute it into art" (111). Given the scope of the story, the critical attention it has received seems appropriate; Allen Josephs, William Braasch Watson, and

James Plath have all written perceptively about it. Plath argues insightfully that Hemingway was considering F. Scott Fitzgerald when he crafted the character of the flit king. While Fitzgerald may have figured in that characterization, however, this essay will argue that the story can be read as an allegory for the Hemingway-Dos Passos friendship, as Hemingway's unsatisfying conclusion to the story reflects his clumsy, self-justifying ending of that relationship and a shift in his conception of the aesthetics of an "ending."

On the surface, the story would seem to have very little to do with John Dos Passos. Indeed, the history of Hemingway's break with Dos Passos is well known and will not be recounted here. Hemingway composed "The Butterfly and the Tank" right after "The Denunciation," which he wrote, in turn, as Michael Reynolds notes, just after "Hemingway's own denunciation of John Dos Passos in a *Ken* essay" (Reynolds, *1930s* 290). Yet the recklessness of Pedro, the flit king of "The Butterfly and the Tank," mirrors the perceived recklessness of Dos Passos, whose persistent questioning of officials about the death of José Robles was viewed by Hemingway as naïve and sentimental. Like Pedro, Dos Passos behaved like a butterfly, unaware of the tanks around him.[2]

The story begins with the first-person narrator walking "home from the censorship office" to the Florida Hotel. It is raining. The persistent rain of chapter one of *A Farewell to Arms* has continued; the brutalities and meaningless death of World War I have been extended through the Spanish Civil War. Alone in the rain, the narrator of this story, like Frederic Henry in *A Farewell to Arms,* is walking back to the hotel. Sick of the rain, he stops into Chicote's for a "quick one," which he instantly regrets. Unlike the pristine, sacred bars of Hemingway's earlier short fiction—the exemplar being "A Clean Well-Lighted Place"—this bar is crowded, "full of smoke, singing, men in uniform, and the smell of wet leather coats" ("Butterfly" 429).

The narrator orders a gin and Angostura and "put[s] it down against the rain" ("Butterfly" 429). The sanctuary of Chicote's substitutes for the exhausted, bankrupt sanctuaries of religion, politics, marriage, and family. The only fortification for the narrator is the drink, but the sanctuary of the bar has been contaminated; the girl at his table is "pretty terrible looking" (429), the fellow with her is "not very forceful looking" (429), but the girl is forceful enough for both of them, as she is "built like a lion tamer" (430). The attractive, companionable, and demure women that populated the short fiction of the 1920s have disappeared. Moreover, this unappealing twosome and their leather coats are dry; they have been cowardly in avoiding the permanent rain of the war outside. The masculine leather coat is the one "becoming" thing about the ugly woman (430), and the timid man's domination by her is signaled to the reader by the fact that he "looked as though he ought to be wearing an old school tie" (430)—he is British and still nostalgic for his undergraduate days—a sure sign of inadequacy and effeminacy.

Then the "flit king" emerges, a civilian in a white shirt and brown suit, squirting the waiters with a flit gun filled with perfume. "Flit gun" was "a trade name for a small, hand-pumped, insecticide spray gun, used to kill flies [and] mosquitoes" (Johnston 184), but as James Plath notes, citing Berry and Van Den Bark's *American Thesaurus of Slang,* "by 1936, 'flit' ha[d] already worked its way into American dictionaries of slang as referring to an 'effeminate man' or 'male homosexual'" (78). Plath writes: "Hemingway's otherwise inexplicable use of the phrase 'flit king' to describe the practical joking civilian suggests that he is, in fact, alluding to slang usage"(78).[3] An indignant waiter protests "'*No hay derecho*,' . . . 'You have no right to do that'" ("Butterfly" 431). . The waiter, a dignified old man, had worked at Chicote's for ten years. His lips tremble. Silence ensues. Three uniformed men, "serious, tough, and very righteous," punish the flit king for violating the sanctity of the bar and insulting the high priest, the waiter ("Butterfly" 431). Forcing him back between two tables, they execute him with a single shot.

The flit king's life is sacrificed to preserve a revered place; Chicote's represents the best of Spain, which Loyalists and Republicans alike believe they are fighting to preserve. A clean, well-lighted place of dignified, ritualized drinking and companionship. The levity, the foolishness of the flit king cannot be tolerated, especially after he insults the waiter, the guardian of the code of conduct within Chicote's. If the year had been 1927, rather than 1938, and Hemingway had been working at the height of his powers, the story would have ended there, its meaning submerged within the iceberg but intuitively grasped by the reader; in the midst of the civil war, comic behavior was intolerable in Chicote's, a place that represented apolitical, areligious Spain. The naïve, irreverent, unsoldierly flit king must pay for his sin of desecrating the bar and disrespecting the seriousness of the war.

Yet in 1938, Hemingway was at an artistic and personal crossroads; he did not end the story there. Hemingway goes on to describe first the indifferent police investigation, resulting in no arrest, and then his conversation with the forceful girl, who is "very upset and almost hysterical" ("Butterfly" 432). Her companion exhibits no grace under pressure; his panic at the shooting makes him appear "ten years younger" (433). The flit king lies on the floor, diminished, with no undershirt and worn shoes, "looking like a grey wax caricature of himself" (433). The narrator proclaims that "the whole thing was a pretty good story and that I would write it sometime" (433). The forceful girl declares that to do so would be disloyal to the cause of the Second Spanish Republic.

The next morning the rain, so persistent the day before, has stopped; it is a "fine, bright, cold early winter day" ("Butterfly" 433). The narrator returns to Chicote's, and, rather than talking to a mismatched, misinformed couple, he talks to the manager, who describes the wife of the flit king, whom we now know to be named Pedro, dramatically weeping and asking,, "Who has done this to thee?" (436). Like Marie Morgan weeping over Harry in *To Have and Have Not,* an ending that Hemingway had recently composed in 1937, Pedro's wife will have to live without her flawed husband. If in the hardboiled Harry Morgan, as one man alone, did not have a chance, then surely the silly, inappropriate flit king did not have a chance either.

Of course, at this time Dos Passos is coming to terms with the Spanish Civil War, his disillusionment with socialism, and the execution of José Robles—who was, like Pedro and Harry Morgan, dramatically mourned by his devoted, loving wife. Dos Passos is also coming to terms with the fact that his intimate, supportive twenty-year friendship with Hemingway has ended. In a well-known letter, dated 26 March 1938, Hemingway wrote to Dos Passos:

> But I want to speak to you about something that seems to me to be serious. A war is still being fought in Spain between the people whose side you used to be on and the fascists. If with your hatred of communists you feel justified in attacking, for money, the people who are still fighting that war I think you should at least try to get your facts right. . . . The only reason I can see for your attacking, for money, the side that you were always supposed to be on is an unsuppressable desire to tell the truth. Then why not tell the truth? The thing is that you don't find out the truth in ten days or three weeks and this hasn't been a communist run war for a long time. . . . You know all people are not cowards, many people will fight and not give a damn about dying to save their country from a foreign invasion and war was not invented by either the communists or the fascists and for you to try constantly to make out that the war the government is fighting against the fascist Italian, German Moorish invasion is a communist business imposed on the will of the people is sort of viciously pitiful. (*SL* 463–64)

By calling the Harvard-educated Dos Passos cowardly, greedy, and misinformed, Hemingway begins to construct the parallel character of the public-school-educated, leather-jacket-wearing journalist of the story. Dos Passos is the naïve outsider; Hemingway is the cyncial insider. Yet he was not finished.

In an article for *Ken* magazine, published 30 June 1938 and entitled "Treachery in Aragon," Hemingway wrote of Dos Passos's unwillingness to believe that Robles was a spy, calling it "as good an example as any of the good hearted naiveté" of American liberals, adding, "I happened to know this man had been shot two weeks before as a spy after a long and careful trial in which all the charges against him had been proven" ("Treachery" 26). Paul Smith dates the composition of "The Butterfly and the Tank" to precisely this period, between July and September 1938 (*Reader's Guide* 375).

Dos Passos's occasionally autobiographical novel, *Adventures of a Young Man,* would be published in the fall of 1938, soon after Hemingway finished "The Butterfly and the Tank." Dos Passos's idealistic protagonist, Glenn Spotswood, has wandered from New York City to the Midwest to the Appalachian Mountains in support of socialism, in support of the people, but when he travels to Spain to fight for the Republicans against the fascists, like José Robles, he runs afoul of the Communist Party. The Republican fortification is overrun before he can be executed, and the cowardly Russians and Communist Party lackeys depart in a rush, agreeing to free Glenn if he will take on the suicide mission of delivering water to artillery men in a pillbox on a distant mountain. Still idealistic, Glenn agrees, belatedly impressing his corrupt captors with his commitment to the cause. Dos Passos writes: "He was halfway up the hill before they brought him down. For a second he had no pain. He thought he'd stubbed his toe on a stone. Too bad the water was all spilled in so much blood. Must get out of this, he said to himself, and started to drag himself along the ground. Then suddenly something split and he went spinning in blackness. He was dead" (342). The end. Dos Passos's matter-of-fact treatment of Spotswood's death underscores his conclusion that the Spanish conflict had manipulated idealistic young people into the service of corrupt professional soldiers, who placed little value on their lives.

Like Frederic Henry, like Harry Morgan, like Pedro, like José Robles, Glenn Spotswood is alone, without a chance, a victim of and participant in an overwhelming war. Spotswood's life, like Dos Passos's idealism, remains unredeemed. David Sanders notes that Spotswood, through his anarchism, is a "characteristic Dos Passos hero" (131). Just prior to this final scene, Spotswood, awaiting his death sentence, scrawls on the wall, "I, Glenn Spotswood, being of sound mind and imprisoned body, do bequeath to the international working class my hope of a better world . . . [yet] he suddenly felt ashamed and rubbed it all out with the palm of his hand" (339). The novel's conclusion underscores the bitter lesson: the class that Spotswood sacrifices himself for seems little worth the sacrifice.

It is illuminating to contrast the ending of Dos Passos's novel with the compelling, perfect drama of the death of Hemingway's fully integrated protagonist, Robert Jordan—no longer alone, no longer an island—who feels "his heart beating against the pine needle floor of the forest" (*FWTBT* 471). Hemingway was able to write that ending in 1940, just fifteen months after struggling to reach a much different conclusion in August 1938, when he finished "The Butterfly and the Tank."

Yet he would struggle to find a compelling conclusion to the short story. Why, at this personal and artistic crossroads, was the ending to this story so challenging for Hemingway? Paul Smith calls this a "troublesome imperfection" (*Reader's Guide* 375), and the Hemingway Collection at the John F. Kennedy Presidential Library holds four different typescripts for it, providing ample evidence of Hemingway's struggle to place, once again, his deepening, expanding experience of war into the now-too-restrictive form of the short story.

Typescript 301 ends with the narrator thinking of the kneeling wife, saying "Pedro, who has done this to thee?" Typescript 302 adds an additional line to this, as the narrator responds to the question, stating, "And I thought the police would never be able to tell her that even if they had the name of the man who pulled the trigger." Typescript 303 continues with dialogue between the manager and the narrator, in which the title "The Butterfly and the Tank" is suggested and debated. And the final line reads: "So that is how it came to be called 'The Butterfly and the Tank.'" Typescript 304 ends with essentially the same five final lines, in which the manager, fulfilling his dream of becoming a writer by collaborating with the narrator, declares writing to be easy.

Of course Typescript 302, the most satisfying, ambiguous, and least cynical of the endings, is the one Hemingway selected, as the vast forces that have infected Spain, infected Chicote's, are really what pulled the trigger, killing Pedro and the lighthearted comic dimension of Spanish culture.

The real dilemma of the ending is this: how should a writer approach the horror and meaninglessness of war? Irony, the strategy employed in the 1920s by a younger Hemingway to write about World War I, is no longer adequate to the task. Indeed, in his essay "Hemingway's Senses of an Ending: *In Our Time* and After," Paul Smith calls attention to a pattern in the endings of Hemingway's early short stories, those written before 1925. This pattern involves the following:

> First, an *associative act,* one in which a character moves or gestures toward another in an act of agreement or reconciliation—some gesture of inclusion;
>
> Then, a *dissociative act,* one in which a character moves away from another, in an act of disagreement or separation—some gesture of exclusion;

> And finally, an act, often a speech-act by a character or narrator, [that] . . . usually serves a prospective or retrospective function, predicting the character's future or commenting on their final moments together and apart. (12–13; emphasis in original)

In this essay Smith does not discuss "The Butterfly and the Tank," but he does note the conclusion of "Old Man at the Bridge," a story emerging from the same period, writing: "The story's ending suggests that in that bone-weary state Hemingway drew one last time on the pattern that he knew so well," the "old pattern from his first collection of short stories" (16). He continues, "In those fifteen remarkable years [between 1922 and 1937], Hemingway [had] exhausted a relatively limited conception on the art of the story, and then was exhausted in turn when it did not serve his reaching vision of the boundaries of fiction, a vision beyond the grasp of his imaginative art" (16). The form of realism Hemingway employed in *To Have and Have Not*—boiling details down to their essence, without narrative intrusions—likewise proved unequal to the task of describing the idealistic war. The cause of the Second Spanish Republic, the people, seems to have demanded a strategy that more directly engages the reader's emotions.

Robert Paul Lamb delineates four different strategies for the end of a Hemingway story. The first, according to Lamb, is what he terms a "*disjunctive bump*" (144, emphasis in original), in which "the story concludes before the narrative sequence has run its full course, leaving the reader to wonder how that sequence will play out" (145). Lamb finds examples of this technique in "Cat in the Rain," "A Natural History of the Dead," and "The Undefeated." Lamb calls a second variation "*a rounded closed ending,* in which the narrative sequence has played out, all the necessary actions of the episode have been reported, and the suspense has been resolved" (145–46; emphasis in original). The third strategy he identifies is a "*float-off,*" in which, "whether or not the episode is completed, the author floats the reader temporally past the ending into some undefined point in the future (or back into the past, as in Fitzgerald's *The Great Gatsby*) or spatially past the ending onto a larger landscape, which has the effect of undercutting the suddenness of the disjunctive bump by merging the story into something larger outside the sequence" (149). In "The Butterfly and the Tank," Hemingway finally settled on the fourth strategy, what Lamb would call "*a seeded closed ending.*" In this strategy, "although the narrative sequence has run its full course, some strands remain that merge into something greater: a time outside the text, an element of nature, an ongoing process. These tend to expand the story slightly past its formal conclusion" (147). Thus, with the flit king's death, the absence of a moral becomes the moral, a time outside the text: there is no answer to who has done this to Pedro, but the expansion comes to the reader as he or she recognizes that modern warfare—senseless war without end in a permanent rain—has done this to Pedro, and, by extension, to us. The only shelter for the narrator, and the reader, is the gin and tonic and the view through a sandbagged window at a broken world.

And what to make of the title? Clumsy symbolism is inadequate to the task of deepening the story, as the title surely proves. As Kenneth Johnston notes, "One is not surprised to discover that the metaphor of the butterfly and the tank relates not only to the dead civilian in the story, but also to the narrator-writer" (184). Watson writes:

> The published version reveals that although the realist is willing to surrender the title to the symbolist, he will corrupt nothing else. The title then becomes ironic, almost mocking. The flit-gun man was no butterfly, and although titles may be elegant and literature beautiful, life is not. The ending brings us back to the first and main subject of the story: the unexpectedly violent tension in a war-torn city. . . . Although the ostensible subject of "The Butterfly and the Tank" is still the war in Spain, its most important subject is its affirmation of a writer's autonomy and integrity. ("Other Paris Years" 152)

Of course, Dos Passos was likewise "no butterfly," and if Hemingway was trying to teach him something about warfare, he failed, as the only thing that the story would reveal is how smug Hemingway the insider could be. Yet Watson is correct that the story is a rejection of literature as propaganda; Hemingway is not trying to manipulate the reader into the service of the Second Spanish Republic, as he would do very soon in *For Whom the Bell Tolls.*

The unanswered question, then, is, why did Hemingway create these four extraordinarily different conclusions to a relatively straightforward story? Of course, it took ten years for the experience of World War I to gestate and become *A Farewell to Arms,* so what happened to transform Hemingway's thinking about narrative, the Spanish Civil War, and warfare in general so quickly? By the fall of 1938, before "The Butterfly and the Tank" was even in print, Hemingway was ready to begin *For Whom the Bell Tolls.*

The answer, I believe, is that in the midst of this personal and artistic crossroads, Hemingway finally extended the ideas he explored in writing about the natural world—what Terry Tempest Williams calls "wild nature" (111)—to the brotherhood of mankind. The frontier of *Green Hills of Africa,* in which man alone stalks an adversarial prey, has given way. The isolation of the bullfighter in *Death in the Afternoon* has been transcended. Fishing the Gulf Stream, living it, since 1932, Hemingway has now recognized the integration of mankind in an extended brotherhood, one that foreshadows Santiago's brotherhood and unity with the marlin. When Hemingway came back from the war in Spain in the spring of 1937, he did not return to Key West. He went to Bimini. To fish.

Hemingway quickly digested the lessons of the Spanish Civil War as he confronted the rejuvenating natural world of the Gulf Stream. Ironically, in *For Whom the Bell Tolls,* he reached a different conclusion from what he perceived as the idealistic and naïve Dos Passos of *Adventures of a Young Man.* Hemingway, in the end, is able to see beyond the flit king's senseless death and the clumsy symbolism of "The Butterfly and the Tank," and to believe that no man is an island; amidst the senseless slaughter of modern warfare, our common humanity, along with our integration with and understanding of the natural world, may yet redeem us. As Hemingway, in love with Martha Gellhorn and at the height of his artistic powers, began writing the novel *For Whom the Bell Tolls,* he would leave the short story behind.

Notes

1. Hemingway drew on the same anecdote used in "The Butterfly and the Tank" in his play, "The Fifth Column," bringing in many of the same details. Langston Hughes also related the essence of the story in his autobiographical *I Wonder as I Wander.* Carlos Baker, Jeffrey Meyers, and Michael Reynolds indicate that the evidence is inconclusive as to whether Hemingway actually witnessed the shooting.

2. William Braasch Watson argues in an unpublished article on "The Denunciation" that there is a close connection between that story and "Treachery in Aragon," which was written 15–25 May 1938. Watson sees the story as a near allegory for Hemingway's final break with Dos Passos. See Paul Smith, *A Reader's Guide to the Short Stories of Ernest Hemingway* (369).

3. Plath argues that the story "supports a reading of the characters in the story as rough composites of Scott and Zelda [Fitzgerald]" (79).

Works Cited

Baker, Carlos. *Ernest Hemingway: A Life Story.* New York: Collier Books, 1969.

Belkind, Allen. *Dos Passos, the Critics, and the Writer's Intention.* Carbondale: Southern Illinois UP, 1971.

Dos Passos, John. *Adventures of a Young Man.* New York: Harcourt, Brace, 1939.

Hemingway, Ernest. "The Butterfly and the Tank." In *The Complete Short Stories of Ernest Hemingway: Finca Vigía Edition.* New York: Scribner, 1986. 429–36.

———. "Butterfly and the Tank" Manuscript and Typescripts. Files 301-4. Hemingway Collection. John F. Kennedy Library, Boston.

———. *Ernest Hemingway: Selected Letters, 1917-1961.* Ed. Carlos Baker. New York: Charles Scribner's Sons, 1981.

———. "Treachery in Aragon." *Ken* 30 June 1938: 26.

Hughes, Langston. *I Wonder as I Wander: An Autobiographical Journey.* New York: Hill and Wang, 1993.

Johnston, Kenneth G. "'The Butterfly and the Tank': Casualties of War." *Studies in Short Fiction* 26.2 (1989): 183–86.

Josephs, Allen. "Hemingway's Spanish Civil War Stories, or the Spanish Civil War as Reality." In *Hemingway's Neglected Short Fiction: New Perspectives.* Ed. Susan F. Beegel. Ann Arbor: UMI Research P, 1989. 313–27.

Lamb, Robert Paul. *Art Matters: Hemingway, Craft, and the Creation of the Modern Short Story.* Baton Rouge: Louisiana State UP, 2010.

Meyers, Jeffery. *Hemingway: A Biography.* New York: Harper and Row, 1985.

Plath, James. "On a Fairy's Wing: Hints of Fitzgerald in Hemingway's 'The Butterfly and the Tank.'" *Journal of the Short Story in English* 43 (2004): 75–85.

Reynolds, Michael. *Hemingway: The 1930s.* New York: Norton and Co., 1997.

Sanders, David. "The 'Anarchism' of John Dos Passos." In *Dos Passos, the Critics, and the Writer's Intention.* Ed. Allen Belkind. Carbondale: Southern Illinois UP, 1971. 122–35.

Sanderson, Rena, ed. *Blowing the Bridge: Essays on Hemingway and* For Whom the Bell Tolls. Westport, CT: Greenwood Press, 1992.

Smith, Paul. "Hemingway's Senses of an Ending: *In Our Time* and After." *Hemingway Review* 12:1 (1992): 12–18.

———. *A Reader's Guide to the Short Stories of Ernest Hemingway.* Boston: G. K. Hall, 1989.

Watson, William Braasch. "Joris Ivens and the Communists: Bringing Hemingway into the Spanish Civil War." In *Blowing the Bridge: Essays on Hemingway and* For Whom the Bell Tolls. Ed. Rena Sanderson. Westport, CT: Greenwood Press, 1992. 37–57.

———. "The Other Paris Years of Ernest Hemingway: 1937 and 1938. In *French Connections: Hemingway and Fitzgerald Abroad.* Ed. J. Gerald Kennedy and Jackson R. Bryer. New York: St. Martin's Press, 2008. 141–58.

Williams, Terry Tempest. *Red: Passion and Patience in the Dessert.* New York: Vintage, 2002.

11

The Education of Henry: Politics and Context in Hemingway

Scott D. Yarbrough

FRENCHY: Why are you doing this, Harry?
HARRY MORGAN: I don't know. Maybe because I like you, maybe because I don't like them.
FRENCHY: I'm glad you are on our side, Harry.
HARRY MORGAN: No kissing, Frenchy.

—from Howard Hawks's screen adaptation of *To Have and Have Not*; screenplay by William Faulkner and Leigh Brackett

Hemingway's short stories about the Spanish Civil War, such as "Under the Ridge," "Night Before Battle," "The Denunciation," and "The Butterfly and the Tank," occupy a peculiarly ironic middle ground in Hemingway's fiction. Through most of his career, Hemingway was known as a largely apolitical writer, yet the existence of these stories constitutes a kind of political statement. They appear to join with the script he cowrote for the documentary *The Spanish Earth,* his play *The Fifth Column,* and his classic novel *For Whom the Bell Tolls* in denouncing Franco and his fascist forces in favor of the Republicans. Despite their seemingly committed, pro-Republican stance, however, the icebergs lurking beneath the Spanish Civil War short stories subtly subvert the very notion of political commitment. The stories consistently demonstrate how ideological extremism leads at best to an incompetent, inefficient, and bureaucratic leadership, and at worst to a blind and unreasoning form of mob mentality, wherein individual rights are denied, individual hopes dashed, and individuals' lives destroyed. The paradoxical, contradictory, and evolving themes of Hemingway's works on the Spanish Civil War are complicated even further when one considers the autobiographical Hemingway avatars that narrate the short stories and star in *The Fifth Column.*

Several books and articles have addressed Hemingway's ideological stance in his writing about the Spanish Civil War, and a narrative of a sorts has developed: initially apolitical, he first intended to write antiwar correspondence that would dissuade the United States from becoming entangled in another European mess (Cooper 89). Already opposed to fascism because of his experiences covering the rise of Mussolini in the early 1920s and his personal affiliation with many members of the Second Spanish Republic, he threw his favor behind the Loyalists. Perhaps, as William Braasch Watson has argued, he was manipulated by the Communists (including Joris Ivens, his Dutch collaborator on the documentary *The Spanish Earth*) into a naïvely pro-Republican stance. Caught up in an anti-Franco fervor, he began writing *The Fifth Column* while still involved in covering the war (Cooper 91); the play is a banal work of propaganda and one of the worst things Hemingway every wrote. Or perhaps, even if he was never blind to the dangers of Stalinism, as Stephen Cooper argued, Hemingway was nevertheless willing to put up with the Russian military machine because of the discipline they forced onto the anarchic and politically disparate Republican forces (92).

As Hemingway gained a little distance from the war, however, he began writing stories that showed, in some cases, a more balanced and nuanced view of the conflict. Allen Josephs has argued that the stories—based heavily on events covered by Hemingway in his roles as correspondent and documentary filmmaker—served as a catharsis that allowed him to leave behind the real war and create a more artful fictionalized version of it in *For Whom the Bell Tolls*. Other critics, like Kenneth Johnston, have portrayed the stories as indictments of the United States' isolationism and as autobiographical self-indictments of the author's inability to commit fully to the cause.[1] Still other writers have focused on Hemingway's work in transforming journalistic dispatches into art.[2] As the narrative of Hemingway's artistic interest in the Spanish Civil War continued, he would go on to write *For Whom the Bell Tolls*, which, as Josephs notes (echoing Hemingway's own contrast between the novel and "Night Before Battle"), is a wholly invented work that eschews the reportage of the short stories and is "rounded rather than flat, invented rather than recalled" (325).[3] *For Whom the Bell Tolls* achieves in art what Hemingway couldn't quite achieve in journalism: moments of compassion and understanding for Franco's forces; in fact, the novel succeeds so well here that it earned the ire of many prominent members of the left.

There is a second peculiar aspect to these stories, however, intertwined with the development of Hemingway's ideology and of his artistic representations of the conflict in his writing—and that is their autobiographical nature. As

Josephs has noted, "The first-person narrator is clearly Ernest Hemingway himself—correspondent, filmmaker, writer, raconteur, personage. There is no making himself up as in the Nick Adams stories, and the occasional use of a fictional name—Mr. Emmunds in 'The Denunciation' and Edwin Henry in 'Night before Battle' and 'Landscape with Figures'—only makes the real identity more obvious" (315). The connection to Hemingway is made even more obvious by the narrators' shared initials of HE and EH.

The obvious use of autobiographical narrators—including the war-weary journalist-spy character Phillip Rawlings in *The Fifth Column,* who more or less seems to serve as an Eric Amblerized version of Hemingway, a better-than-life version of the self-serving author's whim of wish-fulfillment, much as the robust Philip Marlowe stood for the effete Raymond Chandler's masculine ego—would seem to convey a message to the reader . . . but what is that message? Does the act of creating these stories exorcise reportage from Hemingway's system, freeing him to invent, as claimed by Josephs? Or, as critic Mark Van Gunten claims, do the stories reveal a progression in Hemingway's ideology until he, like Robert Jordan, has "transcended the boundary between individual and society, self and other, echoing Donne's 'No man is an Iland' themes in the novel's epigraph" (155)?

Reading the motivation behind Hemingway's almost playful use of autobiographical indicators becomes even more complicated when the reader considers the names of the stories' narrators. In "The Denunciation," as noted earlier, Hemingway's correspondent narrator is named Henry Emmunds; in "Night Before Battle" and "Landscape with Figures," however, Hemingway instead names his fictional analog Edwin Henry. As Josephs has pointed out, the narrators of "Old Man at the Bridge" and "Under the Ridge" are clearly the same as Henry and Emmunds. More to the point, why does Hemingway change the name of his narrator from Emmunds to Henry, using it twice, given the automatic connection drawn by even the most casual readers to Frederic Henry, the protagonist of *A Farewell to Arms?* This choice is made even more interesting when one considers that Frederic Henry, too, is a clearly autobiographical character in ways that Robert Jordan and even Jake Barnes—as biographically based as the plot to *The Sun Also Rises* might be—are not.

The autobiographical nature of these stories serves three purposes. The first, as Edmund Wilson noticed, is to proclaim to the world, in a typically self-aggrandizing maneuver, that Hemingway was a man of action who would put himself in harm's way to get the "true gen."[4] The second purpose is actually to report on the war and show scenes from the war as Hemingway saw them, including not only the casual bombing of civilians carried out by Franco's forces but also the failings of the Republicans: the brutality of the Russian political police, the inefficiency resulting from the internal squabbles between Republican leaders and factions, the quick, unreasoning violence of the Communist Party enforcers, and the detention and execution of former friends.

The third purpose served by the use of autobiographical narrators and the change of Emmunds' name to Edwin Henry is to draw a thematic line between the stories of the Spanish Civil War and Hemingway's earlier work of famously autobiographical fiction, *A Farewell to Arms.* As has been often observed, *A Farewell to Arms* could almost have been titled "The Education of Frederic Henry."[5] Over the course of the novel we see Frederic's transformation, under the tutelage of Catherine Barkley and the Austrian invaders, from a callow, self-absorbed young man to someone who takes his duties more seriously, and then to an individual who makes his own "separate peace" rather than become a victim to bureaucratic inefficiency and wartime patriotic zeal. Alliances are personal, not national. The narrators of Hemingway's Spanish Civil War short stories, Emmunds and Henry, follow similar progressions, and point the way toward Hemingway's most nuanced and politically involved protagonist, Robert Jordan of *For Whom the Bell Tolls.*

Many readers believe that in most important ways Robert Jordan's views mirror Hemingway's own. In *The Politics of Ernest Hemingway,* Cooper writes, "Even though [Robert Jordan] does not share their ideology . . . he is willing to follow Communist leadership because they are the most organized and disciplined party on the Republican side." Cooper aligns the source of Robert Jordan's perspective with Hemingway's, noting that "during the war [Hemingway] said to Joe North, [editor of *New Masses,*] 'I like Communists when they're soldiers, but when they're priests, I hate them'" (92).

Allen Josephs's belief that the writing of the Spanish Civil War stories served as a cathartic rite enabling Hemingway to put the facts of the war behind him may apply equally to *The Fifth Column;* although it would have been too early for Hemingway to realize that the Republican cause was doomed when he wrote the play in 1937, the act of typing it out night after night in Madrid's Hotel Florida, while the war raged about him, might well have vented his need to help the cause. I believe that the stories with the Emmunds/Henry narrator (a group that excludes "Nobody Ever Dies") serve in some sense as Hemingway's repudiation of his digression into political zealotry, reflecting his reasserted individualism and informing our reading of *For Whom the Bell Tolls.*

It is important to bear in mind the context of Hemingway's other works. For example, Hemingway completed the assemblage and reworking of *To Have and Have Not* between trips to war-ravaged Spain. When Harry Morgan discusses the revolution with the boy Emilio, he thinks, "I want a drink. . . . What the hell do I care about his revolution. F—his revolution. To help the working man he robs a bank and kills a fellow works with him and then kills that poor damned Albert that never did any harm. That's a working man he kills. He never thinks of that. With a family. It's the Cubans run Cuba. They all double-cross each other. They sell each other out. They get what they deserve. The hell with their revolutions" (*TTHN* 168). Compare this to Robert Jordan's view of Spaniards before he decides to "censor" himself: "Of course they turned on you. They turned on you often but they always turned on every one. They turned on themselves, too. If you had three together, two would unite against one, and then the two would start to betray each other" (*FWTBT* 135). And, just after Hemingway wrote in his dusty Hotel Florida room that Phillip Rawlings's time was the party's time, he inserted these new final lines for Harry Morgan into the galleys of *To Have and Have Not:* "No matter how a man alone ain't got no bloody fucking chance" (*THHN* 225; Reynolds, *1930s* 259). We could read Morgan's statement, as convincingly argued by some critics, as a farewell to individualism and a rallying cry for the necessity of linking arms with our comrades,[6] or we could read it as a last, defiant protest against the twentieth century's grinding progression of causes, ideologies, and movements that churn individuals between their wheels. I suggest that the Spanish Civil War stories and *For Whom the Bell Tolls* indicate the second reading.

Let us examine, by way of example, "Under the Ridge," which may be the best of the Spanish Civil War stories (not a grand endorsement, given "Landscape with Figures"). While seeking shelter and rest from a barrage during a battle, the filmmaker Emmunds/Henry narrator (unnamed in this story) is challenged by an Extremaduran soldier, who explains that he "hates all foreigners." Josephs explains the scene, stating that

> Hemingway has created or observed (or both) in this strange being a kind of historical compendium of centuries of violence perpetrated on the Spanish people by foreign powers. In the eighteenth and nineteenth centuries a devastating proportion of European wars was fought on Spanish soil, not the least of them—as Goya so horrifyingly recorded—the Napoleonic conflict. Now in 1937, Russia was squared off against Italy and Germany, rehearsing for the coming world war on Spanish soil. The Extremaduran surely had a perverse kind of right to his fierce politics. (323)

While the narrator, the Extremaduran, and other soldiers speak, they watch a French volunteer from the International Brigade walk by, slowly and with dignity, having reached his own separate peace in the face of a futile attack. When the Russian political enforcers arrive in search of the deserter, the narrator lies, stating that he has not seen "such a comrade" walking by ("Ridge" 464), thereby claiming some form of comradeship with the deserter. Nevertheless, the hunters find their quarry and execute him. When the narrator attempts to make excuses for the "battle police," citing the necessity for discipline in war, the Extremaduran tells him, "There is one kind of discipline and another kind of discipline" (466). The Extremaduran goes on to tell the story of Paco, who injures himself to leave the front, and loses his hand, but then does all he can to aid the cause; two months later, the battle police bring him back to the front—which has not significantly moved, since they are still occupying the same place where he shot himself—and execute him. The Extremaduran then asks the narrator, "You understand my hatred?" and the narrator replies, "I understand your hatred" (468). As effective as the story is at subverting the same idea of wartime discipline that Robert Jordan initially embraces in *For Whom the Bell Tolls,* it is even more effective when taken in the context of Frederic Henry's actions during the retreat sequence in *A Farewell to Arms.*

Having drafted two sergeants who are presumably separated from their unit, Frederic tries to engage their help in rescuing his ambulances. The two decide that the task is too dangerous and flee from Frederic and his men. Dutiful officer that he is, Frederic attempts to force them to stay:

> "Halt," I said. They kept on down the muddy road, the hedge on either side. "I order you to halt," I called. They went a little faster. I opened up my holster, took the pistol, aimed at the one who had talked the most, and fired. I missed and they both started to run. I shot three times and dropped one. The other went through the hedge and was out of sight. I fired at him through the hedge as he ran across the field. The pistol clicked empty and I put in another clip. I saw it was too far to shoot at the second sergeant. He was far across the field, running, his head held low. I commenced to reload the empty clip. Bonello came up.
>
> "Let me go finish him," he said. I handed him the pistol and he walked down to where the sergeant of engineers lay face down across the road. Bonello leaned over, put the pistol against the man's head and pulled the trigger. The pistol did not fire.
>
> "You have to cock it," I said. He cocked it and fired twice. He took hold of the sergeant's legs and pulled him to the side of the road so he lay beside the hedge. He came back and handed me the pistol.
>
> "The son of a bitch," he said. He looked toward the sergeant. "You see me shoot him, Tenente?" (204)

Frederic's mistake and the ironic absurdity of this event are spelled out clearly soon after, when he wakes after they've taken shelter in a barn to find that the same man so intent on executing the deserter has, in fact, deserted. Frederic himself is then accused—by the battle police—of being a traitor and a spy and is lined up in a queue that will surely end in his execution. His education in groupthink and political ideology has reached its apogee.

Similarly, a reading of "The Denunciation" benefits greatly from a contextual reading of "The Butterfly and the Tank." As Kenneth Johnston implies in his consideration of the story, there is a strategic disconnect between the Hemingway analog narrator in "The Butterfly and the Tank" and the actual author; Johnston argues that the "story is sharply critical of the writer-narrator for his lack of curiosity and for his failure to respond to the human tragedy" ("Casualties of War" 185). The narrator in "The Butterfly and the Tank" tries to deal with the murder of the flit-gun prankster by showing that he is battle-hardened and indifferent to needless suffering; the waiters at the Chicote—who seem to serve as truth-sayers in the Spanish Civil War stories—refuse to allow him his ironic distance. This sense of remove—call it journalistic objectivity, a failure to commit, or self-indulgence—is exactly what cloaks the narrator in "The Denunciation" (called Emmunds in this story). Eager to show his loyalty for the cause and yet to retain his sense of independence, he aids the waiter in denouncing Delgado by providing him the phone number for the security headquarters; thinking about his act, he says, "I had given him the shortest cut to having Delgado arrested in one of those excesses of impartiality, righteousness and Pontius Pilatry, and the always-dirty desire to see how people act under an emotional conflict, that makes writers such attractive friends" ("Denunciation" 426). In the next paragraph, Emmunds tries to "undo" his betrayal by telling the waiter that he "would never denounce [the spy] myself" (426), because Emmunds is a foreigner and the war is the waiter's war. In his discussion of "The Denunciation," Johnston writes that the text is "sharply critical of the narrator for his failure, his refusal, to assume the responsibilities which come with commitment. His policy of moral aloofness, which helps neither friend nor foe, provides the rationale for his evasion of duty as a professed and loyal supporter of the Loyalist cause" ("Aloof American" 372). I agree that the story is critical of Emmunds and that again we see a distance between Hemingway and his analog that we do not see in *The Fifth Column* or "Landscape with Figures." However, the self-loathing that tears at the narrator is not because he evades his duty as a Loyalist but because he evades his duties as a human being. In his heart he knows that his friendship with Delgado—as attenuated as it is—is still more important to him than his loyalty to the cause, and that he could have served both the cause and his friendship with a simple warning. The waiter, following his heart, has not betrayed Delgado; Emmunds, in his need to appear the insider and the Loyalist, has. One is again reminded of *A Farewell to Arms,* when Frederic Henry wakes to find that Bonello has deserted. Piani tries to explain Bonello's desertion, saying, "You see we don't believe in the war anyway, Tenente." When Henry asks, "Why didn't you go?" Piani replies, "I did not want to leave you" (*AFTA* 217).

Writing of *For Whom the Bell Tolls,* Mark Van Gunten contends that in the end Robert Jordan merges his "individual self with a cause, with humanity, with history," which "completes Jordan's 'education' at the end of the novel." He goes on to say that the novel places an emphasis on "resolving a polemic of the individual versus the collective . . . [affirming] Jordan's desire to dismantle differences" (155). My reading of the novel is almost exactly the opposite. *For Whom the Bell Tolls* shows us repeatedly that Jordan's commitment to the cause is shaky; when Pilar asks him if he has a "religious" level of faith in the Republic, Robert Jordan replies, "'Yes,' *hoping* it was true" (91, italics mine). When he considers his relationship with the Communists, he admits that he has to accept them for their ability to win the war, but he refuses to share their politics. He goes on to ask himself, "What were his politics then? He had none now, he told himself. But do not tell any one else that, he thought. Don't ever admit that" (*FWTBT* 163). Early in the war he believed "all the nonsense" and is shocked to find how much lying attends the cause, although he has learned to accept that there "was always lying in war" (230).

Robert Jordan is "integrated" in the end and "committed" to a cause, but his cause is less the cause of the Republican army and more the cause of Maria. His first and last affiliation is not to an ideology but to people trapped beneath the oppressive weights of the machinery of ideology. He thinks how the rhetoric of the Communists has caused him to be "as bigoted and hide-bound about his politics as a hard-shelled Baptist and phrases like enemies of the people came into his mind without his much criticizing them in any way. Any sort of *clichés* both revolutionary and patriotic. His mind employed them without criticism. Of course they were true but it was too easy to be nimble about using them. . . . Bigotry is an odd thing" (*FWTBT* 164). Reading this passage in the context of *A Farewell to Arms* illuminates it for the reader; the webs of propagandistic clichés must sound just as "obscene" to Robert Jordan as they do to Frederic Henry when he thinks about the "'shouted words" and "proclamations that were slapped up by billposters over other proclamations" (*AFTA* 185). Rather than ideology, it is his physical, concrete connection to Maria, his sleeping with her and loving her, that has helped free Robert Jordan from his ideological blinders and made the struggle real for him, just as "numbers of roads" and "names of rivers" speak of real people and true losses to Frederic Henry (*AFTA* 185). In considering his new compatriots, Robert Jordan wonders, "Was there ever a people whose leaders were as truly their enemies as this one?" (*FWTBT* 163). The cause he is fighting for—like many of his newfound comrades—is rooted less in the Republican cause than in a desire to alleviate human suffering and privation.

As is so often the case in Hemingway, the use of point of view in *For Whom the Bell Tolls* helps us understand his thematic concerns. The focus through Lieutenant Berrendo's perspective at El Sordo's last stand demonstrates how the soldiers of Franco, too, are in the thrall of a faceless and emotionless ideology and bureaucracy. This distance between the causes espoused by ideologues and the day-to-day lives of individuals may best be spelled out by Andrés's rumination that "if our father had not been a Republican both Eladio and I would be soldiers now with the fascists and if one were a soldier with them then there would be no problem" (*FWTBT* 367). His goal is to get back to the "affair of the posts and the bridge" after he delivers his message (366); not because he wants to strike a blow for freedom and liberty but because his "brother Eladio is there, who is of my own bone and flesh. Anselmo, Primitivo, Fernando, Augustín, Rafael . . . the two women, Pablo and the *Inglés,* though the *Inglés* does not count since he is a foreigner and under orders" (366). Andrés fights for the people he knows.

Pablo, on the other hand, when caught up in the first zealous throes of love for the cause, shows no mercy for the enemies—real and imagined—that he sends over the cliffs. His story is told by Pilar, not by himself; in a way we see again a distance between narrator and protagonist—just as we see one between Hemingway and Robert Jordan.

Robert Jordan does have some biographical connections to Hemingway, of course, especially with respect to his father and grandfather. Mostly, Hemingway seems to have based Robert Jordan on the former professor who fought for the Republic, Californian Robert Merriman (Reynolds, *1930s* 277–78). Hemingway started composing *For Whom the Bell Tolls* in first person but quickly switched to third person, achieving one level of distance (that he frequently violates throughout the narrative through use of free-indirect discourse and the second person). Moreover, throughout *For Whom the Bell Tolls,* Hemingway consistently refers to his protagonist by both his first and last names; he never calls him "Robert" or "Jordan" but always "Robert Jordan." He does not allow the familiarity of the first name, "Robert," that he uses with each of the native Spaniards, nor does he allow the distancing that would occur with the use of the last name alone.

Like Frederic Henry, Robert Jordan is a character who has not achieved his fullness of self for the majority of the narrative; he is, rather, in the act of becoming. Even as he destroys a bridge for the Republic he builds one between himself and the people of Spain, as shown through his love for Maria. His sacrifice at the end of the novel is for her. Like the people of the country, he has been betrayed by the inefficiency and aloofness of his leaders, as demonstrated through Andrés's fruitless attempt to deliver the message to Golz in time to stop the assault.

At the same time, it is interesting that Robert Jordan's single intention—should he survive the war—is to write another book. "And what are you going to do afterwards?" he asks himself. "I am going back and earn my living teaching Spanish as before, and I am going to write a *true* book. I'll bet, he said. I'll bet that will be easy" (*FWTBT* 163, italics mine) When he thinks of his Gaylord's education in ideology, hypocrisy, and manipulation, he promises himself that "some day they would tell the truth to every one" (230). In this way, Robert Jordan is just like the narrator of "The Butterfly and the Tank," who is warned by the woman at his table that he "could not write it because it would be prejudicial to the cause of the Spanish Republic" ("Butterfly" 433). And, although the narrator tells the manager that he doesn't "like this story very well," the manager—a civilian—insists, "You must write a story about it" (435).

Similarly, in "Under the Ridge," the Hungarian general friend of the narrator says to the narrator, apropos of nothing, in an almost accusatory tone, "You are supposed to be a writer." The narrator—discouraged, perhaps, by the Russian battle police, or the Extremaduran, or the day's losses, or all of the above, responds, "I can't write now." He is, again, avoiding the duty of the writer: to write one true sentence, to somehow impose order through the fog of propaganda and selective memory. The general, like the manager of the Chicote, refuses to let him off the hook: "Write it afterwards. You can write it all afterwards" ("Ridge" 469). He then urges the writer twice to not get killed, for if the writer dies, who will carry forth the truth of the events they have all witnessed and lived through? If we are to believe that the "first casualty of war is truth,"[7] then the role of the individual artist in telling the truth is never more paramount than when ignorant armies, caught up in the darkling plain of modern ideologies and political zealotry, clash by night.

Notes

1. See Johnston's "'The Butterfly and the Tank': Casualties of War" and "Hemingway's 'The Denuniciation': The Aloof American."

2. See Kvam. See also Watson's "'Old Man at the Bridge': The Making of a Short Story," *Hemingway Review,* 7.2 (1988): 152–65.

3. In March 1938, Hemingway wrote enthusiastically to Max Perkins about his new novel: "It is 20 times better than that Night Before Battle which was flat where this is rounded and recalled where this is invented" (*SL* 482).

4. I am indebted to William Braasch Watson essay "'Old Man at the Bridge': The Making of a Story" for calling my attention to Wilson's essay (157).

5. When playing with possible titles for *A Farewell to Arms,* Hemingway himself considered such titles as "Education of the Flesh," "The Carnal Education," and "The Sentimental Education of Frederick [sic] Henry" (Reynolds, *First War* 296), and Robert Lewis sees the novel as "fundamentally a story of [Frederic's] education" (30).

6. See, for example, James Meredith, "Hemingway's Spain in Flames, 1937," in this volume (146–51).

7. This quotation is attributed to a number of sources, but most often to progressive California Senator Hiram Johnson, 1866–1945.

Works Cited

Cooper, Stephen. *The Politics of Ernest Hemingway.* Ann Arbor: UMI Research Press, 1987.

Hemingway, Ernest. "The Butterfly and the Tank." In *Complete Short Stories of Ernest Hemingway: Finca Vigía Edition.* 429–36.

———. *The Complete Short Stories of Ernest Hemingway: Finca Vigía Edition.* New York: Scribner, 1987.

———. "The Denunciation." In *Complete Short Stories of Ernest Hemingway: Finca Vigía Edition.* 420–28.

———. *Ernest Hemingway: Selected Letters, 1917–1961.* Ed. Carlos Baker. New York: Charles Scribner's Sons, 1981.

———. *A Farewell to Arms.* 1929. New York: Scribner and Sons, 1995.

———. *For Whom the Bell Tolls.* 1940. New York: Scribner and Sons, 1968.

———. *To Have and Have Not.* 1937. New York: Scribner Classic/Collier, 1987.

———. "Under the Ridge." In *Complete Short Stories of Ernest Hemingway: Finca Vigía Edition.* 460–69.

Johnston, Kenneth G. "'The Butterfly and the Tank': Casualties of War." *Studies in Short Fiction* 26.2 (1989): 183–86.

———. "Hemingway's 'The Denuniciation': The Aloof American." *Fitzgerald/Hemingway Annual* (1979): 371–82.

Josephs, Allen. "Hemingway's Spanish Civil War Stories." In *Hemingway's Neglected Short Fiction: New Perspectives.* Ed. Susan F. Beegel. Tuscaloosa: U of Alabama P, 1992. 313–27.

Kvam, Wayne. "Hemingway's 'Under the Ridge.'" *Fitzgerald/Hemingway Annual* (1978): 225–40.

Lewis, Robert W. A Farewell to Arms*: The War of the Words.* New York: Twayne Publishers, 1992.

Reynolds, Michael. *Hemingway: The 1930s.* New York: Norton, 1998.

———. *Hemingway's First War: The Making of* A Farewell to Arms. Princeton: Princeton UP, 1976.

Van Gunten, Mark C. "The Polemics of Narrative and Difference in *For Whom the Bell Tolls.*" In *Blowing the Bridge: Essays on Hemingway and* For Whom the Bell Tolls. Ed. Rena Sanderson. New York: Greenwood Press, 1992. 143–57.

Watson, William Braasch. "Joris Ivens and the Communists: Bringing Hemingway into the Spanish Civil War." *Hemingway Review* 10.1 (1990): 2–18.

———. "'Old Man at the Bridge': The Making of a Short Story." *Hemingway Review* 7.2 (1988): 152–64.

Wilson, Edmund. "Hemingway and the Wars." *The Nation* 147 (10 Dec. 1938): 628 and 630.

12

Foreign Bodies

Documenting Expatriate Involvement in "Night Before Battle" and "Under the Ridge"

MICHAEL MAIWALD

Ernest Hemingway's *For Whom the Bell Tolls* casts a long shadow over his shorter fiction from his Spanish Civil War period, and the relative critical neglect of this material can be said to have been authorized by Hemingway himself. In a letter to his editor, Maxwell Perkins, dated 25 March 1939, Hemingway offered an invidious, and critically influential, comparison between his novel-in-progress and one of his longer Spanish Civil War stories: "It is 20 times better than that Night Before Battle which was flat where this is rounded and recalled where this is invented" (*SL* 482). Unfortunately, Hemingway's own comparative judgment here, buttressed by his eventual abandonment of his immediate plans to publish his Spanish Civil War stories—and his later opposition to their inclusion in a planned 1959 collection—has legitimized subsequent critical neglect of these stories. When they are discussed, they are mainly seen not as valuable in their own right but only as precursors to *For Whom the Bell Tolls.*

Martin Light and, more recently, Allen Josephs have produced the most sustained and insightful discussions of the Spanish Civil War stories, but both of these critics are more interested in the way these stories chart the progression of Hemingway's active engagement with his wartime material than they are in the stories' ability to stand on their own as satisfying aesthetic statements on the war. For Light, Hemingway's stories from this period "deserve notice . . . because in them Hemingway gives expression to his major preoccupations and his perennial themes and because they exist as significant records of the Spanish experience out of which came his major novel, *For Whom the Bell Tolls*" (64).

Light views the stories as "records of the Spanish experience," raw material that Hemingway will later process, use, and ultimately transcend in his more successful novel, since these stories alone "do not transmit that special excitement, sympathy, and pity that emanates [sic] from Hemingway's best fiction" (64). In a more detailed and comprehensive assessment of Hemingway's work from this period, Allen Josephs borrows directly from Hemingway's own dismissive judgment of "Night Before Battle" and expands it into a critical paradigm for distinguishing between the different types of work from this period. Josephs correctly points to the "crossing over of fact and fiction" (34) between the news dispatches and the short fiction from this period, and he clearly values the "invented" character of Hemingway's novel more highly than the "recalled" experiences of his short stories. The main value of these stories, for Josephs, is their purgative function, allowing Hemingway to drain the partisan politics from his writing to the benefit of his later, more aesthetically successful work: "What these stories did . . . precisely because they were autobiographical and political, was to purge the real war and the real loss of the Spanish Republic from Hemingway's fiction" (38). This process is particularly important for Josephs, as he has a strong investment in a staunchly libertarian Hemingway, who, he earlier proclaims, "never had a 'Red rash,' nor was he ever remotely a Stalinist" (32). Paradoxically, Josephs does acknowledge that the stories as a group "show very clearly that [Hemingway] could write accurately and well—despite what his Spanish and American critics have said—about the war and about the politics of the war" (39), thereby implying, presumably, that the stories maintain a critical edge despite being intimately related to Hemingway's own wartime experiences while he was aligned with the Republican side.

Josephs's ambivalence over the political meanings of Hemingway's Spanish Civil War stories and their potential to tar Hemingway ideologically begs the question, what exactly does Hemingway say about the war and its politics in these stories?[1] To answer this question more fully, the self-reflexive, autobiographical elements in the stories—the formal features that have been held out by critics as evidence of their relative weakness—must be examined afresh, with the proviso that the lack of authorial distance from the material is not a priori a critical liability. Hemingway's most interesting stories from this wartime grouping, "Night Before Battle" and "Under the Ridge," are presented through the perspective of a narrator who films the war to raise funds for the Republican side, and who is, in the latter story, explicitly identified as a writer named Edwin Henry. The autobiographical references to Hemingway himself are obvious, given his participation in the propaganda film *The Spanish Earth*, directed by Joris Ivens, and his additional work as a war correspondent, while the preponderance of pseudonyms and variations of Hemingway's name within the overall group of Spanish Civil War stories indicates that Hemingway was eager to capitalize on his insider status within Republican Spain. In "Night Before Battle" and "Under the Ridge," however, Hemingway transforms this absence of authorial distance into a critical device that destabilizes the certainties about the war that had marked Hemingway's earliest artistic representations of it: the script he cowrote with John Dos Passos for *The Spanish Earth* and his own play, *The Fifth Column.* While these two earlier works are united in presenting a uniformly simplistic view of the Republican war effort, they nevertheless offer contradictory visions of the political meaning behind the Spanish Civil War and the Republican resistance to the military coup eventually headed by Franco and supported by Nazi Germany and fascist Italy: while Ivens's film posits the war effort as an organic resistance of native Spaniards against foreign interference, Hemingway's play prioritizes foreign contributions to the Republican cause and even suggests that the current struggle in Spain is significant primarily as the first episode of an ongoing international struggle against fascism. By revisiting and revising the claims of these early works about the role of foreign involvement in the Spanish Civil War, Hemingway's two later stories complicate the reductive, though not always complementary, logic present in his earlier treatment of this material. While Hemingway uses the filmmaker-as-narrator as a device to critique the distortions of *The Spanish Earth,* he nevertheless borrows from Ivens's cinematic valorization of an indigenous Spanish folk in order to question the moral efficacy of an international Republican war effort potentially at odds with local values. As a result, the cosmopolitan radicalism of Hemingway's play is increasingly presented as a compromised and limited position in Hemingway's later stories, and Hemingway, by aligning himself with a narrator who is conscious of his own complicity in producing a somewhat fraudulent record of the war, distinguishes himself from the doctrinaire foreigners who misapprehend the Spanish milieu. By drawing attention both to deliberate and accidental misunderstandings by foreigners fighting for Republican Spain, Hemingway creates a critical self-reflexivity that establishes his own foreign perspective as one worth hearing.

Hemingway began his artistic engagement with Republican Spain in *The Spanish Earth,* an ostensibly collaborative project under the direction of Joris Ivens, a respected Dutch modernist filmmaker. As Stephen Koch has pointed out, Ivens was a Comintern, or Communist International, agent, and Koch believes Ivens the director settled momentarily on the plight of Republican Spain as part of his long-term mission to produce political propaganda for Russian aims (44–49). However, recent work by Alex Vernon has thrown serious doubt on the accuracy of Koch's assertions about the degree to which Ivens was taking his artistic cues from Moscow. While Vernon acknowledges Ivens's leadership role in the production of the film, he persuasively argues for Ivens's artistic integrity and independence, as well as for a more collaborative account of the film's genesis and evolution (97–106). Most important, Vernon makes a strong case for the idea that Hemingway was not a pro-Communist dupe recruited by Ivens, but rather an antifascist supporter of the Second Republic who sought to support Spain's fledgling democracy through his work on Ivens's film (106–10).[2]

What is beyond dispute, however, is Hemingway's involvement with the rewriting of the narration and his stepping in for Orson Welles after the latter's reading of the script was deemed a failure. Through the script and voice-over narration that he contributed to a project already extensively mapped out by Ivens and others, Hemingway presents the war as a struggle between the Spanish folk and foreign mercenaries under the Nationalist banner. While not entirely ignoring international contributions to the Loyalist movement, the film equates the Spanish earth of the title with the anonymous peasants who work the fields in the idyllic village setting that opens the picture. As Hemingway intones, people in the village of Fuentedueña "work for the common good," and the idealized rural peasantry—whose seemingly instinctual communitarian tendencies are well-served by the democratic, populist nature of the Republic—grow food for Madrid's besieged population. When, near the end of the film, a Republican counterattack secures a key bridge along the Jarama River on the Madrid-Valencia road, Hemingway's narration underscores the special bond that these amateur soldiers share with the land for which they fight: "This is the moment that the rest of war prepares for, to walk across a stretch of land when six men go forward into death, and by their presence on it prove, this earth is ours." Hemingway takes pains to portray the Republican fighters as civilians pulled into combat to protect the land that is their birthright, and Ivens reinforces this point visually by juxtaposing images of troops successfully advancing across a barren landscape with images of water running into the irrigation trenches in the same village that opened the film. Ivens's montage here emphasizes that the blood spilled from these soldiers is as nourishing to the Spanish soil as the water that gives life to fallow earth in the Spanish countryside, and that the soldiers may themselves be equated with the earth for which they fight.[3]

In contrast, Hemingway portrays the right-wing Nationalist cause as essentially foreign in all its aspects. The "professional soldiers" who fight for the Nationalists are Moors—referring to Franco's invasion with forces from the

Spanish Sahara—and Hemingway also emphasizes the Italian and German contributions of men and arms to Franco's forces. When a shot of flies on dead Italian troops around Madrid is followed by narration that claims these men "thought they were fighting in Ethiopia," Hemingway tacitly identifies their presence in Spain as an instance of imperial aggression. Likewise, "German artillery" is identified as the source of the bombardment that terrorizes the Spanish people, and the death from the sky above the village of Fuentedueña comes via German-made and German-piloted Junker planes. Though foreigners likewise played a large role in the Republican cause in Spain, this fact is impossible to glean from Ivens's film, in which Soviet involvement is neither depicted nor referenced and only the participation of a single foreigner, the German writer Gustav Regler, is mentioned. Ivens's images and Hemingway's narration equates the Republican cause with Spanish cultural purity, a purity that can best be expressed by the anonymous rural folk characters that populate *The Spanish Earth*'s opening sequences.

In his first solo artistic engagement with the Spanish Civil War, however—his play, *The Fifth Column*—Hemingway presents a very different view of the conflict. Written in 1937, the year that *The Spanish Earth* was screened for several elite audiences (including Franklin and Eleanor Roosevelt at the U.S. White House), *The Fifth Column* diverges strikingly from the perspective of Ivens's film, although the two works are linked by their overtly propagandistic qualities. In an article on the play, John Raeburn asserts that "while *The Fifth Column* did not dramatize the Spanish Civil War as simplistically as had *The Spanish Earth,* neither did it encourage recognition of its extraordinary political complexity. Indeed, the play's focus on counter-espionage in Madrid actually masked the most significant political developments in the Republic in favor of a rousing if vaporous statement of the righteousness of the Loyalist cause and a celebration of the intrepid commitment of those who embraced it" (10). Raeburn's diagnosis of the play's political naïveté is accurate, but his focus on its unsophisticated content somewhat downplays its eccentric character. The play focuses on Hemingway's thinly disguised authorial stand-in, Philip Rawlings, and the conflict between his romance with a comely and high-spirited American reporter, Dorothy Bridges, and his selfless commitment to the Republican political struggle. The play centers on the sexual lives and consumerist excesses of expatriate reporters and friends of the Republic in Madrid's Hotel Florida, and the studied absence of Spanish characters in the play, coming after the valorization of the rural Spanish folk in *The Spanish Earth,* seems decidedly odd. Virtually all the Spanish characters in the play are presented for broad comic effect: the drunken electrician who babbles political slogans, the hotel manager who continually begs for food in tortuous English that seems like a bad translation exercise gone awry, and the hotel maid who warns Bridges about Philip and offers fluttering pronouncements about his "badness" (48) and the sexual potency of Spanish men. The vast majority of Spaniards in the play are the anonymous citizens of Madrid who become victims of the fascist bombardment of the city. Hemingway does, however, present us with Antonio, the somewhat sinister Spanish head of Seguridad, the secret police who maintain Republican military discipline and ferret out civilian traitors to the cause. While jointly interrogating, with Philip Rawlings, an International Brigade soldier caught sleeping at his post, Antonio learns the value of mercy and compassion from Rawlings, who cites Abraham Lincoln and Union discipline during his own country's Civil War as justification for pardoning the young soldier. The other major Spanish character is a fascist politician who controls the subversive "Fifth Column" terrorist resistance in Madrid and whose capture by Rawlings and interrogation by Antonio yield three hundred arrests of fascist operatives within Madrid's citizenry. The inclusion of characters such as Antonio and the politician hardly balances the play's predominantly cosmopolitan slant, however.

This ultimately self-referential, inward focus is reflected in the fact that *The Fifth Column*'s abiding dramatic concern resides in what amounts to a symbolic love triangle between Philip Rawlings, Dorothy Bridges, and Max, a German International Brigade agent who, with Philip, engineers a daring (and entirely implausible) behind-the-lines kidnapping of the aforementioned enemy politician. Max's horribly mangled face, courtesy of his earlier torture at right-wing German hands, contrasts both aesthetically and morally with Dorothy's wholesome American good looks: his physical deformity signals his self-sacrifice and political commitment, while her unblemished beauty reveals a naïve American innocence for which Hemingway evinces much contempt. This romantic and ideological triangle is represented visually by the war poster that hangs in the space of the interior door connecting rooms 109 and 110 in the Hotel Florida, where Dorothy and Philip respectively reside and where, in Act Two, Max's physical presence in Philip's bed (while resting before and after a mission) causes Philip, while in Dorothy's room next door, to vacillate between dutiful self-denial and an escapist fantasy of domesticity.

At the opening of Act Three, Dorothy retreats to her own room over Philip's objections when Max appears, and Max, Iago-like, engenders doubts in Philip's mind about the feasibility of squaring his romantic and political lives. By the end of this scene, Max once again occupies a symbolic position in Philip's bed while entreating him to minister sexually to Dorothy's needs: "I lie down now for a while here. Go in to her now" (*Fifth Column* 68). At the play's conclusion, the doubt that Max has implanted in Philip's mind results in a role reversal, as Philip now insists on breaking off a relationship that Max ironically defends: "I tell you truly I see no signs that she interferes with your work in any way" (81). Having poisoned Philip's romance with Dorothy, Max can now play the emotionally wounded torture victim and caution Philip to "remember to be kind" (81) before Philip barrels into Dorothy's room to break up with her. Cruelly taunting her with a travelogue vision of global expatriate leisure that they could have shared together, Philip then dumps her, despite her last-ditch effort to highlight her sexual use-value. This effort is to no avail: Philip's libidinal energies can be directed toward either private satisfactions or political virtues, and his political romance with Max, the "fifty years of undeclared wars" still to come against the forces of fascism (80), steels his resolve. Despite Philip's political commitments, Hemingway's ending emphasizes that in *The Fifth Column,* the Spanish Civil War is finally just the backdrop to Philip Rawlings's interior battle between his need to project a public façade of brawling, womanizing machismo and his private need for comfort and love. This battle is won by the former because of its more seamless integration into his work as an agent for Republican Spain. As John Raeburn succinctly states, "Philip Rawlings was a caricature of a caricature, Hemingway's public personality of the 1930s touched up and heightened here and there and burnished with the luster of a righteous cause" (9). If the play is a successful work of propaganda on any level, it merits notice not for its political rhetoric, but rather as an instance where Hemingway's fiction merged into an advertisement for his own two-dimensional public persona.

The Fifth Column's sharp departure from *The Spanish Earth* should not be all that surprising, given that the thematic content of the film had been sketched out before Hemingway joined the project, and that this content differed substantially from the predominantly military focus of his own reportage and subsequent fiction on the war. Some critics have suggested that John Dos Passos was largely responsible for the film's focus on the collectivist utopia of Fuentedueña, and that Hemingway was far more interested in capturing the military exploits of Republican forces than dwelling on land reclamation and Spanish peasants.[4] If so, Hemingway's work on the film necessarily diverged from the more personal artistic expression of his interests in wartime Spain contained within the play. However, the rather obvious differences between these two works belie an important similarity: both works are resolutely confident in their ability to depict the reality of Republican Spain. While Ivens's documentary hides its constructed and rather selective view of reality through the emotional power of its imagery and the authenticity of its war footage,

Hemingway's play presents a seamless interpretation of political realities in Spain that never allows for any questioning of its tidy rationalizations on behalf of state-authorized torture and purging of suspected traitors.

These self-confident representations contrast starkly with the short fiction that Hemingway would write about the war in Spain, work that he produced between May 1938 and February 1939. In particular, the stories "Night Before Battle" and "Under the Ridge" find Hemingway questioning the international composition of the Republican side and drawing attention to the difficulties of representing the Republican war effort while being embedded in its military apparatus. By advancing the idea that both mercenary and idealistic foreign involvement was problematical not only for the right-wing Nationalists (as *The Spanish Earth* implied) but for also for the Republican cause, Hemingway manages both to question the possibility of telling the truth about the war in Spain as an outside observer and to foreground the problem of representation through a narrator who is both a documentary filmmaker and a writer—a figure not unlike himself. While the device of the autobiographical narrator can be seen as evidence that Hemingway remained too close to a partisan perspective and still functioned as a documentary propagandist, his focus on the fraught act of representing the war allowed him to create a two-fold dynamic: he critiques the limitations of the foreign-authored visual documentary and its concomitant ideological fealty to a triumphant vision of the Spanish Republic while simultaneously positing his own fictional endeavor as one that uses this self-reflexivity about the nature of, and problems associated with, representation to produce a more complete understanding of the war. Far from constituting an aesthetically flawed or limited engagement with the ailing Spanish Republic, these stories use the raw material of Hemingway's experiences as a war correspondent for NANA and his work on the Joris Ivens film to construct a suitably ambiguous and nuanced version of the war's moral dimensions, and to announce a brisk retreat from the political rationalizations earlier offered in *The Fifth Column*.

In "Night Before Battle," Hemingway's narrator, the thinly veiled autobiographical figure, Henry, accompanies his American friend, Al Wagner, a Republican tank man, on a night of drinking, eating, and gambling on the eve of what the narrative strongly implies will be the tank captain's death in combat. The story begins with Hemingway foregrounding the act of representation during wartime. His narrator, Henry, is a documentary filmmaker who, along with a crew of two, risks his life to create a propagandistic simulation of Republican triumph that ignores the real outcomes of the battles he films. For Henry, the act of filming creates emotional distance and conceptual abstraction, so the "tanks looked like small mud-colored beetles bustling in the trees and spitting tiny flashes and the men behind them were toy men who lay flat, then crouched and ran, and then dropped to run again, or to stay where they lay, spotting the hillside as the tanks moved on" ("Night" 111). The miniaturization occasioned by the camera's distance from the battle creates an experience of unreality for Henry, and the death and destruction below him seems strangely inconsequential. The narrator's emotional distance disappears and the acuity of his judgment returns only after he has finished filming, when he faces the fact that "we had been too far away and any fool could see the offensive was a failure" (111), and concludes that "this was just another blood bath like the Somme" (112). Faced with aesthetic vistas that conceal concrete outcomes and human tragedies, Henry's momentarily blinkered understanding seems largely a product of his documentary aim.

The disjunction between appearance and reality that Henry experiences is not limited to the documentary filmmaker; Hemingway demonstrates how it also afflicts the combat soldier. As the leader of a tank battalion with limited equipment and inexperienced personnel, Al Wagner is already disoriented by the deceptive appearance of the men under his command: "They look like tank men when you see them by the tanks with the helmets on. They look like tank men when they get in. But when they shut the traps down there's really nothing inside. They aren't tank men" (118). These simulacral tank men serve Henry's purposes better than Wagner's, as Henry claims the Twelfth Brigade enabled his crew to film "some good tank shots" during "that attack last week by Pingarrón" (116). Henry responds to Al's retort—"The tanks were no good there"—with the pragmatic confidence of the propagandist who knows he must only capture images that can stir people: "I know . . . but they photographed very well" (116).

Henry's response reveals the cynicism of a filmmaker motivated by propagandistic aims, since he knows that even battlefield disasters can still yield impressive footage; truth here is subsumed by appearance, and appearance is a function of clever editing. For Wagner, however, his disappointment at learning how appearances can deceive in an International Brigade tank battalion is tempered by his belief that he could train his recruits to become real tank men, if only he were given adequate time. What these men in the tanks fear, and what Wagner has attempted to condition them out of, is death, a fear that he has almost eradicated within himself, though the germ of this story is its recurrence within him on the eve of battle and his successful struggle to quell it. (The deliberate omission of the definite article in the story's title indicates Hemingway's emphasis on a particular psychological state, and not merely a chronological moment.) Yet Wagner contradicts his military philosophy of nurture when he asserts that you need a sense of "vocation" to be an effective tank man: "It's sort of like being a priest. You have to be cut out for it" (119). Here, battle readiness is something more than a function of time and training, approaching an intrinsic attribute of human character.

But what is most unusual about this moment—about the use of a religious simile by a Communist atheist—is that it implies something essentially priest-like in Wagner's person, suggesting that his adherence to the Republican cause has a doctrinal character. Certainly his comment here signals where his real anxieties concerning the nature of reality lie: while he can stomach the failings of would-be priests who find their faith wanting on the battlefield, Wagner is deeply shaken by the revelation that Republican military leadership is incompetent. When he hears a tirade in a restaurant against Largo Caballero, at one point both the prime minister and war minister of the Spanish Republic, by a bespectacled Spaniard with the self-important air of the politically well connected, Wagner seems irritated by his posturing, but admits that the diagnosis of the recent failed offensive by this would-be insider is accurate. The appearance of the bespectacled man both at Chicote's and at the restaurant where the narrator buys Wagner an extravagant meal (by wartime Madrid standards) takes on the function of a recurring temptation, through which the faith in the Republic of the priest-like Wagner is repeatedly tested. The extent of Wagner's crisis is highlighted by periodic references to how the bespectacled man has upset and depressed him, culminating in an understated admission that hinges on a single "but": "What he said sounded pretty sensible. . . . I've been thinking it over. But my duty is to do what I'm ordered to do" (127). Confronted with the reality that his life may be lost in a doomed offensive, Wagner momentarily considers the possibility of not fighting, of deserting the cause that has become his life, before recommitting himself to the military discipline that constitutes his faith. When, at the end of the story, he presents the narrator with some letters and personal effects to send to a brother in New York in case he is killed the next day, Wagner shows him a picture of his brother's wife, a fitting symbol of his own monastic devotion to the political cause he serves and of his acceptance of his near-certain death in its service. Without a wife or family of his own, Wagner can only find a surrogate, perhaps a fitting analogy for his decision to devote himself to a political cause far from his home.

Al Wagner's status as a foreigner accentuates his rootless status, but more important, his status as a cultural outsider makes him an isolated figure in Republican Spain, disturbed by the all-too-human fallibility and outright incompetence of the Republican military and political leadership and curiously detached from the human virtues of the actual people for whom he supposedly fights. For Wagner, the moral universe of Republican Spain is a projection of his own ideological template, and his inability to see the decent virtues of its ordinary citizens and the self-serving nature of its supposed military heroes renders his implied sacrifice all the more poignant. Meeting a waiter outside Chicote's, the bar where he and the narrator had been drinking, Wagner placates this worried father, who asks the two men whether they have seen the 145th Brigade, in which his twenty-year-old son serves. The waiter asserts, "I am of no party. . . . But my boy is a Communist" (121); his heartfelt interest in the military situation that involves his son comes from understandable familial concern. Unlike the politically minded Al Wagner, the waiter is less interested in the overall status of the offensive than in the local conditions that affect "my boy." After being reassured by Wagner, the waiter offers a decidedly apolitical benediction: "God bless you . . . God guard you and keep you" (121). Once outside, Wagner observes to Henry, "Jees he's kind of confused politically, isn't he?" (121). Henry, however, does not concur with his friend's judgment, instead averring that the waiter is a "good guy" whom he's "known . . . for a long time" (122). By asserting personal considerations ahead of political pronouncements, the narrator seems to be correcting Al, who is quick to incorporate his friend's judgment even while reasserting his initial bias: "He seems like a good guy. . . . But he ought to get wise to himself politically" (122).

Al Wagner, a self-declared communist, may view the waiter's blessing as a de facto assertion of fascist sympathies or allegiance, as the Left in Spain was overtly hostile to the Catholic Church and organized Christianity, since priests had traditionally been a reactionary force and had allied themselves with the broad coalition of anti-Republican forces clustered around General Franco. Hemingway, however, further subverts Wagner's judgment by having his two characters walk into a "dark street" (121) after their conversation with the waiter, signaling Wagner's failure to recognize this native moral touchstone. Later, at the Hotel Florida amidst the drinking, carousing, and gambling of foreign mercenaries and journalists, Wagner will engage in yet another misrecognition, failing to see the drunk, belligerent, and vaguely ridiculous-looking figure of Baldy Jackson as a fighter hero, fresh from shooting down a German Junker bomber. The man he calls "you rummy fake Santa Claus" (130) is mobbed upon his drunken return by fellow mercenary pilots eager to hear of his exploits, and Wagner quickly reverses himself and attempts to placate Jackson, who hams up his wounded feelings while his fellow flyers make cutting comments about the inadequacy of the tanks and the men who operate them.

Baldy Jackson's status as an unqualified hero is questionable for a number of reasons, however, beginning with his association with the mercenary flyers, who fleece the poorly paid Al Wagner not once but twice, through a dice game that may or may not be fixed. The ambiguity of Jackson's heroic status is also hinted at several times during his self-aggrandizing narrative, most notably when he admits that after being shot down and parachuting behind Republican lines, "there was a tendency to regard me as a criminal fascist due to my inability to master the Lanish Spanguage" (131). Jackson's inability to speak proper Spanish categorizes him momentarily, however incorrectly, as an enemy of the Republican state, but the slight stigma of the original accusation draws attention to his peripheral relationship to Spanish culture and life. Insulated within a corps of foreign flyers mainly intent on gambling and carousing, Jackson proclaims himself "a potential ace of the people's army" (136), but the hollowness of his boast is underscored by the emptiness of his rhetoric: having downed only a single plane, Jackson is as far from being an ace as he is from being physically and symbolically integrated into the ranks of Spanish soldiers who fight for country and cause. Unlike his countryman Al Wagner, who has at least "got politics" (132), Jackson is motivated largely by greed for the relatively high pay he receives for the risky task of piloting a Republican fighter plane.

While Jackson seems to serve primarily as a foil for the altogether modest and more authentically heroic Wagner, his curious behavior in the story establishes his additional symbolic role as an amalgamation of the foreign documentary filmmaker and the wartime correspondent. Unlike Wagner, who remains focused on battlefield strategy and the logistical forces that have diminished the strategic value of tanks, Jackson approaches the war from the stance of participant-spectator, and the cinematic vocabulary of *scene* and *spectacle* recurs repeatedly in his drunken, narcissistic, rambling attempts to narrate his adventure. When he finally completes his first attempt, the strained and obvious metaphors that he uses echo some of the descriptive language that Hemingway sometimes employed in his NANA dispatches.[5] He likens viewing the burning cockpit of the crippled Junker to "looking into a blast furnace" and compares the group of parachutes created by the escaping crew to "great big beautiful morning glories opening up" (134).[6] The other flyers are unimpressed by this account, and one of them sarcastically responds to Jackson: "You're a writer all right. . . . You ought to write for *War Aces.* Do you mind telling me in plain language what happened?" (135). In fact, the entreaty from another to "Tell us what happened, really" (135), confirms that Baldy's account is nothing more than fiction to the flyers until it is rendered in the flat technical language of formations and maneuvers, an account the drunken Jackson finally, if only temporarily, achieves. While Hemingway's comic portrayal of Baldy Jackson as a would-be storyteller at odds with his audience seems like a self-deprecating nod to the well-worn figure of the dissolute expatriate writer, this overdetermined figure also facilitates Hemingway's autocritique of the pursuits of documentary filmmaker and war correspondent, while in addition suggesting that the military campaign conducted by the Republican forces is marked by tactical flaws and inadequate personnel.

"Night Before Battle" remains then at cross-purposes with its ostensible point: its celebration of the purity in Al Wagner's dedication to the Republican cause so distant geographically from his home is undermined by Wagner's doctrinaire thinking and failure to perceive his doomed role within the historical moment he inhabits. Through the contrast between the stoical tank captain's quiet, unsung heroism and the garish self-promotion of the Republican flyer, Hemingway seems almost inadvertently to have told a story of haves and have-nots within the framework of Republican Spain, but even this message is more optimistic than the darker moral that lurks behind this apparent opposition. The narrator of the story—who, until the final moments of the narrative, has withheld overt judgments—ends the piece by asserting that the superficial appearance of anger in Al Wagner as he strides off to meet his destiny is actually indicative of a deeper anger "somewhere inside of himself" that the narrator attributes to Wagner's possible recognition that he may soon be "dying uselessly" (139). While the narrator's privileged speculation seems to carry with it the weight of Hemingway's own convictions, the overall tenor of the story invites us to read the conclusion not merely as a response to the pointless death of a brave man in a foolish military action but also as an indirect critique of Wagner's continued faith in a Republican cause perhaps fatally undermined by local political shortcomings and self-interested foreign involvement.

As in "Night Before Battle," "Under the Ridge" finds Hemingway questioning, through the figure of a documentary filmmaker-narrator, the documentary form and the tactics employed by Republican forces, and offering an even more overtly critical depiction of foreign involvement in the Republican cause. As in the previous story, the narrator is engaged in filming an attack by an International Brigade column, while native Spanish troops, described as "soldiers only in name" ("Ridge" 141), sit inactive behind the lines as reservists. In "Under the Ridge," Hemingway takes great pains to imbed his narrator in the action, and the foreign filmmaker-narrator's wartime authenticity is established by his willingness to risk his own life: "twice during the early part of the attack we should have been killed and were not" (142). The story's central action is the human tragedy created when a French International Brigade soldier, tired of fighting a futile and dangerous offensive, literally walks away from the war and is hunted down and killed by two Soviet military police officers, who are unsympathetically characterized as "hunting dogs" and whose guns' "jerky barking" confirms the inhuman nature of the military discipline they enforce (146). The narrator has a conversation with an Extremaduran from amongst the reserve troops who claims to "hate all foreigners" (143). Although Hemingway initially positions the reader's sympathies in line with the narrator's increasing contempt for his ignorant adversary, Hemingway later cedes narrative authority to the Extremaduran's voice, as he tells a story that justifies his hatred for foreign meddling in the Republican cause. A young soldier, Paco, lost a hand as a result of an injury he inflicted on himself to avoid combat. Although the story strongly implies that Paco's loss of his hand and his subsequent humble service to Republican troops is atonement enough for his cowardice, the Soviet military police execute him in a peremptory manner. After the Extremaduran finishes the story, he asks the narrator, "You understand my hatred?" (150); the narrator can only reply respectfully in the affirmative. Having presented us with numerous foreign characters who manipulate spools of film and conjure words in order to create misleading depictions of the war's progress, Hemingway has now turned his story over to another narrator, whose searing narrative of injustice offers a truth about the war from the perspective of and in the voice of the Spanish people, folk that Joris Ivens and his collaborators have previously objectified for their own propagandistic purposes. Now the narrator's firsthand knowledge of combat and his willingness to risk his life for documentary footage is supplanted by a greater authenticity: a broader historical experience of suffering over centuries of time and perpetrated by a long list of foreign invaders that is the birthright of the Extremaduran. Linked to the soil and untainted by cosmopolitan influences—as the unnamed man proudly informs our narrator, there are no foreigners in this Spanish province—the Extremaduran destabilizes the narrator's own authority within the story.[7]

Despite the power of Hemingway's secession of narrative authority to the biased Extremaduran, the poor Spaniard's tale of foreign meddling in his homeland is not the final word in the story. When the narrator, upon his return, is queried by his cameraman as to what he had been doing during the latter's lengthy nap, his minimalist exchange with the cameraman is telling:

> "Were you talking all that time?"
> "Listening."
> "Hear anything interesting?"
> "Plenty."
> "What do you want to do now?"
> "Get back to Madrid."
> "We should see the General."
> "Yes," I said. "We must." (150)

The narrator here confirms his status as the passive recipient of a privileged narrative, yet his role as a mute witness of this story within his own story seems to propel him back into an active role: his urgency to return to Madrid appears to be a direct consequence of his encounter with the Extremaduran. The narrator's emphasis on what he has heard instead of what he has seen subordinates his witnessing of the Frenchman's death at the hands of the military police to the Spanish soldier's recounting of Paco's execution. As a result, the narrator seems to be tacitly acceding to the Spaniard's philosophical premise that foreign intervention in Spain has been uniformly detrimental and exploitative. The narrator, in effect, becomes a more successful version of the French International Brigade soldier: he flees the site of the battle he has filmed, similarly convinced of the futility of the offensive, but with military approval for his action that the soldier lacks.

His visit to the General initially replicates his experience with the Extremaduran: he is once again put in the position of the passive listener while the General rants about the failed offensive—doomed by insufficient forces and poor battlefield discipline—that the narrator had helped film. When the narrator finally speaks, it is to ask the following question about the disastrous battle: "What can I write on it?" (151). The General's answer—"Nothing that is not in the official communiqué" (151)—creates a parallel between the narrator's circumstances and those of the French soldier who deserted: both men are trapped by a war that threatens to extinguish selfhood, a selfhood that is, for the narrator, inextricably bound up with the act of writing. The narrator himself concedes to the General, "I can't write now" (151), an admission that renders his previous question moot. Rather than responding to a single localized instance of censorship, the narrator's open-ended statement also seems to suggest a practical component—he cannot find the time to write as long as he is shooting propagandistic documentaries—as well as a philosophical one: he cannot find the necessary space in which to write during war. The General's final suggestion, presented almost as a military order, authorizes both the narrator's flight from the front and his written account of the war that will transcend the partiality and inaccuracy of his documentary filmmaking efforts: "Write it afterwards. You can write it all afterwards. And don't get killed. Especially, don't get killed. Now, get out of here" (151). While the narrator asserts that "the nearest any man was to victory that day was probably the Frenchman who came, with his head held high, walking out of the battle" (151), the fact that, with his cameraman, he walks by the Frenchman's corpse on his own way out of the war via a staff car to Madrid establishes the narrator as the real victor. While Hemingway's ending accentuates the parallel between the narrator and the Frenchman, this moment is preceded by one final meditation by the narrator on the documentary footage he has helped to film, a reflection that is prompted by the ironic nature of the General's advice: "He [the General] could not take his own advice because he was killed two months later. But the oddest thing about that day was how marvelously the pictures we took of the tanks came out. On the screen they advanced over the hill irresistibly, mounting the crests like great ships, to crawl clanking on toward the illusion of victory we screened" (151). The narrator marvels at the incongruity between the arresting images he has captured and the reality that they mask, but he does so in terms that foreground the public and polemical nature of the documentary form. The narrator's reference to "the illusion of victory we screened" seems inseparable from Hemingway's own participation in the initial screening of *The Spanish Earth* at Carnegie Hall and in subsequent screenings at several Hollywood locations, including the home of actor Fredric March, and may represent the closest thing to Hemingway's public exposure of the distance between the optimism of the film's message and the hopelessness of the Republican military position. By envisioning these images in the live, on-screen rhetorical setting that is their intended end, the narrator maximizes the tank-like "clanking" tone of the film's inauthenticity, against which his own observations, soon to be presented in the story we have just read, may be contrasted. Having opened the story by establishing his narrator's proximity to combat, Hemingway presents his autobiographical narrator as having survived a military ordeal that claimed both the French soldier and the narrator's friend, the General. If the story ends with the narrator's subtle triumph and the story itself acts as evidence that the narrator has found the space in which to produce an account of the war that includes everything, including his own compromised activities as a filmmaker/propagandist, then the story also documents, in an understated way, the narrator's interior change of consciousness, one that causes him to turn from an apologist for Republican military police to a man who, like their quarry, must flee the war and its seductive simplifications.

Both "Night Before Battle" and "Under the Ridge" find Hemingway adapting the trope of Spanish folk authenticity from *The Spanish Earth* while nevertheless thoroughly discrediting the documentary form from which it emerged and the political aims that occasioned the use of that form in Ivens's film. But what finally differentiates these stories—and what perhaps accounts for Hemingway's own strong preference[8]—is the more thorough rejection in "Under the Ridge" of the foreign role in the Republican cause. Whereas in "Night Before Battle," the narrator remains separate from a foreign soldier whose ideological commitment wavers but does not ultimately collapse amidst an ambiguous and morally confused expatriate Republican environment, "Under the Ridge" finds the narrator's own education becoming the story's subject, in which fleeing the war becomes an unquestioned good. This shift results in a short story finally able to dramatize compellingly the futility of this war.

Notes

1. For the most comprehensive assessment of the political implications of Hemingway's involvement in, and artistic engagement with, the Spanish Civil War, see Cooper (81–113). Cooper nevertheless reproduces the standard line on Hemingway's work during the war itself—that it was hindered by his own ideological allegiances, and he needed to escape the war before he could write freely about it—even though Cooper thoughtfully exposes the numerous ways in which *For Whom the Bell Tolls* is still permeated by partisan political views, thereby effectively undermining the progression he hopes to chart.

2. This brief account of Ivens's and Hemingway's reasons for working on the film necessarily ignores the full story of the film's genesis and subsequent evolution. For the most authoritative and comprehensive account of the many hands that had a role in the film's development into its final form, see Vernon (73–110).

3. For the most detailed discussion to date of the film's structure and meanings, as well as an insightful consideration of its critical reception and place within the documentary film tradition, see Vernon (111–41).

4. For a more detailed discussion of this point, see Cooper (85–86) and Koch (126–27).

5. In his introduction to the edited collection of the NANA dispatches, William Braasch Watson discusses the diversity of subjects Hemingway wrote about in the dispatches, and the plurality of styles he used to relate them. For Watson, while "war was [Hemingway's] theme and combat his most persistent and dramatic subject, Hemingway's mind and eye engaged a wide range of topics and he wrote about them in ways that were appropriately varied" (4). In particular, Watson mentions the descriptive "word-paintings" peppered throughout the dispatches, and how these vivid descriptions, while being congruent with "that objective, third-person, fact-filled way appropriate to most American newspapers," nevertheless "were really poetry disguised as prose" (5).

6. Hemingway's use of a flower metaphor in Baldy Jackson's description of the crew parachuting out of the falling plane echoes an image he uses in "Dispatch 21-Defense at Tortosa": "Black puffs of anti-aircraft bursts blossomed around them and showed they were Government planes" (74). Hemingway's own imagery is subtler than that of his fictional character.

7. The realization that Hemingway presents in this story is echoed somewhat in his final dispatch for NANA, where he discusses "the regionalism of the Spaniard" as a characteristic that allowed the Republican war effort to continue in the face of Nationalist territorial gains and the increasing fragmentation of Republican military resistance ("Madrid Fighting" 91). While Hemingway's observation pertains solely to the fighting of the war, its presence in the final dispatch suggests not only that Spanish regionalism

was on Hemingway's mind but also that his favorable estimation of its effects could have led to the realizations present in his short story.

8. In a letter to Arnold Gingrich dated 22 October 1938, Hemingway mentions that he has "another swell story done that [he] only need[s] to go over (maybe best ever wrote, anyway one of them)" (*SL* 472). Carlos Baker's editorial note identifies "Under the Ridge" as the story that Hemingway most likely had in mind.

Works Cited

Cooper, Stephen. *The Politics of Ernest Hemingway.* Ann Arbor: UMI Research Press, 1987.

Hemingway, Ernest. "Defense of Tortosa." In "Hemingway's Spanish Civil War Dispatches." Ed. William Braasch Watson. *Hemingway Review* 7.2 (1988): 73–75.

———. *Ernest Hemingway: Selected Letters, 1917–1961.* Ed. Carlos Baker. London: Granada Publishing, 1981.

———. *The Fifth Column.* In *The Fifth Column and Four Stories of the Spanish Civil War* 1-87.

———. *The Fifth Column and Four Stories of the Spanish Civil War.* New York: Charles Scribner's Sons, 1969.

———. "Hemingway's Spanish Civil War Dispatches." Ed. William Braasch Watson. *Hemingway Review* 7.2 (1988): 13–121.

———. "Madrid Fighting Its Own War." In "Hemingway's Spanish Civil War Dispatches." Ed. William Braasch Watson. *Hemingway Review* 7.2 (1988): 90–92.

———. "Night Before Battle." In *The Fifth Column and Four Stories of the Spanish Civil War* 110-39.

———. "Under the Ridge." In *The Fifth Column and Four Stories of the Spanish Civil War* 140-51.

———. Voice-over narration. *The Spanish Earth.* Dir. Joris Ivens. Contemporary Historians Inc., 1937. Film.

Josephs, Allen. For Whom the Bell Tolls*: Ernest Hemingway's Undiscovered Country.* New York: Twayne Publishers, 1994.

Koch, Stephen. *The Breaking Point: Hemingway, Dos Passos, and the Murder of José Robles.* New York: Counterpoint, 2005.

Light, Martin. "Of Wasteful Deaths: Hemingway's Stories about the Spanish War." In *The Short Stories of Ernest Hemingway: Critical Essays.* Ed. Jackson J. Benson. Durham: Duke UP, 1975. 64–77.

Raeburn, John. "Hemingway on Stage: *The Fifth Column,* Politics, and Biography." *Hemingway Review* 18.1 (1998): 5–16.

Vernon, Alex. *Hemingway's Second War: Bearing Witness to the Spanish Civil War.* Iowa City: U of Iowa P, 2011.

Watson, William Braasch. "Hemingway's Spanish Civil War Dispatches: Introduction." *Hemingway Review* 7.2 (1988): 4–13.

13

Bulls and Bells

Their Toll on Robert Jordan

Lawrence R. Broer

My relationship with *For Whom the Bell Tolls* dates back to the year I was twelve, when my family had moved from Baltimore to Woodland Hills, California, and I was befriended by a precocious thirteen-year-old I think of as my personal Stephen Dedalus. It was Ronald Anthony Cross who placed a copy of *For Whom the Bell Tolls* in my hands, and that, as they say, has made all the difference. Ronnie, by the way, went on to become a successful fantasy and science fiction writer, and I was able to reunite with him and thank him not long ago.[1] What held me spellbound in that first reading of *For Whom the Bell Tolls* was Hemingway's ability—which I still believe no writer has ever done better—to make you see, feel, and hear the way it was, to write *so* truly, to project felt experience with *such* vitality and immediacy "that it becomes part of the experience of the person who reads it" (Baker 314). We should of course recognize "taste" among those physical senses that not only feed Hemingway's art but heighten our own capacity for sensuous pleasure as well. I love Ann Putnam's account of a heated exchange between two colleagues, Mary Gordon and Frank McCourt, over whether Nick Adams in "Big Two-Hearted River" had spaghetti or beans for dinner. It was an intriguing commentary, Ann says, on the power of Hemingway's evocative prose "even on those female readers like Gordon who said she could not stand to read him yet believed so strongly in her memory of what a single character ate for dinner" (qtd. in Putnam 119). Hemingway had in fact become so excited by the vividness of his own prose in the last chapter of *For Whom the Bell Tolls* that, reading it over, he said, "I was as limp and dead as though it had all happened to me" (*SL* 506).

Ray Vince is probably right that the real hero of Hemingway's Spanish work is the Spanish earth itself, not only as a source of artistic inspiration but also as a moveable feast to the senses (77). To Robert Frost's "Earth's the right place for love: I don't know where it's likely to go better" (122), Hemingway might have added, "especially in Spain." After my publication of *Hemingway's Spanish Tragedy* (1973), subsequent trips to Spain reminded me why Hemingway identified with and was fortified by the Spaniard's fiesta concept of life—the hearty drinking, and the mostly male camaraderie among aficionados. In tracing the Spanish influence on Hemingway's life and work, however, I had paid too little attention to the unspoiled Spanish countryside that influenced Hemingway so deeply: the sensual delights of the Spanish Pyrennees, with their clear air, ancient beech and pine forests, and trout-filled streams around Burguete; and the bracing water of the sea at San Sebastian, which proved as cathartic for Hemingway as for Jake Barnes. It is the fertility, abundance, and beauty of the Spanish earth, embedded in Hemingway's ecstatic prose, that causes Bill Gorton in *The Sun Also Rises* to proclaim, "This is country" (122).

Perhaps only on the Gulf Stream did Hemingway find another place that equally made him feel his primitive relatedness to the world around him, that equally intensified that wondrous capacity for elemental experience he evokes so enticingly that we too dread the prospect of its reduction and loss. Carlos Baker says that when Hemingway was writing *Death in the Afternoon,* the author lamented not having time "to name over all the sights and sounds and smells, like a miser in his countinghouse: the wheat-colored fields of Navarre, the 'small, careful stepping horses . . . rope-soled shoes . . . the loops of twisted garlics; earthen pots; saddle bags carried across the shoulder; wine skins; the pitchforks made of natural wood' with branches as tines; the tall papyrus grass along the littoral; the baked clay hills, red dust, white sand. The tinny sound of churchbells in the villages; the clop of mules and burros; the rustle of the sea-wind in the palms; the smells of olive oil and dust and hot paellas and of early morning in the freshly swept cafés" (Baker 224). Hemingway, Baker reports, "would have liked to set down in words, as Goya did in paint, all that he had 'seen, felt, touched, handled, smelled, enjoyed, drunk, mounted, suffered, spewed-up, lain-with, suspected, observed, loved, hated, lusted, feared, detested, admired, loathed, and destroyed'" (224).

We need not look far in *For Whom the Bell Tolls* for evidence of what, according to Baker, Hemingway wanted most: total immersion in the sensuous experience of living. "Robert Jordan stood looking across the high mountain meadow with the trout brook running through it. There was heather growing where he stood. There were gray boulders rising from the yellow bracken that replaced the heather in the lower part of the meadow and below was the dark line of the pines" (*FWTBT* 96). Jordan's recitation of the smells he loves reminds me of Mary Hemingway's response when Ernest said to her, "I'm not a phony but I'm a terrible braggart." "No," thought Mary fondly. "Just full of joy" (qtd. in Baker 518).

> Which would you rather smell? Sweet grass the Indians used in their baskets? Smoked leather? The odor of the ground in the spring after rain? The smell of the sea as you walk through the gorse on a headland in Galicia? Or the wind from the land as you come in toward Cuba in the dark? That was the odor of the cactus flowers, mimosa and the sea-grape shrubs. Or would you rather smell frying bacon in the morning when you are hungry? Or coffee in the morning? Or a Jonathan apple as you bit into it? Or a cider mill in the grinding, or bread fresh from the oven? You must be hungry, he thought, and he lay on his side and watched the entrance of the cave in the light that the stars reflected from the snow. (*FWTBT* 260)

I cannot but think that Jordan has such elemental delights in mind at the end of the novel when, his death a certainty, he says, "I hate to leave it, is all. I hate to leave it very much" (467). How appropriate it is that Jordan dies with his heart pressed against the Spanish earth, a last communion both tactile and spiritual.

In as complete and instructive a study of this novel as exists, For Whom the Bell Tolls: *Hemingway's Undiscovered Country,* Allen Josephs cites the novel's remarkable verisimilitude as precisely the quality that makes it a masterpiece, a gift of invention he calls Hemingway's personal religion and a key to understanding the author's notions of truth-telling in fiction. Yet this central expression of Hemingway's artistry is something I had also neglected in my study of Hemingway and Spain. Just as reviewers were correct that I had not paid sufficient attention to Hemingway's *humanismo,* and to the wonders of the Spanish landscape, so were they right that I had argued too exclusively that Hemingway's personal tragedy, increasing machismo, and diminished creative possibilities had come to him inexorably because of his adoption of "Spanishness," his apotheosis of the obsessively masculine rituals of the bullfight. I find myself now in the unenviable position of the British economist Mitchel, whose writing on Spain was regarded by Robert Jordan as "too clear and simple and too open and shut . . ." (*FWTBT* 239). So this essay is my mea culpa, an opportunity to rectify a thesis that obscured as much as it illumined.

Multiple layers of new scholarship have changed my view of Hemingway's Spain and enlarged my understanding of the author's late fiction—in particular, a recognition that the complex characters and complicated moral issues of *For Whom the Bell Tolls* are anything but "open and shut," rendering all critical generalizations suspect, and that the technical virtuosity of this novel and the works that follow signify not artistic decline, but creative advance. In what has now become a commonplace in Hemingway criticism, I argued in *Hemingway's Spanish Tragedy* that Hemingway's fictive mask contributed to what I believed was the most important and least understood of tensions in Hemingway's work—the creation of divided, contradictory selves within Hemingway and his protagonists, the mask, and the man beneath the mask: the former, brutish, superstitious, and often irrational and cruel; the latter, vulnerable, sensitive, caring, subtle, and articulate—the artist-protagonist who struggles to prevail in the author's posthumous fiction.[2]

It was because I had discovered startling parallels between this unsettling emotional paradox within Hemingway and his later heroes, and within the Spanish character as explained by Unamuno and other prominent Spanish critics, that I was led to make the case that Hemingway's identification with the primitive laws and forces within the world of the corrida had produced this diabolical internal struggle. The spirit of the Spaniard is "dualistic and polarized," argues Unamuno. "Don Quixote and Sancho Panza travel together, they help one other, they love one another, but they can't unite." According to Unamuno, the conflictive nature of Spain and all things Spanish is the single but powerful source of her fundamental tragedy: angry voices blended with sane words, fierce cruelty linked with deep charity, all the composed shreds of the anarchist and absolutist character. There can be no harmony, Unamuno contends, in that war which each Spaniard wages against himself and his antagonists, but only perpetual strife, interminable contradiction, and continual incivility (qtd. in Broer, *Spanish Tragedy* 78).

Subsequent studies of Hemingway's Spain confirm my argument that Hemingway's embrace of the dualistic and contradictory Spanish spirit and his identification with the Spaniard's extraordinary interest in violence and death had helped him isolate and crystallize the fundamental spiritual attitude at the core of his life and work, particularly showing what the ritual of the corrida and the code of the matador had meant to Hemingway and his heroes.[3] Most notably, Allen Josephs asserts that Hemingway's work is simply not conceivable without Spain and Spanish values, observing that even the author's non-Spanish fiction is marked with the imprint of the matador and the corrida ("Spanish Sensibility" 227). Not by coincidence had the corrida harmonized with Hemingway's own tragic sense of the way things are. He watched the destruction of 1,500 bulls in the decade before he published *Death in the Afternoon* (*DIA* 238), and as early as 1924, in a particularly autobiographical passage in "On Writing," he could write of Nick Adams that "his whole inner life had been bullfights all one year" (216). In *Death in the Afternoon,* his spiritual autobiography and what I continue to see as the critical turning point of his life and career, Hemingway sums up the grim lesson he has learned: that "there is no remedy for anything in life," that "Death is a sovereign remedy for all misfortunes" (*DIA* 104). As Jackson Benson argues of Hemingway's vision, "There can be no happy end to love [or to life] because in some way or another, life *must* break through what man has built in order to destroy it—if not through death, then through separation, loss of affection, or physical degeneration" (101; emphasis in original).

Hemingway takes comfort in the fact that the Spanish not only accept death as an inescapable reality but seek it out as often as possible in the corrida, experiencing a feeling of tragic catharsis afterward if the matador gives his best effort. Having been wounded both physically and psychologically in childhood and in the war in Italy, Hemingway identifies with the torero in particular, as a man who must learn to live with fear and death, just as the crippled soldier has had to learn.[4] Sitting in a barrera seat at a bullfight was like having a ringside seat at the war, except that, as Jake Barnes explains to Brett in *The Sun Also Rises,* violence and death now become "more something that was going on with a definite end, and less of a spectacle with unexplained horrors" (*SAR* 171). It is not the wounded hero now who is "attainable," who has been pulled to his knees in fear and despair, but the bull, whose defeat seems a victory over death itself. Throughout *Death in the Afternoo*n, we see Hemingway mesmerized by the way the skillful matador controls the terrain in which he moves, because it creates the illusion of managing the violence that once wounded and humiliated him. The matador must dominate the bull by knowledge and science, the narrator of *Death in the Afternoon* declares. "In the measure in which this domination is accomplished with grace will it be beautiful to watch" (*DIA* 21). The ability to dominate one's adversary is a quality exhibited repeatedly by Hemingway's heroes in his post-1930s fiction, heroes I argued were largely modeled after his stoical and defiant matadors. From *Death in the Afternoon* on, Hemingway would define himself and his literary aspiration in exclusively masculine terms, a man indistinguishable from his next three protagonists.[5] In the view of Reynolds, Hemingway invents the man he wished to be or have people believe he was from his earliest days in Oak Park—"a warrior, an outlaw, a rough character capable of extreme violence" (*Final Years* 206), never uncertain, self-doubting, weak, or afraid of anything. Not to be virile would be womanly. What would his father say? What would Oak Park say?

Critics like Mike Reynolds, and John Peale Bishop before him, stress my concerns that from the 1930s on, Hemingway increasingly plays the part—the masculine tough guy—that he had invented for himself in fiction.[6] "He appears," Bishop wrote, "to have turned into a composite of all those photographs he has been sending for years: sunburned from the snows, on skis; in fishing get-up, burned dark from the hot Caribbean; the handsome, stalwart hunter crouched smiling over the carcass of some dead beast. Such a man could not have written Hemingway's early books. . . . It is hard not to wonder whether he has not, hunting, brought down an even greater victim" (40). Reynolds suggests that Hemingway exaggerated his personal history in heroic terms to the point that real life lies became inseparable from his fictional reproductions—by us, but, more disturbingly, by Hemingway himself. Reynolds worries that "these fabrications," playing to the tough guy image, distanced Hemingway from his better self, increasing what Mark Spilka calls Hemingway's "deadlier leanings" and "devalu[ing] his very real and serious work" (Spilka 11; Reynolds, *Final Years* 222). Although I will offer a counterargument later in this essay, Reynolds joins numerous recent Hemingway scholars who believe that the author's failure to examine this contradictory "inner part of him where the writer lived" (*Final Years* 158), the source of his best and most personal stories, was his ultimate personal tragedy.

What now seems clear to me, however, from *The Young Hemingway*, Reynolds's marvelously authoritative biography of Hemingway's early years, is that there were more obvious underlying sources for the author's darker side and his obsession with bravery and correct bearing than the mask of torero. As Reynolds suggests, there were plenty of self-destructive models of manly behavior available in Oak Park, Illinois, before Hemingway ever saw a bullfight. There was his early reading of romantic fiction. There was the family glorification of hunting and the rugged out-of-doors represented by his father and grandfather, including his grandfather's Civil War experience. There was Oak Park's staunchly conservative cultural milieu, which encouraged, if not legislated, aggressive, self-conscious manly behavior and heroic comportment, symbolized by the character and philosophy of Teddy Roosevelt and his emphasis upon vigorous physical exhibitions of manhood. Roosevelt's influence on Hemingway's early character seems especially telling, a surrogate father whose call for "'rougher, manlier virtues,' for physical and moral courage" (Reynolds, *Young Hemingway* 14), had an influence perhaps deeper, certainly earlier, than that of all the bullfights Hemingway ever watched. Not insignificant, of course, among the forces encouraging the author's brutish tendencies, Reynolds cites the genetically based inherent disposition of the Hemingway family to madness, erratic emotional behavior, and depression that produced anger and violence and eventual suicide.

From Allen Josephs's *Undiscovered Country* (1994) and Thomas Strychacz's *Hemingway's Theaters of Masculinity* (2003), I learned why my readings of Hemingway's treatment of machismo—of death, violence and male aggression that I associated with recalcitrant bulls and matadors—were never as absolute as I had reported, but were subject to the destabilizing effects of Hemingway's prose that Strychacz calls Hemingway's "aesthetic of complexity" (142) and Josephs describes as the author's "higher order of truth" (*Undiscovered Country* 60), a process of complex invention that produces real but always ambiguous characters and themes. Strychacz explains that even when Hemingway's fiction appears to affirm a particular concept of masculinity, as in Robert Jordan's authoritarian impulse to dominate and control those around him as the matador does his bull, or to sanction the enjoyment of killing that Jordan calls the Spaniard's "extra sacrament" (*FWTBT* 286), the author's ironic artistic methods critique the very codes of masculinity the text appears to exemplify, inviting multiple and conflicting interpretations.

No effect in *For Whom the Bell Tolls* more ingeniously undermines masculine authority than that of the epistemological uncertainty that extends to all the novel's characters, even to that imperfect knowledge that dooms the Republican offensive.[7] In a typical moment of self-doubt, Jordan thinks, "The things he had come to know in this war were not so simple" (248), including his faith in the Spanish people and the purity of the Republican cause, notably the trustworthiness of what Agustín calls the "lunatic asylum" of guerrilla fighters around them (211), and the insane leadership of officers like André Marty, whose incompetence represents the futility of the war effort in general. About his orders to blow the bridge, Jordan laments, "What do I know about why this attack is made? Maybe it is only a holding attack. Maybe they want to draw those troops from somewhere else. Perhaps they make it to draw those planes from the North. Maybe that is what it is about. Perhaps it is not expected to succeed. What do I know about it?" (333). "You follow orders," he decides. "Follow them and do not try to think beyond them" (335).

Particularly important to me is the way the novel's problematizing of truth illuminates the separate selves of Robert Jordan's inner world. However much Jordan desires to dominate and control those around him, his every opinion and every assertion of truth is complicated by an opposing or qualifying truth, "riven" with contradictions, as Strychacz puts it (144). Try to fix the meaning of any one of the novel's tangled moral issues or to stereotype any of its multidimensional characters, and we find that, as Strychacz demonstrates about Hemingway's fiction in general, the appearance of truth is systematically "modified, supplemented, metaphorically displaced, and contradicted" (141). When, for instance, Jordan chastises himself for "shaking, like a Goddamn woman," the appearance of misogyny is displaced when, referring to Pilar, Jordan reminds himself, "I'll bet that Goddamn woman up above isn't shaking" (*FWTBT* 437). The blurring of gender lines shows us that courage is an attribute of character, not of sex.

Sometimes Jordan's truth is purely pragmatic, serving his needs at a given moment. As much as he wants to believe that "now"—*ahora*—is all that matters, and that one can have as good a life in three full days as in a lifetime, his innate skepticism causes him to wonder if "that is *really* nonsense" (*FWTBT* 166). "Try to believe what you told her," he says about his efforts to console Maria. "That is the best" (466). When Jordan tries to convince himself, as well as Pilar, that "we can beat them," telling her that her doubts about the doomed Republican cause "will dissipate . . . like a mist," she answers, "If you want it that way" (89). He recognizes that truth fluctuates with time and the bias of the observer. Questioning his faith in his own brand of anarchy—"all people should be left alone and you should interfere with no one" (163)—he thinks, "So he believed that, did he?" (163). Wondering if "patriotic imagination" hasn't skewed his perceptions, he thinks, yet "Karkov said it was true. But then he had written it for Russian papers so he probably wanted to believe it was true after writing it" (237). Jordan reflects that "the talk that he had thought of as cynicism when he had first heard it had turned out to be much too true" (228). He says he would like to know "how it really was" but knows his "belief" is all he has, what he holds "to be true" (230). Maybe Lope de Vega's play, "'Fuente Ovejuna' was the greatest play ever written, . . . but he, Robert Jordan, did not think so" (231). An immature Jordan, boarding the train to college, feels "so much older than his father," yet when before battle he says goodbye to Maria, he reflects on how he told the brakeman on the train that he didn't mind leaving home: "It would not have been true before but it was true that minute and it was only now, at this parting [from Maria] that he ever felt as young again as he had felt before that train left" (406).

That Jordan, the "windy bastard" (43), as he calls himself, is his own severest critic mitigates against an otherwise unnerving authoritarian manner.[8] Confessing that there are so many things he knows nothing of that he thought he knew (380), he worries that "he had gotten to be as bigoted and hide-bound about his politics as a hard-shelled Baptist," and that his mind employed "*clichés* both revolutionary and patriotic . . . without criticism" (164; emphasis in the original). "To be bigoted," he thinks, "you have to be absolutely sure that you are right and nothing makes that surety and righteousness like continence." Then he asks himself, "How would that premise stand up if he examined it?" (164) Arguing that it is bad for his work," Jordan would like to put his conscience on hold for the duration of the war, to suspend all thinking that might undermine his ideals and clash with what he perceives to be his soldierly responsibilities, "instruments to do your duty" (43).[9]

As the war effort worsens and he admits to lying more and more about things he no longer believes, Jordan in fact develops a strategy of conscious exaggeration and deceit that he not only rationalizes as necessary for the war's prosecution, but also comes to enjoy, calling into question "the always ridding of self that you had to do in war" (447).[10] Jordan's pretend "self" encourages the self-deception that he must resist to become the writer he aspires to be after the war is over and that presently makes unreliable his more elevated thoughts of his connection with Maria that he describes as "la Gloria." Recognizing how little he really knows, he thinks that he is "oversensitized because of the shortness of time" (381), and scoffs internally at his feelings about "the *gloria* and all that nonsense that you had. . . . You had this world all taped, didn't you?" (386). Jordan confesses to Maria that he knows her "very little from talking" (341), and despite what I will cite as Maria's function as a Jungian religious archetype, Jordan's attraction to her seems to me more sensual than reverential, excited as he is by her beautiful face and lovely long body, her hair that "rises like a wheatfield in the wind" when he passes his hand over it, and her small, erotic breasts. Jordan in fact admits to "lying to his girl and to himself to pass the night. . . . He liked to do it" (345). When Jordan tells Pilar he has not found a woman before Maria that truly moved him, and she replies, "I think you lie," he agrees, "Maybe a little" (91). He reminds himself to avoid "slipping into make-believe again" (345). Eventually Jordan's evolving moral sense, which forces him to visit his conflicted inner life as never before, causes him to recognize that he has "no right to shut [his] eyes" to the complexity or impurity of "any of it nor any right to forget any of it nor to soften it nor to change it" (304). The ugly realities of war teach him that "there was no purity of feeling for those who survived the fighting and were good at it" (235). He learns that anger, emptiness, and deceit are an inevitable consequence of soldiering, that soldiers must turn sadness to hatred to continue fighting.

Despite Jordan's understanding that he must make difficult moral choices that are always subjective and personal—what Kierkegaard calls the existentialist's "earnestness"—he is forced to question his most passionate convictions about war, killing, religion, and the brutality of the Spanish people. In my rereading of *For Whom the Bell Tolls* I am even more convinced of my view, stated in *Hemingway's Spanish Tragedy,* that the hero's obsession with and inner struggle against aggression—and killing in particular—is the primary moral concern of Hemingway's work. In the tortured debate between Jordan and Anselmo about the right to kill, Jordan wants to ease his conscience by believing that killing the "enemy" is the only means of ensuring the cause of peace, while the wiser, gentler Anselmo argues that killing teaches "nothing," that it only breeds hatred and a desire for revenge (42). The two men agree that killing in Spain is often done too easily, and that, as Anselmo says, "in those who like it, there is always a rottenness" (197–98). In fact, Anselmo says, nobody likes it "except those who are disturbed in the head" (39).[11] Jordan recognizes that calling killing "successful assassination" makes it no more palatable (165). Though he struggles to believe in the rightness of the Republican cause, his attempts to rationalize killing as a necessary means to a noble end wear thin. He confesses that liking to kill is something that has tainted him for a very long time (287). He knows that the killing he feels required to do will harden him even more, much as bullfighters are warped over time. Pilar explains to Pablo, "You think I lived years with bullfighters not to know how they are after the Corrida?" (128).[12]

Hemingway connects the blood and gore of the bullring with the horrors of war through the slaughter of fascist prisoners organized by Pablo. We recognize the blood lust common to the killing of men and animals alike when the massacre begins and someone yells, "Let the bull out!" (109). When Don Faustino, a former aspiring matador, announces that he is coming out, we hear that "it was the same impulse that had made him announce himself for the bullfight" (113). Jordan recognizes too that the absurdity of war requires the killing of people labeled "enemy" whom one might otherwise befriend, people divided only by arbitrary political alignments. "If our father had not been a Republican," Andres reasons, "both Eladio and I would be soldiers now with the fascists . . ." (367). Anselmo likewise observes about the fascists at the bridge, "I have watched them all day and they are the same men that we are" (192). Anselmo's remark, "It is only orders that come between us" (192–93), further undermines Jordan's wavering defense of killing as a soldier's responsibility. Jordan remains equally unpersuaded by his generalization that the Spanish people are particularly barbaric, realizing that there are "as many sorts of Spanish as there are Americans" (205). As Josephs explains, Pilar's tale of the cruel and hateful execution of the fascists has its "precise counterpoint in Jordan's account of the Ohio lynching of [a] black man" (*Undiscovered Country* 100). The novel's title might have been "A Meditation on Inhumanity." Nothing confounds Jordan's efforts to simplify the Spanish people more than the character of Pablo, who is sometimes cowardly and cynical but at other times brave and sincere. Pablo, Jordan concludes, is "all of them" (*FWTBT* 370).

The fact is that in my first analysis of Jordan, I demonstrated no Hemingway protagonist to date had been more willing to examine the darker side of his nature, and showed that it was Hemingway's focus on Jordan's painfully conflicted nature—complex, divided, contradictory, and tragic—that made him such a convincing character. However, what I had not seen in that first analysis was what the female scholars in *Hemingway and Women* and critics like Spilka and Eby have clarified as the deepest and most personal part of the multifaceted nature of Hemingway and his protagonists: the buried or suppressed feminine. I had recognized the existence of contradictory or disharmonious selves, but not that the mask and the man beneath the mask would have been more revealingly described as the mask and the *woman* beneath the mask: Jung's "Eternal Feminine." This woman, as Susan Beegel explains, is a persona that contradicts the machismo hero of myth from Nick Adams to Santiago and that struggles to become the dominant force in Thomas Hudson, David Bourne, and the narrating Hemingway of *Under Kilimanjaro.*

For a psychoanalytic voyeur like myself, Spilka's probing of Jordan's "androgynous wound" (13), a manifestation of the more personal and delicate sexual depths of Hemingway's iceberg, was enticing, but, more importantly, it deepened my awareness of the pre- or non-Spanish source of the hero's psychic split: a flight from women and the female within, Jung's "anima," that Spilka equates with a fear of loss and death. In *For Whom the Bell Tolls,* Spilka explains, Hemingway had begun to explore the taboo sexuality—incest and the transformation of gender roles—that anticipates the gentler, more feminized Santiago and the more gender-integrated figures of Thomas Hudson and David Bourne. In Maria, for instance, we see a sisterly female with whom Jordan desires to merge identities, and in Pilar an inversion of the hated, emasculating mother for whom Jordan may have Oedipal feelings (Spilka 246–47, 221).[13] In the erotic threesome, Spilka detects a desire for the ménage à trois of *The Garden of Eden* and the hero's interest in playing the female role (154).

Yet while Spilka contends that these buried tensions were always there for the discerning and willing reader to uncover, he believes, as I once did, and as a majority of critics argue about the posthumous works, that the defensive mask of machismo prevented Hemingway from exploring his inner world fully enough, pushing far enough, as Burwell and Fleming suggest, to achieve a vigorous self-examination of conflicts that might have added even more to the stature of his life's work.[14] We think too of Virginia Woolf's quip that

Hemingway lets his "dexterity" prevent him from standing "close up to the bull and let[ing] the horns—call them life, truth, reality, whatever you like—pass him close each time" (91-92), and, of course, Stein's indictment: "What a book . . . would be the real story of Hemingway, not those he writes but the confessions of the real Ernest Hemingway" (216–17).

Given Jung's reminder of the "dark incalculable power of the unconscious" (87), the argument that a more overt, more conscious articulation of things omitted, feelings of guilt or suppressed androgynous longings, would have made better fiction is moot at best, fallacious at worst, even if the thawing of the iceberg is basically what the posthumously published works are about: a very different kind of self-conscious fiction, calling for new forms of literary expression. Spilka's own argument for the importance of the unsaids in a novel like *For Whom the Bell Tolls* demonstrates that, as always, Hemingway's meanings are more powerfully suggested than stated, omissions that in Strycachz's words, guide the reader to an "ideal plentitude" (141). But it is in the more comprehensive and inclusive analyses of what Ann Putnam calls "the dark place that holds the entanglements of the feminine" (113), or simply "all things 'fearful, gloomy, [and] entangling'" (Westling, qtd. in Putnam 113), residing in Hemingway's secret hidden depths, that she and critics like Carl Eby, Debra Moddelmog, and Susan Beegel answer Spilka's call for the more discerning and willing reader.

In their respective discussions of the hero's feminized consciousness in "Big Two-Hearted River," and *The Old Man and the Sea,* Putnam and Beegel show why it is so important to understand that Spain, the Spanish people, the battlefields of war, or Spain's bulls, and matadors (or, for that matter, the Gulf Stream or the jungles of Kenya) were not Hemingway's primary subjects any more than the South was Faulkner's, but a landscape anyone can know. In agreement with Spilka that Hemingway's efforts to resolve the feminine-masculine duality in himself was always at the heart of Hemingway's work, they explain its ancillary relationship to Hemingway's still larger, more mythically resonant theme of the happiness of the garden a man must lose, Hemingway's quintessential metaphor for his and his heroes' knowledge of the impermanence of all things. What Putnam describes as the hero's quest for wholeness, across paradisiacal landscapes from "Indian Camp" to *Under Kilimanjaro,* constitutes the basis for what A. Carl Bredhal and Susan Lynn Drake call the author's "creative evolution" (24), in which each new hero assimilates the lessons and creative energy of his predecessor. In this process of discovery and recovery of lost Edens, and their interior counterpart, the effort to access the denied or split off feminine, it is the hero's habit of associating the feminine with the darker, destructive aspects of nature, the "fearful other" (Putnam 114), Putnam and Beegel explain, that poses his greatest challenge, learning to embrace the feminine rather than view it as a landscape to be avoided, taken, or destroyed (113).

Despite Spilka's criticism that Hemingway relegates Robert Jordan's struggles with machismo to the novel's subtext, it is precisely Jordan's acceptance of the duality of nature and, by extension, the duality within himself—what Josephs cites as the creative and fertile overthrow of the authoritarian masculine (*Undiscovered Country* 98)—that defines Jordan's moral progress in relation to earlier heroes. In reference to Jordan's remark, "Christ, I was learning fast there at the end" (*FWTBT* 467), nothing guides Jordan to the integration of self and "other" more than his hard-earned knowledge and subsequent cultivation of what I call Hemingway's "doctrine of plentitude," the knowledge that for every rapture there is an offsetting dread. There is, for instance, the "plenty" Jordan says he believes in, and the "plenty" that he does not (305), the life-affirming "plenty" Maria offers him in the form of transcendent love-making—"hot-aching, rigid, close together" (346)—and the deathly "plenty" that had been done to her by fascists (162). Reflecting the complex and contradictory nature of Hemingway's own art, Jordan, for instance, hears singing inside the cave about nature's bounty—the beneficence of sun and moon, the "spending" of which is "never done" (59)—yet in the space of a few minutes, his buoyant mood is undercut by knowledge of nature's perfidy, a coming frost, the cry of an owl hunting, the sound of distant firing, and the insistence of the gypsy Rafael that Jordan must kill Pablo (61).

The novel's myriad references to fire express nature's duality as a force with both creative and destructive potential; what Joseph Campbell calls the "inexhaustible and multifariously wonderful divine existence that is the life in all of us" (391)—the creative fire of sex, food, drink, love, art—is counterposed with the killing fire of war and of loss, grief, and flux. The scent of the flower market contends with the smell of burned powder (85–86), while Pilar tells Maria, "that is a fire to cook with. Not to burn down a city" (190). For Pilar, Valencia is a moveable feast of delicate pastries, prawns fresh from the sea, fish of an incredible richness, and "melons long as one's arm" (85), yet she is aware that the blowing up of trains has kept her and Pablo from ever seeing and making love in Valencia.

As a sign that Hemingway has grown significantly more aware of the destructive implications of the artist-killer discord inside himself, he increasingly juxtaposes, in his writing from *For Whom the Bell Tolls* on, the forces of Eros and Thanatos, a process by which the creative, life-affirming energy of love is converted to or threatened by the destructive energy of chaos and death.

"Kiss me," Jordan tells Maria. "Nay," she says, "show me . . . the pistol" (170). In bed with Maria, Jordan declares that all of him is as cocked as the pistol against his naked leg, ready to shoot (360). Jordan puts the muzzle of his gun to his lips in the dark and touches the bore with his tongue (410). The good taste of coffee in Jordan's mouth is offset by the bulge of machine-gun clips in his trouser pockets (392). Fascists are slaughtered by tools meant for threshing wheat (107).

If life is the ecstasy of Jordan and Maria's love-making, it is as well the omnipresence of the fascist planes, "shaped like sharks," the "mechanized doom" that kills El Sordo (87), the earth rolling and lurching under him at the moment of his death, a grotesque inversion of "La Gloria," the life-affirming Eros of Jordan and Maria (379). But this is ultimately a novel about creative transcendence, a profoundly mythic tale of new life out of sacrificial death, the saving realization for which comes to Jordan when, envisioning Madrid "just over the hills there . . . rising white and beautiful," he declares, "That part is just as true as Pilar's old women drinking the blood down at the slaughterhouse. There's no *one* thing that's true. It's all true. The way the planes are beautiful whether they are ours or theirs" (467; emphasis in original). Jordan's reconciliation to plentitude's painful duality, a paradox Jordan knows now he carries within himself, allows him to feel, as he says, "completely integrated" (471), first with the Eden, the defiled Spanish earth that has betrayed him even as he reaffirms his love for it by touching the palm of his hand against the pine needles where he lies at the moment of his death, and second, with his Eve, his beloved Maria, the embodiment of ideal plentitude, the reunion with whom represents not only a healing of the hero's masculine-feminine wound, but a reconciliation with all women—lover, wife, sister, even the daughter Jordan and his creator will never have except through the fertility of imagination.[15]

When Jordan finds himself growing cynical about the futility of the war, and morbid with thoughts of his own death, he chides himself that he's learning plenty (136). "You have to take advantage of what time there is" (203), he tells Pilar. Rather than submit to the fatalism of Rafael's "*no hay remedio,*" a theme dramatically reiterated in *Under Kilimanjaro,* their knowledge of the inevitability of loss and death compels both Jordan and his creator to become skilled in the artful management of time, Jordan in life, Hemingway on paper, knowing how to extract the maximum value and pleasure from sensuous experience—what Thomas Hudson, in *Islands in the Stream,* calls the "palliative measures" (*IS* 282)—by paying complete and focused attention. Jordan understands that loneliness and even death may be "abolish[ed]" by the fullness of Maria's "long light body, warm against him," the "simple touching of flanks, of shoulders and of feet" (*FWTBT* 264). He consoles himself that the tragic snowstorm that dooms his mission possesses the paradoxical excitement of battle, and though it will ruin everything, he might as well enjoy it (181–82). Even little pleasures are carefully planned, shaped with artistic finesse, as if nothing were more important than, say, the stirring of the thick milk into your coffee "until it was light brown" (80). So dread converts to beauty, and tragedy to the fiery art of Yeats's "Byzantium," as the tragically short love affair of Jordan and Maria converts to a plentitude of ecstasy and wonder.

As opposed to Spilka's view that the novel ends by "separat[ing] what [Hemingway] could not for long unite—considerate androgynous love between partners of equal strength" (248)—our understanding of Maria as the personification of Jordan's own female nature proves doubly instructive about Maria's complex, even allegorical characterization: that as what Josephs calls the "androgyne of classical mythology" (*Undiscovered Country* 107), Maria completes Jordan's humanity by uniting the two halves of his divided soul. He sees them as one being, "so close that neither one can tell that one of us is one and not the other" (262), and she agrees, "I am thee and thou art me and all of one is the other" (262). If she carries Jordan's child, then, as Beegel says of Santiago's relationship with Manolin, who cares for the old man with feminine tenderness, "the cycle of life [turns] upwards once more," assuring the "continuity of life in the face of destruction" (155). The view of the hero's reincarnation through Maria deepens our sense of her urgent desire to be of service to him, supporting my overview of Hemingway's career as "creative evolution," in which Hemingway uses Maria symbolically (as he does Renata in *Across the River and into the Trees;* Manolin in *The Old Man and the Sea;* Thomas Hudson's boys in *Islands in the Stream;* David as a boy in *The Garden of Eden;* and the resurrected Nick Adams in "The Last Good Country") as youthful female parts of himself who restore the feeling of Eden and refertilize—or, in Burwell's words, "cross-fertilize"—the author's creative imagination (qtd. in Putnam 128–29).[16] Jung explains, "Just as a man brings forth his work as a complete creation out of his inner feminine nature, so the inner masculine side of a woman brings forth creative seeds which have the power to fertilize the feminine side of the man" (98).

In fairness to Spilka, consistency with what we have discussed as the novel's complex aesthetics requires that we no more insist on one reading of this richly problematic text than another. We might well decide to call disingenuous, for instance, Jordan's repeated desire for more time with Maria, in which they would enjoy the prolonged but more muted joys of married life, when in fact it is the very absence of time that enables them to live in the fullness and intensity of the timeless present. The reader knows that a relationship without the erotic/romantic intensity inspired by war will not hold much interest for Hemingway or his protagonists for very long. Such are the complications of Hemingway's richly contradictory art, which baffle our efforts at closure and force us to debate his work's indeterminate moral issues within and among ourselves. Josephs and Strychacz show us that *For Whom the Bell Tolls* is the perfect place to appreciate what Josephs calls Hemingway's "artistic anarchism" (*Undiscovered Country* 27, 32), complicating narrative strategies whose inventiveness not only rivals the acclaimed experimental story-telling of contemporaries like Fitzgerald and Faulkner but also anticipates the self-reflexive polyphonic-texts of postmodernism.[17] Like the characters, says Strychacz, we "*hazard* interpretations" that reflect our own values and interests (165; emphasis in original).

Nowhere is this more apparent to me than in my differences with Hemingway's bullfight apologists, Allen Josephs, Edward Stanton, and Angel Capellán. For these critic-aficionados, Hemingway's artful representation of the bullfight, a living text, so to speak, may be "sacramental," and the killing of the bull a high, religious experience, one that they believe offered Hemingway a semblance of salvation, a cure for postwar angst without which, Stanton says, Hemingway might never have been able to grow beyond his early preoccupation with death to affirm the power of life, nature, and love in a novel like *For Whom the Bell Tolls.*[18] I, on the other hand, being what Hemingway mocks as an "animalarian" in *Death in the Afternoon* (9), see in the corrida less that is spiritually transcendent but more that reminds us of our common inhumanity—a ritual of blood and death that I worry may have done more to brutalize and divide than to calm and heal Hemingway's ailing postwar spirit. I cannot help but associate Hemingway's *afición* with what Jung sees as a reflection of the psyche's darker self, "the existence of a lower level of personality . . . [where] one behaves more or less like a primitive, who is not only the passive victim of his affects but also singularly incapable of moral judgment" (166). In effect, *afición* becomes a masculine "projection" that precludes understanding one's true nature. But, again, how we respond to the bullfight or to any other aspect of Hemingway's complex person and art should be viewed, as Sanders demonstrates, in the context of Hemingway's subjective epistemology. Sanders shows us that in works like *Death in the Afternoon* and *For Whom the Bell To*lls, Hemingway's philosophical stance encourages individuals to discover truth for themselves. By constructing narrative voices who do not claim to be authorities, the author tells readers that they themselves must strive to know what is true in their own lives (78–79).

Though meaning changes from reader to reader, what does not change is that remarkable verisimilitude, the poignancy of Hemingway's perfected *Ars*

Poetica, which first drew me to *For Whom the Bell Tolls,* and which Putnam says draws her in over and over. How else to explain, she asks, "this beauty at the heart of loss, this beauty in the shadow of violence, this heart touching heart?" (130). Perhaps it is that simple sense of wonder in Nick Adams's response, in "Big Two-Hearted River," to his first bite of beans and spaghetti, whose plentitude he cannot wait to cool, which Putnam says is the closest thing she knows to "how theory reconciles with feeling" (130): "'Chrise,' Nick said, 'Geezus Chrise,' he said happily" ("Two-Hearted River" 216).

Notes

1. Ronald's inventive and powerful stories have appeared alongside those of Isaac Asimov, Harlan Ellison, and Stephen King in major fantasy magazines such as *Fantasy and Science Fiction* and *The Berkley Showcase: New Writings in Science Fiction and Fantasy.* He also wrote the *Eternal Guardians* series: *The Fourth Guardian* (1994), *The Lost Guardian* (1995), and *The White Guardian* (1998), and *The First Guardian* (TBP). I also owe my initial attraction to Spain and Hemingway's *For Whom the Bell Tolls* to Carmen Avila, with whom I shared a cubby hole of an office when we were both first-year graduate students at Florida State University. "Any man's death diminishes me"; some, more than others.

2. Apropos of my view of the hero's developing feminized nature in *For Whom the Bell Tolls,* Jung calls the masculine persona a "mask" "between the individual consciousness and society, . . . designed on the one hand to make a definite impression upon others, and, on the other, to conceal the true nature of the individual" (81). In Jung's view, this painfully familiar division of a consciousness between a public persona and a private, submerged identity, two figures often preposterously different, constitutes an incisive psychological operation that is "bound to have repercussions on the unconscious." The subject so "identifie[s] with his [outer] persona that he no longer knows himself," understanding neither demands from within nor those from without (82, 81). In keeping with one's masculine ideals, it becomes easier to deplore what is perceived as feminine weakness, Jung's "Shadow" or "darker self," than to shatter those ideals (84). In Hemingway's posthumously published novel, *The Garden of Eden,* this provides particularly useful insight into David Bourne's rejection of his "devil" Catherine—Jung's "jealous mistress," upon whom the subject projects his own darkness, forcing others into equally unconscious, dishonest roles that reinforce the subject's outward projected masculine identity (Jung 89). In *Strange Tribe,* John Hemingway's exposé of his father's "physical manifestation" of his grandfather's gender ambiguity (34), the author documents the tragic effects upon the entire Hemingway family of the failure of both his father and his grandfather to understand and accept the feminine side of their nature.

3. Allen Josephs calls this split Spain's genius and its devil, "two-Janus-faces of the same being" (*Undiscovered Country* 127). As I had done in *Hemingway's Spanish Tragedy,* Edward Stanton, in *Hemingway and Spain,* questions the notion that Hemingway's "typi-

cally Spanish preoccupation with death" was positive, arguing that in the author's use of the Spanish matador for models of masculine conduct, one can see the "seeds of his own destruction" (95). Hemingway's identification with the Hispanic code of machismo, he acknowledges, leads eventually to disillusion and despair, a self who prefers oblivion to a life without physical strength and sexual potency (207, 211). The obligation to conform to the moral code of the matador, which Hemingway imposes on himself and his characters, leads to a "blind alley." Thus Stanton concludes that Hemingway's suicide was "a personal as well as a Spanish tragedy" (hence, my title).

4. In her discussion of the influence of Kierkegaard on Hemingway's work, J'aime Sanders explains that learning to face the certainty of death through the spectacle of the Spanish bullfight was as necessary to Hemingway as the matador's creation of successful art in the bullring. The bullfight teaches what Kierkegaard calls "the earnestness of life," allows the individual to see life "whole," and promotes "life-force" (Sanders 84–107). Gail Sinclair argues that Maria, in *For Whom the Bell Tolls*, grows to be courageous and wise beyond her years (96); her acceptance of the certainty of death is demonstrated by her calm description to Jordan of how she will, if necessary use the razor blade she carries to cut her own throat. "So she goes around with that all the time," Jordan observes, " . . . as a definitely accepted and properly organized possibility" (*FWTBT* 171).

5. In *Hemingway and Spain*, Stanton echoes my thesis (in *Hemingway's Spanish Tragedy*) that at this stage of his career, Hemingway gave his American protagonists, including Robert Jordan, many of the qualities of the Spanish matadors he had portrayed in the earlier books. The later heroes—Morgan, Jordan, Cantwell, Santiago—are conspicuously self-possessed and more assertive than the deeply impaired protagonists of Hemingway's earlier work—the tentative Nick Adams, the demoralized Frederic Henry, the impotent Jake Barnes. In *Hemingway: The Homecoming*, Reynolds agrees that the emerging Hemingway hero—tough, masculine, self-reliant—represented a radical break from the more vulnerable and haunted figures in Hemingway's earlier work.

6. Among the descriptions Reynolds cites of Hemingway's psychic split—the mask and the man beneath the mask—those by women (the first to feel Hemingway's abuse, yet the quickest to appreciate his contradictions), claiming that he was far more vulnerable than he liked to pretend, stand out. As Jung says, "The wives of such men . . . have a pretty tale to tell" (83). Reynolds explains that whereas Hadley and Pauline suffered from Hemingway's insults, neglect, and need to dominate (a condition Jung describes as the wife's pretense of inferiority in order to provide her husband with proof that he is the masculine hero he projects publicly and not the inwardly more feminine self he is in private [84]), Martha and Mary were less willing to play limiting, self-effacing wifely roles, asserting their independence in ways that angered him, openly challenging him when he became abusive. When the adventurous and independent Martha tells Ernest that "I have to live my way as well as [you] yours or there would not be any me to love you with," he calls her "insane" (*Final Years* 88, 90). Then there was Mary's declaration to Charles Scribner that the reason she planned to leave Ernest was his "program of being a tough guy . . . destroyed what [she] used to think was an inexhaustible supply of devotion" (qtd. in Burwell 205). Reynolds reports that Martha Gellhorn's mother saw clearly that Hemingway was strangely divided, that there was something hidden beneath the surface

that made her feel sorry for him (*Final Years* 27). Gertrude Stein was perhaps the earliest of Hemingway's female admirers to sense, in the words of Reynolds, the precarious "fictive mask" with which Hemingway was "about to enter the public arena" (*1930s* 123).

7. See Sanders's discussion of Kierkegaard and Hemingway as "subjective thinkers" for whom the discovery or creation of "truth" is always an individual experience, dependent upon one's own feelings, perceptions, and powers of observation.

8. See Strychacz's discussion of Hemingway's richly complex management of the "competing possibilities" of a masculine/feminine split in Jordan (my term), in which Jordan's attraction to fascist authoritarianism—e.g., the will to power, aggressiveness and hunger for control—is undercut by a feminine "counter-masculinity" (122). Spilka sees Maria's rape by fascists as a critique of Jordan's authoritarian tendencies. He sees Hemingway creating a conscious or unconscious metaphor for his sense of what he, as arrogant authoritarian, has done to wives and children, a symbolic rape of their innocence and vulnerability. Hemingway himself first suffered such a symbolic rape by an unforgiving, conservative, patriarchal culture that demands total allegiance to its masculine chauvinist norms (108).

9. Jordan's deep-seated fear of repeating his father's cowardice probably shapes his attitudes about following "impossible" orders. Strychacz questions whether Hemingway, through Jordan, isn't indulging fantasies of male power masquerading as historical necessity, though he sees Jordan's "fascist" self to be a "construction" capable of change (106–7).

10. Jung explains that "a man cannot get rid of himself in favor of an artificial personality without punishment," often in the form of unconscious phobias, obsessions, and bad temper, even "a limp sexuality" (83).

11. This offers critical counterpoint to Hemingway's apparent sympathy with the enjoyment of killing chronicled in *Death in the Afternoon,* notably when he observes that the great matador "must have a spiritual enjoyment of the moment of killing," and that killing must be seen as its own reward (*DIA* 232). Whereas in *Death in the Afternoon,* Hemingway scorns people who identify with the pain of animals, in *For Whom the Bell Tolls,* he draws us into a debate about the brotherhood of animals and humans that in my view argues for moral advance. As Jordan and Anselmo inquire into the similarities between men and beasts, they agree that distinctions between animals and humans are negligible.

12. Strychacz cites Bruce Henricksen's remark that the "values implied in the subtext [of *In Our Time*'s bullfighting vignettes] have disturbing affinities with fascist fantasies" (108).

13. In Jung's terms, Hemingway invokes the mythic paradoxical mother of medieval allegories, who both gives life and takes it away. On the negative side, the mother anima connotes anything dark and hidden, someone to whom the subject needs to prove his self-worth. As this neurosis transfers to wives, the subject becomes "truculent and tyrannical" (86). Spilka asks whether the tough, outspoken Pilar, who in many ways resembles Hemingway's mother, is not the mother Ernest would have preferred (246). While Spilka stresses the sexual implications of Jordan and Maria as his "sisterly companion" (247), Jung's view of the "erotic threesome" might well include incest, with the "sacred archetype of the marriage of mother and son" (169). Jung also explains the hidden psychic force that may lead Jordan to exalt Maria to divine status. Such elevation becomes an unconscious means of policing the Id, forcing unruly passions down into the unconscious (84).

14. How we view Hemingway's management of the iceberg's secret depths over the course of his career, which operates with enticingly ambiguous degrees of awareness or unconsciousness, seems to me highly consequential, both aesthetically and morally, especially in considering the value of Hemingway's posthumously published works. The debate about what is omitted purposefully or unconsciously will remain forever unresolved.

15. Maria represents what Jung calls the anima's "extraordinary many-sidednesss" (90), a "shining incarnation" of the female self that Jordan consciously or unconsciously seeks (81). Her fusion of pagan earth goddess and religious icon accounts for her immense emotional and spiritual power, which Jordan calls "La Gloria." Jung explains that the symbolic attributes of the Virgin are unquestionably erotic in origin (24), that the worship of Mary was a vestige of paganism that secured for the Christian church the heritage of the Magna Mater (19), extolled as a "vessel of virtue" (8), associated with the uterus and reflected in nonbiblical allegories as the "fecundation of Isis by the seed of Osiris" (C. W. King, qtd. in Jung 8). As a figure exalted into the heavenly mystical figure of the Virgin Mother (103), a process Jung calls the "spiritualization of eroticism" (21), Maria protects, nurtures, guides, and transforms all that fosters growth and fertility (110). At one point, Maria, Jordan, and the Blessed Virgin become one entity. Praying that Jordan be brought back to her safe and whole from blowing the bridge, Maria says, "But, Oh, Sweet Blessed Virgin . . . Take care of him for me and . . . I will do what he says and what you say" (450). Maria's violation by fascist soldiers equates with the desecration of the Spanish earth, Jung's "unploughed field" (18). Conversely, her fertilizing, transformative powers as a combination of Virgin and Spanish earth goddess register dramatically in a veritable rite of healing and renewal. As Maria presses against Jordan, her breasts are like "small hills that rise out of the long plain where there is a well, and the far country beyond the hills was the valley of her throat where his lips were. He lay very quiet and did not think and she stroked his head with her hand" (341). "I will keep everything clean," she promises Jordan, "and . . . I will obtain olives and salted codfish and hazel nuts for thee to eat" (343).

16. Burwell refers to the "deep, strange merging of identities" that Hemingway sought with Adriana Ivancich as "the most potent instance of his attempting to experience the feminine aspect of his own creative imagination through love for a woman" (130).

17. As a postmodern text, the novel occasionally blurs the lines between reality and illusion or story, foregrounding art and life as playful constructions, ventures in self-creativity. "A rose is a rose is an onion," Jordan quips at one point, " . . . a stone is a stein is a rock is a boulder is a pebble" (289). As an increasingly self-conscious storyteller, Jordan warns himself to stop "making dubious literature" when he finds himself lying about his enjoyment of killing (287). He feels he plays a part from something he has read or dreamed (212), and associates the smell of cyanide with that of bitter almonds in detective stories (238). Jordan's masculine/feminine dichotomy, denial of the feminine, and tendency toward absolutism, vain domination, and occasionally violent behavior reflect Hemingway's essential modernism but also point to a discernible movement toward postmodern narrative strategies throughout his career. The contrary tendencies are manifest in Ihab Hassan's contrast of modern versus postmodern traits. Modern traits align themselves with Jung's "animus"—order, control, predictability, fascism, law—while the postmodern traits equate with the feminine "anima"—disorder, chaos, indeterminacy, anarchy, creativity.

18. Stanton argues that Hemingway's Spanish association was both positive and negative. Though he joins Josephs and Capellán in stressing the bullfight's aesthetic and spiritual qualities, he primarily sees Hemingway's emulation of the matador and Spanish values as "a measure of personal and artistic decline" (200–201) in someone who came to loathe the "whole damned bull business" (205), the position I originally argued but have reconsidered here as too simplistic. Stanton explains that even a majority of Spaniards detest bullfighting as a "culture of death," "an embarrassing, degrading relic of a primitive and 'African' past" (93). He views Hemingway's own need to kill as a symptom of spiritual "desperation," as if "the giving of death postponed his own mortality" (120).

Works Cited

Baker, Carlos. *Hemingway: A Life Story.* New York: Charles Scribner's Sons, 1969.

Beegel, Susan. "Santiago and the Eternal Feminine: Gendering La Mar in *The Old Man and the Sea.*" In *Hemingway and Women: Female Critics and the Female Voice.* Ed. Lawrence Broer and Gloria Holland. Tuscaloosa: Alabama UP, 2002. 131–56.

Benson, Jackson, *Hemingway: The Writer's Art of Self Defense.* Minneapolis: U of Minnesota P, 1969.

Bishop, John Peale. "Homage to Hemingway." *The New Republic* 11 Nov. 1936: 39–42.

Bredhal, A. Carl, Jr., and Susan Lynn Drake. *Hemingway's Green Hills of Africa as Evolutionary Narrative: Helix and Scimitar.* Lewiston, N.Y.: Edwin Mellen Press, 1990. Studies in American Literature.

Broer, Lawrence R. *Hemingway's Spanish Tragedy.* Tuscaloosa: Alabama UP, 1973.

Broer, Lawrence R., and Gloria Holland, eds. *Hemingway and Women: Female Critics and the Female Voice.* Tuscaloosa: Alabama UP, 2002.

Burwell, Rose Marie. *Hemingway: The Postwar Years and the Posthumous Novels.* Cambridge, UK: Cambridge UP, 1996.

Campbell, Joseph. *The Hero with a Thousand Faces.* Princeton: Princeton UP, 1973.

Capellán, Angel. *Hemingway and the Hispanic World.* Ann Arbor: UMI Research Press, 1985.

Fleming, Robert E. "Hemingway's Late Fiction: Breaking New Ground." In *The Cambridge Companion to Hemingway.* Ed. Scott Donaldson. Cambridge, UK: Cambridge UP, 1996. 128–48.

Flora, Joseph M. *Hemingway's Nick Adams.* Baton Rouge: Louisiana State UP, 1982.

Frost, Robert. "Birches." In *The Poetry of Robert Frost.* New York: Holt, Rinehart, and Winston, 1969. 121–22.

Gajdusek, Robert E. "Is He Building a Bridge or Blowing One? The Repossession of Text by the Author in *For Whom the Bell Tolls.*" *Hemingway Review* 11.2 (1992): 45–51.

Hemingway, Ernest. *Across the River and into the Trees.* New York: Scribner, 1950.

———. "Big Two-Hearted River." In *Complete Short Stories of Ernest Hemingway: Finca Vigía Edition.* 161–80.

———. *By-Line.* Ed. William White. New York: Scribner, 1967.

———. *The Complete Short Stories of Ernest Hemingway: Finca Vigía Edition.* New York: Scribner, 1987.

———. *Death in the Afternoon.* New York: Scribner, 1932.

———. *For Whom the Bell Tolls.* 1940. New York: Scribner, 1995.
———. *The Garden of Eden.* New York: Scribner, 1986.
———. *Green Hills of Africa.* New York: Scribner, 1935.
———. *Islands in the Stream.* New York: Scribner, 1970.
———. *The Old Man and the Sea.* New York: Scribner, 1952.
———. "On Writing." *The Nick Adams Stories.* New York: Scribner, 1972.
———. *The Sun Also Rises.* New York: Scribner, 1926.

Hemingway, John. *Strange Tribe: A Family Memoir.* Guildford, CT: Lyons Press, 2007.

Josephs, Allen. For Whom the Bell Tolls: *Ernest Hemingway's Undiscovered Country.* New York: Twayne Publishers, 1994.

———. "Hemingway's Spanish Sensibility." In *The Cambridge Companion to Hemingway.* Ed. Scott Donaldson. Cambridge, UK: Cambridge UP, 1996. 221–42.

Jung, Carl G. *Aspects of the Feminine.* Trans. R. F. C Hull. Princeton: Princeton UP, 1982.

Ortega y Gasset, José. *Obras.* Madrid: Espasa-Calpe, 1936.

Putnam, Ann. "On Defiling Eden: The Search for Eve in the Garden of Sorrows." In *Hemingway and Women: Female Critics and the Female Voice.* Ed. Lawrence R. Broer and Gloria Holland. Tuscaloosa: U of Alabama P, 2002. 109–30.

Reynolds, Michael. *Hemingway: The American Homecoming.* New York: Norton, 1992.
———. *Hemingway: The Final Years.* New York: Norton, 1999.
———. *Hemingway: The 1930s.* New York: Norton, 1997.
———. *The Young Hemingway.* New York: Norton, 1986.

Sanders, J'aime L. *The Art of Existentialism: F. Scott Fitzgerald, Ernest Hemingway, Norman Mailer, and the American Existential Tradition.* Ann Arbor: UMI Dissertation Services, 2007.

Sanderson, Rena, ed. *Blowing the Bridge: Essays on Hemingway and* For Whom the Bell Tolls. New York: Greenwood, 1992.

Sinclair, Gail. "Revisiting the Code: Female Foundations and the 'Undiscovered Country' in *For Whom the Bell Tolls.*" In Broer and Holland. 93-108.

Spilka, Mark. *Hemingway's Quarrel with Androgyny.* Lincoln: U of Nebraska P, 1989.

Stanton, Edward F. *Hemingway and Spain: A Pursuit.* Seattle: U of Washington P, 1989.

Stein, Gertrude. *The Autobiography of Alice B. Toklas.* 1933. New York: Vintage, 1990.

Strychacz, Thomas. *Hemingway's Theaters of Masculinity.* Baton Rouge: Louisiana State UP, 2003.

Unamuno, Miguel de. *Tragic Sense of Life.* Trans. J. E. C. Flitch. New York: Dover, 1954.

Vince, Ray. *War, Heroism, and Narrative: Hemingway, Tolkien, and le Carre, Storytellers to the Modern World.* Ann Arbor: UMI Dissertation Services, 2005.

Woolf, Virginia. "An Essay in Criticism." Review of *Men Without Women,* by Ernest Hemingway. *New York Herald Tribune.* 9 Oct. 1927. Rpt. in *Granite and Rainbow: Essays by Virginia Woolf.* New York: Harcourt, Brace, and Co., 1958. 85-93.

Index